SLOW TRAVEL

Shropshire

Local, characterful guides to Britain's special places

P9-CAL-754

Marie Kreft

EDITION 1

Bradt Travel Guides Ltd, UK
The Globe Pequot Press Inc, USA

Bradt

Shropshire

*Taking it Slow in Shropshire rewards you with a
stronger connection to the here and now;
an ability to live completely in the moment.*

1 In the north, Shropshire has miles of serene, navigable canals. 2 Horseriding near Chetwynd Aston. 3 Treats from the Ludlow Magnalonga. 4 Ellesmere Sculpture Trail installation by John Merrill. 5 Long views over Ludlow Castle.

THE GREAT OUTDOORS

Shropshire is a wanderer's dream; you can spend hours traversing hills, forests, valleys and bogs without encountering any traffic. Sometimes you won't see another human being.

1 The Wrekin, Shropshire's 'little mountain'. 2 Sheep grazing on the Long Mynd. 3 Devil's Chair, a quartzite rock tor on the Stiperstones. 4 Common kingfisher may be spotted near lowland, slow-flowing watercourses. 5 Shropshire is home to the British Hedgehog Preservation Society. 6 Walking in the Shropshire hills.

THE GREAT & THE GRAND

Shropshire is blessed with over 300 churches, each holding its own mysteries and stories. And the county's border with Wales has left a legacy of castles and castle ruins, with countless tales of battles and feuds.

1 Weston Park, ancestral seat of the Earls of Bradford. **2** Lilleshall Abbey ruins. **3** Knight's tomb in St Mary's Church, Acton Burnell. **4** Battle re-enactment, Whittington Castle. **5** Moreton Corbet Castle ruins. **6** St Peter's Church, Melverley. **7** 'Tin tabernacle' church, Maesbury Marsh. **8** Norman arches in Shrewsbury Abbey.

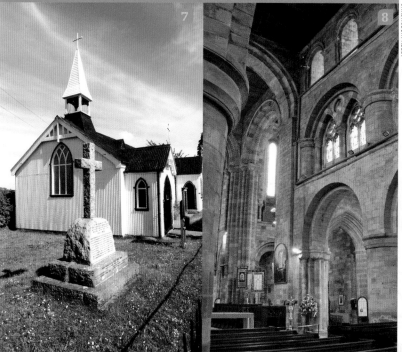

SLOW TRAVEL

Slow is a mindset and one that can be adopted from whichever mode of transport you have chosen that day. Nevertheless Shropshire offers many ways to travel at a speed conducive to peaceful contemplation.

1 Bridgnorth Cliff Railway. 2 Cycling in view of The Wrekin. 3 Sabrina Tours, Shrewsbury. 4 Ironbridge Coracle Regatta.

AUTHOR

Marie Kreft has been writing professionally since graduating from the University of Leeds' School of English in 2004. She's had the travel bug forever. After a year working in Singapore she took the unusual decision to travel home to the UK the Slow (sometimes very Slow) way, via tuk-tuk, train, bus and the occasional pick-up truck. Marie is a previous winner of the Bradt/*Independent on Sunday* travel-writing competition.

AUTHOR'S STORY

I fell in love with Shropshire one October when my husband drove us from our apartment in Birmingham to Stokesay Castle for my birthday. Just an hour from our city life was a revelation: dramatic hills, verdant hedgerows, the scent of woodsmoke in the autumn air. Amid this tranquillity, I discovered, was a county with a history that had changed the world. The Industrial Revolution. The modern Olympics. Clive of India, Charles Darwin, Wilfred Owen. Before them, Bronze Age people, Iron Age tribes, Romans, Saxons and Normans had left their marks in hillforts, earthworks, roads, churches, place names, castles and legends. And long before them, seismic changes in the earth shifted and shaped the landscape: the flat, fertile plains of the north and the hills, valleys and woodland of the south. To think, until that weekend, Shropshire for me had been a rural patch of central England, a farmland vagueness one might hurry through on the way to Wales. I've since discovered this in-betweenness is a vital part of Shropshire's identity.

Now even when away from the county I see its influence everywhere: in the AGA shop (page 119) in the chic 7th arrondissement of Paris; in pubs called the Royal Oak (page 104); on a Shrewsbury Town T-shirt in the spoof rockumentary *This is Spinal Tap*. While Many Shropshire characters captured my imagination, notably the drunken Regency squire John 'Mad Jack' Mytton and poet-novelist Mary Webb. While I find the buzz, multiculturalism and convenience of Birmingham suit my young family, Shropshire is our happy place to which we escape in wellies at weekends. Having celebrated his second and third birthdays in central Shropshire my son thought for a time that the months of the year ran *January, February, Shrewsbury, March* ...

With its fascinating history, idyllic market towns, infinite walking possibilities and exciting gourmet scene, I believe Shropshire offers everything for the discerning traveller. Except the sea. And of course, with the ocean lapping at its borders instead of four other English counties and two Welsh — and the feuds, folklore, strongholds and stories such a landlocked position produces — this quietly bewitching county wouldn't be Shropshire.

First edition published February 2016
Bradt Travel Guides Ltd
IDC House, The Vale, Chalfont St Peter, Bucks SL9 9RZ, England
www.bradtguides.com
Print edition published in the USA by The Globe Pequot Press Inc,
PO Box 480, Guilford, Connecticut 06437-0480

Text copyright © 2016 Marie Kreft
Maps copyright © 2016 Bradt Travel Guides Ltd includes map data © OpenStreetMap
contributors
Photographs copyright © 2016 Individual photographers (see below)
Project Managers: Anna Moores & Katie Wilding
Series design and cover research: Pepi Bluck, Perfect Picture

ISBN: 978 1 78477 006 8 (print)
e-ISBN: 978 1 78477 151 5 (e-pub)
e-ISBN: 978 1 78477 251 2 (mobi)

British Library Cataloguing in Publication Data
A catalogue record for this book is available from the British Library

Photographs
Photographs (c) individual photographers credited beside images & also those from picture
libraries credited as follows: AWL images (AWL), www.flpa.co.uk (FLPA), Shropshire Council
Tourism (SCT), Shutterstock.com (S), Superstock.com (SS), Visit Ironbridge (VI)

Front cover Stokesay Castle gatehouse and garden (Nigel Pavitt/AWL)
Back cover Shropshire Hills open countryside (Andrew Roland/S)
Title page Shrewsbury, Shropshire's county town (SCT)

Maps David McCutcheon FBCart.S and Liezel Bohdanowicz
Typeset by Pepi Bluck, Perfect Picture
Production managed by Jellyfish Print Solutions; printed in Turkey
Digital conversion by www.dataworks.co.in

ACKNOWLEDGEMENTS

Thank you to my fellow Slow guide writers Donald Greig (*Dumfries & Galloway*) and Lawrence Mitchell (*Norfolk*) for their advice and encouragement – and most of all Helen Moat who became a friend as she undertook parallel Slow journeys, physical and metaphorical, in the Peak District. Shropshire Council has been hugely supportive, especially Tim King, and so have the kind people at Shropshire Tourism (thank you). Thank you to my contributors Gladys Mary Coles, Hugh Collins, Amy Douglas, Charlotte Hollins, Rosie Morris, Marc Petty (who also shared with me some of Shropshire's lesser-known literary connections), Katherine Swift and Peter Toghill for adding expertise and fresh voices to this book. For the wonderful walks: Ron Bond, Church Stretton Walkers are Welcome, Keith Pybus and family, Shrewsbury Ramblers and Wellington Walkers are Welcome. Thank you to the walking groups who let me tag along: Market Drayton Ramblers, Severn Strollers and Oswestry Walkers are Welcome (especially Liz Evans). And thank you to everyone else who pointed the way: Kay Dartnell of Wheely Wonderful Cycling, Gordon Dickins, Pat Edgar at PR Matters, Anthony Francis-Jones, Paul Gossage at Ironbridge Gorge Museum Trust, David Harley, Ray Hughes, Caroline Magnus at Stokesay Court, Clive and Cynthia Prior at Shropshire Gold, Andy Richardson, and Twitter's mysterious 🐦 @Shroppiemon. I hope I've done you, and Shropshire, justice.

Thank you to the talented and tireless team at Bradt Travel Guides for supporting and inspiring me, with special thanks to Pepi Bluck, Hugh Collins, Rachel Fielding, Tim Locke, David McCutcheon, Janet Mears, Anna Moores and Katie Wilding for your commitment to making this the best book it could be.

Thanks and love to the Kreft and Wilkes families, my brother Adam Kreft, cousin Trish Smith, friend Andrea Chance-Hill, and all the other friends who accompanied me on Shropshire adventures (especially Lindsay Shaw, who never allows me to do anything silly … alone).

Finally, the biggest thank you of all to Steve and Vincent Wilkes, for being there for the journeys, being understanding, and being the whole world to me.

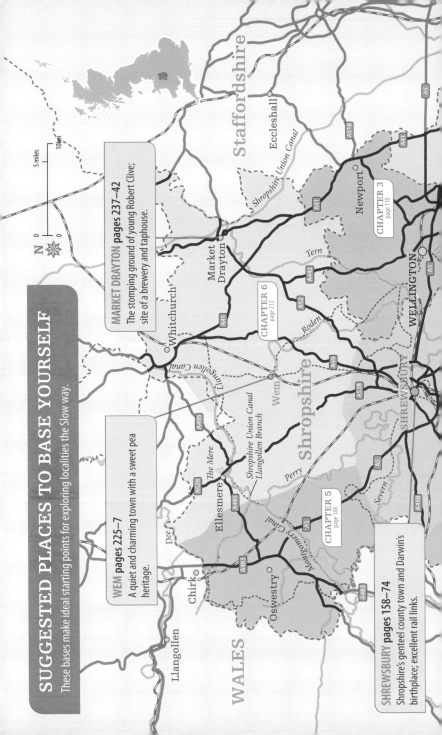

SUGGESTED PLACES TO BASE YOURSELF

These bases make ideal starting points for exploring localities the Slow way.

WEM pages 225–7
A quiet and charming town with a sweet pea heritage.

MARKET DRAYTON pages 237–42
The stomping ground of young Robert Clive; site of a brewery and taphouse.

SHREWSBURY pages 158–74
Shropshire's genteel county town and Darwin's birthplace; excellent rail links.

N

0   5 miles
0   10km

WALES

Staffordshire

Shropshire

Ecclesshall

Newport

CHAPTER 3
page 110

Market Drayton

CHAPTER 6
page 212

Whitchurch

Wem

Shropshire Union Canal

Tern

Roden

WELLINGTON

Llangollen Canal

The Mere

*Shropshire Union Canal
Llangollen Branch*

Ellesmere

Perry

Montgomery Canal

Oswestry

Chirk

Llangollen

Dee

Severn

SHREWSBURY

CHAPTER 5
page 188

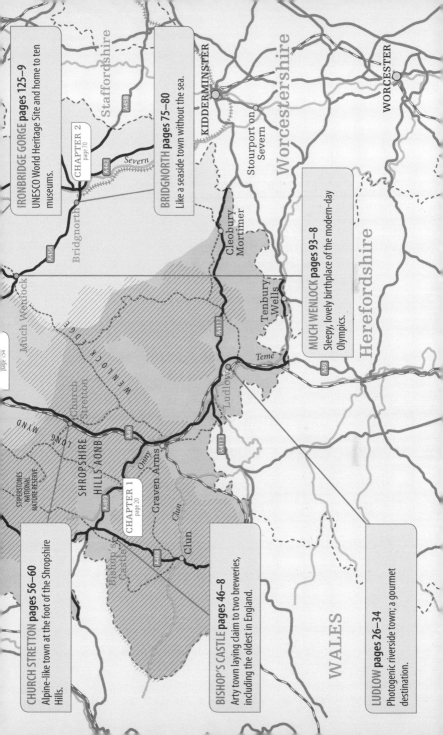

IRONBRIDGE GORGE pages 125–9
UNESCO World Heritage Site and home to ten museums.

BRIDGNORTH pages 75–80
Like a seaside town without the sea.

MUCH WENLOCK pages 93–8
Sleepy, lovely birthplace of the modern-day Olympics.

CHURCH STRETTON pages 56–60
Alpine-like town at the foot of the Shropshire Hills.

BISHOP'S CASTLE pages 46–8
Arty town laying claim to two breweries, including the oldest in England.

LUDLOW pages 26–34
Photogenic riverside town; a gourmet destination.

CHAPTER 2
page 70

CHAPTER 1
page 20

Staffordshire

Worcestershire

Herefordshire

WALES

WORCESTER

KIDDERMINSTER

Stourport on Severn

Bridgnorth

Much Wenlock

Cleobury Mortimer

Tenbury Wells

Ludlow

Church Stretton

Craven Arms

Clun

Bishop's Castle

Severn

Teme

Onny

Clun

WENLOCK EDGE

LONG MYND

SHROPSHIRE HILLS AONB

STIPERSTONES NATIONAL NATURE RESERVE

CONTENTS

SHROPSHIRE ONLINE

For additional online content, articles, photos and more on Shropshire, why not visit ⌚ www.
bradtguides.com/shropshire.

GOING SLOW IN
SHROPSHIRE

Again and again you'll find bits of road, an odd cluster of house and farm buildings, a pool or a coppice not only worth seeing, but good enough to come back and see again. Above all, if you can, learn to use the country to rest in, rather than to pass through.
E Moore Darling, *Seeing Shropshire* (1937)

Canon E Moore Darling's voice isn't the only one which whispered to me down the decades as I researched *Slow Travel: Shropshire*. I read countless other guides and local history books from time long passed, delighting in the fact that – rural and relatively unspoilt as its landscape is – the Shropshire they describe is one I still recognise. And they nearly all endorse slow travel, without knowing of course about our modern-day appreciation (perhaps need) for Slow with a capital S.

For me going Slow in Shropshire isn't only about cycling, walking and using public transport, although I feel keenly the urgent environmental need for us all to burn less fuel. As you will see on page 8, Slow is a mindset and one that can be adopted from whichever mode of transport you have chosen that day. From behind a steering wheel in Shropshire it means being open to the scenery around you; making time to pull over and take a picture, explore an intriguing churchyard or buy honesty-box honey from a makeshift stall. It means waving not frowning when 57 vintage tractors and their drivers of a similar vintage snarl up your route.

Going Slow gives you time and space to appreciate how Shropshire's history has been determined and defined by its varied landscape: how the hills brought defence, the rivers (and later canals) brought prosperity; how the raw materials of Ironbridge Gorge enabled engineers and ironmasters to realise innovations that would change the path of industry and indeed the world.It allows us to understand how Shropshire's liminality and identity are entwined, particularly at the county's Welsh borders, where we find the legacy of the Marches.

A march, of course, is an area of land on the border between two countries or territories. The word derives from the Old English *mearc* (meaning mark, boundary, limit), from which the Anglo-Saxon kingdom of Mercia also took its name. In Shropshire we refer to the **Welsh Marches** – an imprecise borderland between England and Wales incorporating much of south Wales – which in medieval times was controlled not by English monarchs but marcher lords, installed to defend English soil from Welsh invaders. Thanks to the Welsh Marches Shropshire has well-preserved sections of Offa's Dyke (page 199), castles and castle ruins, countless stories of battles and feuds. You can consider yourself in the Marches when you're in the Oswestry area; also in the parts of south Shropshire that border with Wales.

THE SLOW MINDSET

We shall not cease from exploration
And the end of all our exploring
Will be to arrive where we started
And know the place for the first time.
T S Eliot, 'Little Gidding', *Four Quartets*

This series evolved, slowly, from a Bradt editorial meeting when we started to explore ideas for guides to our favourite country – Great Britain. We wanted to get away from the usual 'top sights' formula and encourage our authors to bring out the nuances and local differences that make up a sense of place – such things as food, building styles, nature, geology, or local people and what makes them tick. Our aim was to create a series that celebrates the present, focusing on sustainable tourism, rather than taking a nostalgic wallow in the past.

So without our realising it at the time, we had defined 'Slow Travel', or at least our concept of it. For the beauty of the Slow movement is that there is no fixed definition; we adapt the philosophy to fit our individual needs and aspirations. Thus Carl Honoré, author of *In Praise of Slow*, writes: 'The Slow Movement is a cultural revolution against the notion that faster is always better. It's not about doing everything at a snail's pace, it's about seeking to do everything at the right speed. Savouring the hours and minutes rather than just counting them. Doing everything as well as possible, instead of as fast as possible. It's about quality over quantity in everything from work to food to parenting.' And travel.

So take time to explore. Don't rush it, get to know an area – and the people who live there – and you'll be as delighted as we are by what you find.

I hope you'll enjoy walking in the striding footsteps of those landed barons, reading about their skirmishes, and experiencing for yourself, in places where the landscape remains largely unchanged, the ease at which you can reach back and touch the past.

Conversely, going Slow in Shropshire rewards you with a stronger connection to the here and now; an ability to live completely in the moment. Sometimes, I admit, this state may be imposed upon you: Shropshire's mobile phone and Wi-Fi coverage lag behind the times; some country lanes feel impassable; often you won't find a supermarket for miles. Embrace it all, I say. Take your time to stop and smell the David Austin roses, pick the whinberries, savour a pint or two from one of Shropshire's many breweries.

And that brings me back to the other vital aspect of Slow travel. By embracing Slow joys – eating local and seasonal food, supporting sustainable businesses, buying from artisan producers and craftspeople – we begin, without even trying, to tread more lightly on the planet. I hope you will enjoy your Slow journeys in Shropshire every bit as much I do.

CHANCEL ENCOUNTERS

Whenever I push open the heavy oak door of an unfamiliar English church to reveal the cool and dusty dimness within, I'm newly amazed by the treasures we possess here in the UK. We might fly to China and Southeast Asia in search of sacred temples but at home, in towns and villages across the country, you can find 900-year-old knights' tombs, alabaster effigies, lepers' windows, marble plaques commemorating long-dead heroes, woodcarvings grotesque or beautiful. And often these artefacts are not guarded under lock and key, but in churches open and unattended, whose dwindling communities welcome your footsteps, and your jottings in their visitors' books.

Shropshire is blessed with over 300 churches, each with stories and mysteries, some structures dating to Saxon times. Detailing them all would require a separate tome (and indeed John Leonard has carried out this labour of love with *Churches of Shropshire & their Treasures* from Logaston Press) but I've listed very special ones throughout this book. My favourites include St Laurence's in Ludlow, St Mary's in Shrewsbury, St Mary's in Acton Burnell, St Peter's in Melverley, and the 'tin tabernacle' church of St John the Baptist in Maesbury Marsh.

REVERED HEDGEHOGS & BELOVED BUGS

Wildlife and wildlife lovers are in caring hands in Shropshire. This is the birthplace and home of the British Hedgehog Preservation Society, an organisation whose work includes campaigning for escape ramps to help hedgehogs out of pits beneath cattle grids. (Hobsons Brewery in Cleobury Mortimer created a beer called Old Prickly to commemorate the charity's 30th anniversary.)

Managing 40 varied nature reserves and a membership totalling 10,000 people, **Shropshire Wildlife Trust** is the county's leading conservation organisation. Its headquarters in Shrewsbury are open to visitors and its website (⊘ www.shropshirewildlifetrust.org.uk) is an ideal starting point for learning about the woods, meadows and wetlands that support astonishing levels of biodiversity.

If it's butterflies that make your heart flutter, contact the West Midlands branch of **Butterfly Conservation** (⊘ www.westmidlands-butterflies.org. uk) for events and walks in Shropshire, as well as identification leaflets.

For close-up or even hands-on experiences with animals, you could visit one of several children's farms around the county: **Rays Farm** near Bridgnorth, **Hoo Farm** near Wellington, or **Park Hall the Countryside Experience** near Whittington. If you've always wanted to handle a bird of prey, try the **Hawks Walk** near Shrewsbury.

FESTIVALS & FAIRS

Maybe it's due to the county's rural farming heritage: Shropshire's calendar is illuminated with festivals and fairs, celebrating everything from apples, flowers, steam machinery and ale to sweet peas, coracles and storytelling. On **May Day** in Clun a fight on the packhorse bridge between the Green Man and the Frost Queen determines whether summer comes to the Clun Valley. Nearby Aston on Clun is thought to be the only village that still celebrates **Arbor Day** (or Oak Apple Day), an ancient tree-dressing custom that also commemorates the oak tree which shielded Charles II from Parliamentarians.

I've mentioned the more popular or unusual events under their relevant region chapters but check out the online calendar for more at ⊘ www.bradtguides.com/shropshireevents.

SHROPSHIRE AS INSPIRATION

Artists and writers have been moved by Shropshire's dramatic scenery for centuries: William Turner painted Ludlow Castle; A E Housman wrote poems about Wenlock Edge (despite not holding its intimate acquaintance) and Ralph Vaughan Williams turned them into a song cycle; P G Wodehouse declared the county the 'nearest earthly place to paradise'. Today Shropshire crackles with the creativity of artists, craftspeople, filmmakers and writers: some home-grown; many who've escaped rat races elsewhere in search of peace and space. The result is a plethora of galleries, studios and festivals for us to enjoy in every nook of the county. I've mentioned many under their relevant place listings, but if you're into independent cinema look out for the non location-specific **Borderlines Film Festival** in March (www.borderlinesfilmfestival. co.uk) and **Flicks in the Sticks**, organised year round by Arts Alive (www.artsalive.co.uk/flicks.aspx). To visit artists' studios not usually open to the public, don't miss **Shropshire Hills Art Week** in late May and early June (www.shropshirehillsartweek.co.uk). In Oswestry, **Borderland Visual Arts** (www.borderlandvisualarts.com) holds an annual exhibition in June.

A TASTE OF SHROPSHIRE

It may not seem true when we visit supermarket chains, stocked as they are with air-flown produce and international brands, but in the past decade Britain has undergone a quiet food revolution. We're rediscovering, where practical and affordable, the importance and pleasures of the local, the seasonal and often the organic. We're more aware of the unnaturalness in eating Peru-grown asparagus with our Christmas dinner, and enjoying food and drink in the way it was grown, sold and consumed in the not too distant past.

In parts of Shropshire, where supermarkets are few and far between, one gets the impression that local sourcing has always been the norm; that the rest of the country is simply returning to this older, yet more enlightened, way of thinking. Farmers' markets aren't just a Saturday-morning treat for middle-class hipsters (although I promise you'll find some very rock'n'roll cheese in Shropshire) – rather they're reflective of the way things have always been done. And all around the county you'll find beautifully presented farm shops; food festivals (including the country's first, the Ludlow Food Festival) and innovative chefs pushing at the boundaries of what can be achieved with produce from Shropshire and its neighbouring counties.

I've explored food and drink more comprehensively at ⊘ www. bradtguides.com/shropshirefood, where you'll also find a **guide to farmers' markets** and a recipe for the traditional Shropshire dish, **fidget pie** – a one-time lunchtime staple baked with gammon, onion, potato, apple and cider, named perhaps for its ingredients' tendency to shuffle around in their pastry case when baked.

GEOLOGY

Dr Peter Toghill

Dr Peter Toghill taught geology for 35 years for the University of Birmingham's School of Continuing Education. He is president of the Shropshire Geological Society, which he founded in 1979, and has published the successful books, *Geology of Shropshire* and *Geology of Britain*, both with Crowood Press.

Shropshire displays a greater variety of rocks than any other area of comparable size in the world. The varied scenery, a tangle of hill and dale, is a reflection of an amazing rock sequence – representing 11 of the 13 recognised periods of geological time and covering a period of 600 million years.

The modern study of plate tectonics (the movement of huge rigid plate plates over the earth's hot mantle) shows how Shropshire has travelled a distance of some 7,000 miles, from near the South Pole over the equator to its present latitude in the northern hemisphere. The county has crossed various climatic belts, including the subtropics and the equator, and often been close to plate boundaries. This has created a remarkable sequence of rocks which includes abundant fossils, volcanic rocks, coral reefs, coal seams and desert sandstones. Numerous faults show evidence of abundant earthquake activity, while folded rocks are the result of continental collisions in the distant past.

When Shropshire was near to the South Pole, around 600 million years ago, volcanoes spewed lava and ashes which now form the volcanic hills east of Church Stretton (for example Caer Caradoc and the Lawley) and, further north, The Wrekin. Nearby, the hard sandstones of the Long Mynd were formed at the same time in a shallow sea.

About 500 million years ago Shropshire started its slow northward movement, about an inch a year. As it did so the hard white quartzites of the Stiperstones were formed.

The coral reefs of Wenlock Edge, which uniquely in the fossil record can be compared with modern patch reefs in the Caribbean, were formed in warm subtropical seas as Shropshire drew nearer to the equator 400 million years ago. As the county crossed the equator itself, coal seams were laid down in decaying tropical rainforests 300 million years ago. The exploitation of these coal seams was instrumental to the Industrial Revolution.

Around 200 million years ago Sahara-type desert sands, now hard sandstones, covered the area and primitive lizards walked around north Shropshire, leaving their fossilised remains and footprints at Grinshill. Evidence of rocks with dinosaurs have been removed by erosion but it is probable that dinosaurs did roam the Shropshire countryside around 150 million years ago.

The last important event to affect Shropshire geologically was the Ice Age which started about two million years ago with great ice sheets spreading south and covering many parts of the land. Meltwaters from these ice sheets left behind thick coverings of sand and gravel in north Shropshire, while the presence of the ice also caused the diversion of the River Severn to form Ironbridge Gorge.

When the ice melted herds of mammoths roamed the county. The famous skeletons of one of these, with youngsters, were discovered in 1986 at Condover. The climate has now warmed up but geological processes will continue as usual for countless millions of years.

You'll find more information at ⌀ www.shropshiregeology.co.uk or you could visit the local museums in Shrewsbury, Ludlow and Much Wenlock.

PLANNING YOUR VISIT

For those in the know, Shropshire is considered a bit of a secret. Unjustly, it doesn't possess the international pull of the Cotswolds or Lake District and is often overlooked by holidaymakers whizzing up the M54 to mid and north Wales. While I researched this book at least three Salopians warned me in jest not to do too good a job. 'We don't want everyone suddenly turning up,' they said. Please don't interpret this as

Shropshire being unwelcoming or its tourist industry as flailing, though: it's a friendly county with a healthy annual revenue of over £500 million from visitors. No, I think the truth hidden in my friends' grumbling joke is that Shropshire is quiet (with a population density of just 96 people per square kilometre, according to the Office for National Statistics) and the quietude is a part of its charm. Rest assured that Shropshire will welcome and comfortably accommodate you at any time of year.

One caveat: if you're planning to attend one of the more popular festivals (such as the **Ludlow Food Festival** in September), be aware that nearby accommodation usually gets booked up months in advance.

HOW THIS BOOK IS ARRANGED

I have covered Shropshire in six chapters, more or less representing the five districts or boroughs that existed before Shropshire Council become a unitary authority in 2009, plus the borough still overseen by Telford & Wrekin Council. These district divides are extant in people's minds, so it seemed the logical way for me to map out the county. Where I've taken liberties with the pre-2009 boundaries I've given my rationale in the relevant chapter introduction.

For practical reasons I've kept the scope of this book within Shropshire's borders but, as the largest landlocked county in England, it is inevitably surrounded by sights worth seeing: the Welsh hills, the black-and-white towns and villages of Herefordshire, the rural charms of Cheshire and the industrial heritage of the West Midlands, Staffordshire and Worcestershire. Because I don't know anyone who would refuse to traverse an invisible line while on holiday, several chapters contain brief suggestions for *Just over the border* places of interest.

No charge has been made for the inclusion of any business in this guide (apart from advertisements).

MAPS
Each chapter begins with a map with numbered stopping points that correspond to numbered headings in the text. The relevant Ordnance Survey maps are listed under the *Walking* headings, indicated by the ❋ symbol. The ♀ symbol on these chapter maps indicates that there is a walk in that area, and featured walks are also given sketch maps.

ACCOMMODATION, FOOD & DRINK

At the end of this book I've listed a selection of B&Bs, camping and glamping sites, self-catering cottages, lodges and a few boutique hotels: welcoming, heartwarming and occasionally quirky places I've either stayed at myself, or which have been recommended to me by people in the know. The hotels, B&Bs and self-catering options are indicated by ♠ under the heading for the area in which they are located. Campsites are indicated by ▲. For full descriptions of accommodation providers, visit ⊘ www.bradtguides.com/shropshiresleeps.

Throughout the guide I've shared details of my favourite pubs, cafés and restaurants (and some of those recommended to me), with a preference for independent businesses serving local or organic produce. My listings are nowhere near exhaustive, of course, so I hope you will approach your travels as I've had fun in doing: with curiosity and a big appetite.

ACCESSIBILITY

Wherever possible, I've included accessibility tips for people who use wheelchairs, buggies or prams. This is marked in the text with the symbol ♿. The information isn't comprehensive (intended, rather, to give extra support where I thought it may prove useful) so if the symbol is missing, please don't assume the attraction is inaccessible.

ADDITIONAL ONLINE CONTENT

Slow travel is about getting under the skin of a place and making time for the detail of a location, whether historical, descriptive or simply anecdotal. Sadly, the economics of guidebook publishing mean that there are inevitable restrictions on what can be fitted in a book. Therefore, additional information has been entered online for those who wish to delve further into Shropshire's story. Throughout this guide you will see the symbol ♨ which signifies that there is more information on a particular subject online.

GETTING THERE & AROUND

Slow favours public transport and leg power: not only are these methods of travel kinder to the environment but they allow you to see and experience places at the right pace. I'd be misleading you if I didn't admit to zipping around by car during my research for this book, though, especially when I had my toddler in tow. But my most rewarding journeys were those spent trundling on trains, chatting to local people, weaving through villages on buses, wandering in the hills. If you can leave the car behind, at least for a portion of your trip, I doubt you will regret it.

PUBLIC TRANSPORT

An entirely car-less holiday is possible in Shropshire, but it will take some planning. A relatively large rail network will get you started: 19 National Rail stations on various lines, with direct links to London, Birmingham and mid and south Wales. Trains from Shrewsbury run to Holyhead where there are ferries to Dublin.

Several heritage lines exist too, although the **Severn Valley Railway** is the only one extensive enough to be regarded as a mode of transport as well as offering a fun outing. I've given bus routes where available under each place of interest, and you may find ∂ www.travelinemidlands.co.uk invaluable for checking times and stops. Timetables are also available in visitor information centres.

Sunday is usually a day of rest where Shropshire buses are concerned, although in summer you can catch the brilliant **Shropshire Hills Shuttle Buses** (page 22) which wend their way through some of south Shropshire's best places for eating, drinking, walking and sightseeing. Shropshire Council's extensive ∂ www.shropshiresgreatoutdoors.co.uk offers a wealth of information on all modes of travel.

Public transport, unfortunately, doesn't always work out cheaper than travelling by car, especially if you're in a group. Look for weekly/monthly and group saver fares offered by most of the bus companies and off-peak **Day Ranger** and **Heart of England 7 Day Rover** or **Flexi Rover** tickets from London Midland trains.

The car-sharing social enterprise **Co-wheels** has bases in Ludlow and Shrewsbury (∂ www.co-wheels.org.uk) so another option might be to borrow a car for just part of your trip.

WALKING

Shropshire is a wanderer's dream; you can spend hours traversing hills, forests, valleys and bogs without encountering any traffic. Sometimes you won't see another human being. Several major walking routes pass through Shropshire (including two sections of the **Offa's Dyke Path**), while the **Shropshire Way** – a huge project to link walkers' favourite routes and scenery – offers waymarked footpaths which cross the length and breadth of the county. See ⌀ www.shropshirewalking.co.uk/shropshire-way for downloadable maps and guides. I've given details of other worthwhile routes under the *Walking* heading of each chapter.

Shropshire has ten **Walkers are Welcome** towns, which means each has joined a national initiative (⌀ www.walkersarewelcome.org.uk) to ensure their locales are attractive for walking, offering information on nearby walks and keeping footpaths and signposts well maintained. You'll find many pubs and cafés bearing the Walkers are Welcome window sticker: feel confident they'll not mind your muddy boots and wet-weather gear.

As well as ⌀ www.shropshirewalking.co.uk, Shropshire Council's **LocalView** website is useful (for cyclists and horseriders as well as walkers), allowing you to overlay footpaths, bridleways, cycling routes and places of interest on to a map of Shropshire (⌀ www.shropshire.gov.uk/maps). It doesn't include the area overseen by Telford & Wrekin council.

CYCLING

Shropshire's landscape is diverse and should please every type of cyclist. From quiet lanes in the Weald Moors to downhill trails at Eastridge and Hopton Wood, cycling here is as relaxed or challenging as you want.

I've given tips on Sustrans' National Cycle Network routes and other trails under the *Cycling* heading in each chapter and listed reputable places for hiring and buying bikes and accessories or getting repairs.

Shropshire Council has been proactive in mapping out traffic-free and low-traffic journeys, often with a few historic sights and real ale pubs thrown in. You'll find free leaflets in every visitor information centre. The cycling section of its ⌀ www.shropshiresgreatoutdoors.co.uk website is valuable too – and includes a 'Sports Cycling' page for ideas on biking with added adrenaline.

The national journey planning app ⌀ www.cyclestreets.net allows you to plot out cycling routes graded 'Fastest' or 'Quietest' (or choose 'Balanced' for a sensible mixture of the two).

For social rides and to meet people who cycle in Shropshire regularly, you could contact Cycle Shropshire, the local member group of the national cycling charity CTC: ⌀ www.cycleshropshire.org.uk.

Charlotte's Tandems (⌀) offers the free lending of tandems and tag-alongs for people with disabilities and special needs who are unable to enjoy cycling on their own. Ray Hughes is the organisation's helper for Shropshire and will cheerfully help you get started on the lanes near his home in Easthope. You can contact him via ⊘ www. charlottestandems.co.uk.

HORSERIDING

> In no other way either does one get quite that sense of wild freedom, of being on top of the world, which a canter over the Longmynd [sic] or the Clun uplands can give, with the wind whistling in one's ears, and the curlews flying overhead …

Magdalene Weale, *Through the Highlands of Shropshire on Horseback* (1935)

Shropshire has changed little in landscape terms since Magdalene Weale wrote her 1930s equine travel narrative, in which she urged readers to 'Go thou and do likewise'. We have more traffic on the roads now, it's true, but on the Long Mynd and Stiperstones, or in the Onny Valley and Clun uplands, there is little to stop riders capturing that 'wild freedom' embraced by Weale. We also now have bridleways that include the **Jack Mytton Way**, **Humphrey Kynaston Way** and the **Blue Remembered Hills** trail. I've given information about routes under the *Horseriding* section of each chapter, and listed riding schools, places to hire ponies, and accommodation providers with equine facilities.

Shropshire Tourism's ⊘ www.shropshireriding.co.uk and Shropshire Council's ⊘ www.shropshiresgreatoutdoors.co.uk/horse-riding may provide further inspiration. **Natural England** offers a useful resource for finding permissive routes at ⊘ cwr.naturalengland.org.uk.

FEEDBACK REQUEST & UPDATES WEBSITE

At Bradt Travel Guides we're aware that guidebooks start to go out of date on the day they're published – and that you, our readers, are out there in the field doing research of your own. You'll find out before us when a fine new family-run hotel opens or a favourite restaurant changes hands and goes downhill. So why not write and tell us about your experiences? Contact us on ☏ 01753 893444 or ✉ info@bradtguides.com. We will forward emails to the author who may post updates on the Bradt website at ⊘ www.bradtupdates.com/shropshire. Alternatively you can add a review of the book to ⊘ www.bradtguides.com or Amazon.

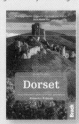

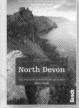
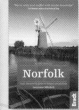

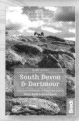
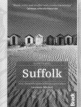

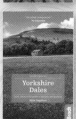

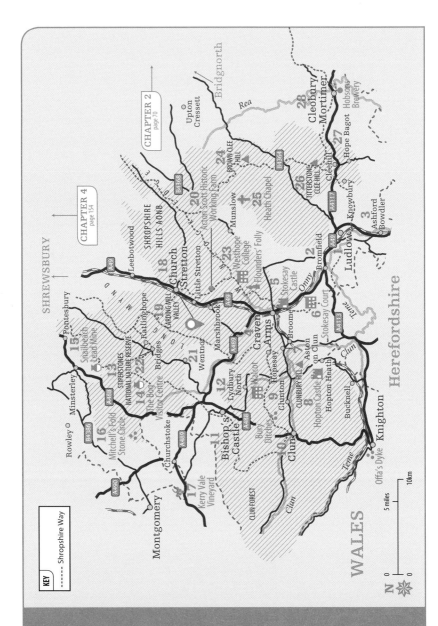

SOUTH SHROPSHIRE

1

SOUTH SHROPSHIRE

For many people, south Shropshire is the definitive Shropshire. Here are the 'blue remembered hills' of A E Housman's poetry; the country that for Mary Webb 'lies between the dimpled lands of England and the gaunt purple steeps of Wales – half in Faery and half out of it'. Much of this region is an Area of Outstanding Natural Beauty (AONB), designated in 1958 to protect and enhance the region's celebrated hills, farmland, woods, valleys and batches, richly varied geology and diverse wildlife. From this natural geography we are given walks and views and abundant opportunities for quiet contemplation. From its conservation we enjoy fresh produce from local farms and smallholdings; the chance to see birds, butterflies and plants whose numbers elsewhere have diminished in the wake of development.

And from the human lives overlaid on the countryside's natural beauty we have castles and market towns, striking black-and-white Tudor buildings, country houses with generations of intrigues. Going back earlier, we have ancient earthworks such as **Offa's Dyke,** and the 'sleeping war' with Wales, sensed by the children in Sheena Porter's 1964 Carnegie Award-winning *Nordy Bank* (named after the Iron Age hillfort on Brown Clee where they camp).

Major attractions in south Shropshire are **Ludlow**, a strikingly well-preserved hilltop town popularly known as a foodie destination, **Church Stretton**, an excellent base for exploring the Shropshire Hills and **Bishop's Castle**, home to **Britain's oldest working brewery. Clun** is a favourite too, with a ruined castle and a literary heritage that punches above the town's villagey character.

Look beyond the obvious, and you'll find a near-perfect **Norman chapel** in an 'abandoned' village, the disused workings of Europe's most productive **lead mine**, and a **late-Victorian mansion** which took a starring role in a Hollywood film.

An excellent place to start your adventure would be the **Shropshire Hills Discovery Centre** in Craven Arms, where you can make a virtual balloon ride over the AONB, a panoramic film narrated by one of Shropshire's beloved adopted sons, the late **Pete Postlethwaite** who spent his last years at Minton near Little Stretton.

When deciding where to shop, eat and drink, look for the **Shropshire Hills Sustainable Business Scheme** sticker. Businesses displaying it have pledged to take action to reduce their impact on the environment; enhance wildlife and landscape; involve local people and visitors; and support the local economy.

GETTING THERE & AROUND

South Shropshire is fairly well served by public transport, with **train** stations at Broome, Church Stretton, Craven Arms, Ludlow and – just over the Welsh border – Knighton. Church Stretton, Craven Arms and Ludlow are on the Welsh Marches line which runs from Newport in southeast Wales to Shrewsbury (sometimes continuing on to Crewe and therefore north Shropshire on the way). The Heart of Wales line intersects at Church Stretton and Craven Arms, taking passengers down to Broome (Aston on Clun), Hopton Heath and Bucknell.

There's a decent **bus** network (I've given particulars where possible under each place listing) and the Shropshire Hills Shuttle Buses run at weekends and on bank holiday Mondays from May to late September, offering two services: Castle Connect (linking Ludlow, Knighton, Clun

---

ℹ TOURIST INFORMATION

Bishop's Castle Town Hall, SY9 5BG ✆ 01588 630023 ◷ 10.00–16.00 Mon–Sat

Church Stretton Church St, SY6 6DQ ✆ 01694 723133 ⬥ www.churchstretton.co.uk ◷ Apr–Oct 09.30–17.00 & Nov–Mar 09.30–12.30 & 13.00–15.00 Mon–Sat

Craven Arms Shropshire Hills Discovery Centre, School Rd, SY7 9RS ✆ 01588 676060 ◷ 10.00–17.00 daily

Ludlow Ludlow Assembly Rooms, 1 Mill St, SY8 1AZ ✆ 01584 875053 ◷ 10.00–20.00 Mon–Sat

Stiperstones The Bog, SY5 0NG ✆ 01743 792484 ◷ Apr–end Oct 12.00–17.00 Mon, 10.00–17.00 Tue–Sun (close at 16.00 in Oct)

and Bishop's Castle) and Long Mynd & Stiperstones (connecting Church Stretton, Bridges, Stiperstones and Pontesbury). The timetables are at ⊘ www.shropshirehillsaonb.co.uk. It's worth knowing that you don't have to wait at a designated shuttle stop: hail the minibus and the driver will pull over for you.

WALKING

Spoilt for choice. That sums it up – especially if you're a hill walker. The highest are the Clee Hills: Abdon Burf on **Brown Clee** just snares the prize, but **Titterstone Clee** is significant enough to be the only hill in Britain depicted on the medieval Mappa Mundi which now hangs in Hereford Cathedral. And height's not everything: the **Stiperstones**, wreathed in mystery and legend, offers a six-mile quest along its craggy ridge, while the moonscape plateau and valleys (known locally as 'batches') of the Long Mynd await your wanderings with a variety of routes.

If you're not a confident navigator or you're heading out with children, the waymarked trails from the **Shropshire Hills Discovery Centre** or **Carding Mill Valley** may prove easy but fun starting points.

In terms of long-distance trails, the **Shropshire Way** and **Wild Edric's Way** will lead you high and low through some of south Shropshire's most beautiful valleys, hills and villages. The Clun Valley in Shropshire's far southwestern tip has some of the best-preserved sections of Offa's Dyke. I've given more information about the **Offa's Dyke Path** on page 199 but see also the 'Walking with Offa' guides produced by Shropshire Hills AONB Partnership (⊘ www.shropshirewalking.co.uk/walking-with-offa). The 18 walks and four 'days out' leaflets feature hillforts, woodland, castles and former castle sites along the Welsh–English border, with a few real ale pubs to keep you refreshed.

I've given more ideas for walks under place listings throughout this chapter – and do also visit the walking section of the Shropshire Hills AONB website ⊘ www.shropshirehillsaonb.co.uk. To plan your own explorations of the region, it may help to use ✻ OS Explorer map 217.

CYCLING

The great thing about south Shropshire for cyclists is the variety: gentle, quiet country lanes for Sunday-afternoon outings, exhilarating off-road tracks (for example at Carding Mill Valley and on the Long Mynd) and fast downhill tracks for mountain biking (including at Hopton Wood near Hopton Heath and Bringewood just west of Ludlow). The cycling section of the Shropshire Hills AONB website (www. shropshirehillsaonb.co.uk) has suggestions for all types of riders.

Ray Hughes, a keen cyclist and Active Travel and Road Safety Officer for Shropshire Council, recommends for novices the **short, quiet route** from Dinham Bridge in Ludlow to Ludlow Food Centre at Bromfield along Halton Lane, passing through Oakly Park and under the subway to cross the A49. 'We've even taken little ones on balance bikes on this route,' he said. A circular extension is the seven-mile **Lady Halton Loop,** returning to Ludlow Castle on the side of the Mortimer Forest (leaflet available to download from www.shropshiresgreatoutdoors.co.uk). Very new cyclists and people with accessibility needs could try the **inclusive track** at Shropshire Hills Discovery Centre.

The first **Ludlow Cycling Festival** took place in 2014, raising money for Macmillan Cancer Support, and looks set to become an annual event (see www.ludlowcc.org.uk).

 ## BIKE HIRE

Shropshire Hills Mountain Bike and Outdoor Pursuit Centre (MTB Shropshire)
Marshbrook nr Church Stretton SY6 6QE 01694 781515 www.mtb-shropshire.co.uk. This is a huge operation: four acres' worth, in fact. As well as hiring out a fleet of Scott bikes and supplying trail maps (even a guide, if you'd like one), the people behind MTB Shropshire have their own pub, the **Station Inn**, where the beer line-up includes Woods Blazing Bikes Trailblazer. Marshbrook is just minutes away from some excellent downhill courses, in the form of Minton Batch and Pole Bank on the Long Mynd. The site also has a campsite and camping pods.

Wheely Wonderful Cycling Petchfield Farm, Ludlow SY8 2HJ 01568 770755 www.wheelywonderfulcycling.co.uk. The ever-helpful Chris and Kay Dartnell provide everything you need for a perfect day's cycling, including bike and tandem hire; hire of children's bikes, trailer bikes, seats and helmets; route guides and maps. They also organise cycling holidays, for which they've won an Excellence in Tourism award from Enjoy England.

New Street Cycles New St, Bishop's Castle SY9 5DQ 01588 638060. This friendly shop stocks bikes, electric bikes, parts and accessories, and carries out repairs. It's an ideal place to hire a pedal bike (adult size only), helmet and puncture-repair kit and then head for the countryside around Bishop's Castle or alternatively the Clun Valley. For e-bike riders: meet at New Street Cycles from 18.00 on Tuesdays in summer for a 10–15 mile group ride.

BIKE SALES & REPAIRS

Blazing Bikes Marshbrook, near Church Stretton SY6 6QE ✆ 01694 781515 ⌨ www.blazingbikes.co.uk. Part of MTB Shropshire (see above), Blazing Bikes sells mountain and road bikes and accessories.

Epic Cycles Weeping Cross Lane, Temeside, Ludlow SY8 1PA ✆ 01584 879245 ⌨ www.epic-cycles.co.uk. More than 12,500 square feet of shop space devoted to bikes, from sportive and road racing bikes to commuting and cross bikes. Free sizing and set-up sessions.

Go Cycling Shropshire ✆ 07950 397335 ⌨ www.gocycling-shropshire.com. Church Stretton-based mobile bike mechanic Will Baugh offers a collection and drop-off service in South and mid Shropshire, with no call-out fee.

Islabikes Ltd Bromfield SY8 2JR ✆ 01584 856881 ⌨ www.islabikes.co.uk. One of the top manufacturers of children's bikes just happens to be based in south Shropshire. Fittings by appointment only (and bikes are custom made so not available to take away immediately).

Pearce Cycles Fishmore Rd, Ludlow SY8 3DP ✆ 01584 879288 ⌨ www.pearcecycles.co.uk. For bikes, accessories and full servicing facilities (book in advance if possible). Big on mountain biking, the team runs uplift days and downhill events. The Pearce XC trail at Hopton Wood (page 42) was built in partnership with Pearce Cycles.

Plush Hill Cycles 8 The Square, Church Stretton SY6 6DA ✆ 01694 720133 ◷ closed Wed. For new bikes, accessories and repairs; plus bike hire and training on the Long Mynd.

HORSERIDING

South Shropshire is the richest region in Shropshire for waymarked bridleways. The **Jack Mytton Way**, celebrating a rakish county squire (page 218), focuses on the Clee Hills and Wenlock Edge in the east, with the final two sections heading towards Clun and the Offa's Dyke Path. The Clun Forest in the southwest of the county is where you'll find the 38-mile circular **Blue Remembered Hills** trail (also suitable for walkers and cyclists). You can ride on the Long Mynd from Carding Mill Valley (page 60) or head up to the Stiperstones on horseback. You'll find more inspiration at ⌨ www.shropshireriding.co.uk.

HORSE HIRE & RIDING LESSONS

Long Mountain Centre Rowley, Pleasant View SY5 9RY ✆ 01743 891274. Organises riding lessons, hacks, pony camps, bridleway riding and riding holidays. The eco-friendly centre has two-bedroom log cabins and can accommodate your horse on site (non-riders are also welcome).

North Farm Riding North Farm Riding, Whitcliffe, Ludlow SY8 2HD ✆ 01584 872026. A riding school owned by the same people since 1968. Riding instruction takes place in the Mortimer Forest straddling the Herefordshire border. ♿ Caters for riders with disabilities.

WET-WEATHER ACTIVITIES

Land of Lost Content (page 37)
Parish Church of St Laurence, Ludlow (page 31)
Shropshire Hills Discovery Centre (page 37)

LUDLOW & BROMFIELD

Ludlow is arguably the UK's Slow Food capital and known as a gastronomic destination, at one time holding three Michelin stars, the greatest number per capita in Europe. As Shropshire historian Keith Pybus points out in *Blue Remembered Hills*, Ludlow's foodie reputation makes it 'a brand-name capable of extension into the hills and down the A49'. That's why we're able to have the Ludlow Food Centre in Bromfield, over two miles away.

The Birmingham artist H Thornhill Timmins described Ludlow's surroundings as being 'full of the charm of secluded, rural beauty; while rustic villages and smiling homesteads are to be met with on every hand'. His book *Nooks and Corners of Shropshire* was published more than a hundred years ago but, so unspoilt is this quiet countryside by the River Teme, it's as though he speaks as our contemporary.

1 LUDLOW

🏠 **The Bindery Flat** (page 247), **Castle House Apartments** (page 247), **Charlton Arms** (page 247), **Fishmore Hall** (page 247), **Redford Farm Barns** (page 248)

> And who that lists to walk the Towne about
> Shall find therein some rare and pleasant things.
> Thomas Churchyard (1581)

It was Ludlow that first inspired me to write this book. Thomas Churchyard is one of many writers who have praised its elegance (Sir John Betjeman in 1951 described it as 'probably the loveliest town in England', while Henry James in 1884 imagined it a place where 'Miss Burney's and Miss Austen's heroines might perfectly well have had their first love affair'). And indeed Ludlow is picturesque, with a majestic church, castle ruins, rivers and bridges and around 500 listed buildings. This is an affluent town, founded on wool and cloth, which was by the 16th century a major administrative centre governing Wales and Shropshire's border counties. Some of its medieval defensive walls remain and one of its seven gateways (Broad Gate on Silk Mill Lane) is complete with drum towers and portcullis arch. Naturally, handsome inns and well-to-do houses grew up here too. The Jacobean Feathers Hotel on Bull Ring, the very model of a black-and-white timbered coaching inn, is one of the most photographed hotels in England.

But the beauty of Ludlow runs deeper than stone, water and history. Today many people make concerted efforts to protect and nurture what makes this market town unique, in order to improve the quality of life in Ludlow and beyond. Ludlow was the UK's first Cittaslow town, an accreditation stemming from the Slow Food movement, which recognises the community's commitment to making its place in the world 'healthier, greener, happier, slower'. Ludlow is no longer a Cittaslow member (I have never unknotted the local politics behind this) but what remains is an enduring communal belief that supporting local suppliers, artisan producers and traditional skills is the key to a thriving town.

"The beauty of Ludlow runs deeper than stone, water and history."

Ludlow station is half a mile northwest of the town centre, on Station Drive. It's on the Welsh Marches line between Shrewsbury and Hereford and offers decent connections from Manchester, Cardiff, Chester and the North Wales coast. One to two trains run every hour in each direction from Monday to Saturday.

There are several options for **buses**. You can catch the 2L Diamond Bus service from Kidderminster which travels via Cleobury Mortimer (page 68): don't miss the view over the Malvern Hills in Worcestershire as you travel through Cleehill village and its sheep-grazing common. The Minsterley Motors service 435 travels from Shrewsbury on Saturdays only. From the west, the 738 and 740 Arriva bus services bring you into Ludlow from Knighton, travelling via Bromfield. On weekends and bank holidays from May to the end of September, you can catch the Castle Connect shuttle bus (see *Getting there & around* on page 22). If you're driving it's worth knowing about the cheap and frequent **park and ride** scheme from Ludlow Eco Business Park just off the A49 (use SY8 1ES or follow signs from the main approaches into Ludlow), which will drop you off by Ludlow Assembly Rooms. Once you arrive, you'll find Ludlow to be a compact town, ideal for exploring on foot.

♿ An excellent **accessibility guide** to shops, services and places of interest can be downloaded from ⬡ www.ludlow.org.uk/access.

Museums, tours & Ludlow visitor centre

By the time you read this, Ludlow should have a new town museum in **The Buttercross**, the honey-coloured, open arcaded building (designed by local architect William Baker, c1746) straddling Broad Street, King Street and High Street.

CELEBRATING LOCAL FOOD

Established in 1995, the **Ludlow Food Festival** (⌗ www.foodfestival.co.uk) in September was the UK's first food festival and is still perhaps the most famous. It was originally set up in response to the building of a supermarket on the outskirts of town, understandably taken as a threat to Ludlow's independent shops and producers. 'The local Chamber of Commerce couldn't fight the supermarket development so a group of us looked instead for a way to showcase everything great about our region's food and drink,' one of the founders, Phil Maile, told me. 'No big companies are allowed in, and everything seen at the festival comes from Ludlow and the Marches.' The festival is centred on the grounds of Ludlow Castle where revellers can sample treats and enjoy more substantial dishes from producers, restaurants, farms and smallholdings from the region, listen to live music and watch demonstrations from celebrated chefs. Trails take visitors into shops and pubs around Ludlow, in search of the best sausages, artisan bread and real ale. Look out for Slow Food workshops, organised by **Slow Food Ludlow** (⌗ www.slowfoodludlow.org.uk). If you're arriving by car, take advantage of the festival park and ride service: simply follow signs on your approach to the town. Ludlow gets very busy that weekend, with hotels and B&Bs fully booked months in advance.

An offshoot of the September celebration, the **Spring Festival** in May (⌗ www.ludlowspringfestival.co.uk) is described accurately as a 'beer festival but better'. It runs in tandem with the former Marches Transport Festival, ensuring a brilliant display of vintage and classic cars in the castle grounds. August sees the annual (⌗ www.greenfestival.co.uk) and the exciting **Ludlow Magnalonga** (page 30).

For Christmassy beer, cheer and feisty battle re-enactments, look out for the **Medieval Christmas Fayre** (⌗ www.ludlowmedievalchristmas.co.uk), which is held in the last weekend of November.

At any time of year, you can enjoy the fruits of this region's farms and hills and support local businesses by shopping at Ludlow's **markets**: one takes place in Castle Square on most days except Tuesday. General markets are on Monday, Wednesday, Friday and Saturday. Ludlow Local Produce market is on the second and fourth Thursday of the month, showcasing food and drink produced within 30 miles of the town (⌗ www.localtoludlow.org.uk). Antique and flea markets are every first and third Sunday. Other craft, local food and antique markets are held on the days in between.

The splendid Victorian building on the corner of Mill Street is **Ludlow Assembly Rooms** (✆ 01584 878141 ⌑ www.ludlowassemblyrooms. co.uk). The 1840 building was modernised and reopened in 1993, incorporating a cinema, theatre, café and plenty of space for community events. **Ludlow's visitor information centre** is on the third floor.

For a lively introduction to the history and architecture of the town you can join a **guided tour** on Saturdays, Sundays and bank holidays, generally from April to November. Meet at the cannon outside the castle at 14.30; tours last approximately 90 minutes.

Two ways to tap into Ludlow's current happenings are via ⌑ www.theludlowguide.co.uk and the *Ludlow Ledger*, a good-humoured, high-quality independent free newspaper available from various venues around town. And for a rare peep into Ludlow's private terraces, flowerbeds, orchards, borders and lawns, try the **Ludlow Secret Gardens** weekend in June; it's been a staple in the town's summer calendar since 1990. Tickets are usually available from the Assembly Rooms.

Ludlow Castle
✆ 01584 873355 ⌑ www.ludlowcastle.com ⌚ daily (except Jan to mid-Feb when it's w/ends only); dogs allowed on leads

Daniel Defoe, writing in 1772 on his *Tour of Great Britain,* described the ruins of Ludlow Castle as the 'very perfection of decay'. This Norman castle and fortified royal palace does indeed make for romantic ruins: the outer bailey embraces almost four acres, while the inner bailey, protected by a thick curtain wall, includes four flanking towers and the surviving circular nave of the chapel of St Mary Magdalene. On a quiet day you won't have to work your imagination too hard to populate the courtyards with people, relight the fireplaces, and hang the chambers with bright tapestries. For children there are stone steps to scale, pillars to ambush from, and wooden swords and shields available in the gift shop.

The information boards dotted around the castle grounds focus mainly on architecture and masonry, largely ignoring the colourful stories that the walls themselves hold. Ludlow Castle began life in the late 11th century as the border stronghold of marcher lord Roger de Lacy and was enlarged by Roger Mortimer in the 14th century, becoming a magnificent palace. The walls withstood the War of the Roses, embraced the two sons of Edward IV (before history consigned them to be known forever as the Princes in the Tower) and to this day keep the secrets of the honeymoon of 15-year-old Prince Arthur and his bride, Catherine of Aragon. Mary Tudor, who would later be Queen of England, spent three winters at Ludlow Castle, while in 1634 it provided the stage for the earliest performance of John Milton's court masque *Comus.*

LUDLOW MAGNALONGA

Hugh Collins

Marie believes, as maybe you do, that a perfect Sunday involves a long walk followed by lunch and a pint in a country pub. The combination of leg-stretching exercise, an amble through Britain's countryside and a traditional meal, can't be beaten. Can it?

That's what I thought too, at least before visiting Ludlow for its annual Magnalonga event. An idea copied from Ludlow's twinned city – and Slow Food capital – San Pietro, the Magnalonga is an annual walk through the Shropshire countryside where, at a number of refreshment stops *en route,* you are treated to food and drink from local producers. Rather than simply the welcome nourishment at the end of a country walk, the Magnalonga integrates local food so that it becomes part of the journey too.

Beginning in the shadow of Ludlow Castle with a bottle of water and crumbly chocolate biscuit, the eight-mile route wound slowly up from the town into the Shropshire Hills. At the first stop, perched on hay bales with chickens pecking at my feet, I tucked into a soft Scotch egg from The Handmade Scotch Egg Company and fortified myself for the miles ahead with half a pint of ale from the town's Ludlow Brewing Co.

Three miles or so later, after a lung-bursting climb and regrets over eating my Scotch egg quite so quickly, the walk's 'main course' was a delicious pork, cider and turnip stew accompanied by local cider. Sitting on the grassy lawn and shaded by one of the many apple trees, it made for the perfect pastoral picnic, connecting you and your food to the landscape in which it was produced.

As the walk continued so did the food and drink, and at a rather staggering rate. A raspberry and chocolate brownie, salted caramel ice cream, a cheese board and, with a nod to Shropshire's westerly border, a Welsh cake, followed in quick succession.

Refreshed with an elderflower liqueur cocktail and a perry from Oliver's in Herefordshire, I became glad that the final stretch to the finish was all downhill. I was full enough that I could have rolled down it.

Ludlow is lucky to have so many people committed to promoting the region's local, seasonal and traditional food, including the Slow Food Ludlow group. The terrific and unusual Magnalonga gives you the chance to support the area's local producers, and I guarantee by the end, you'll certainly be Slow too.

The Magnalonga is organised by the Ludlow Food Festival team – tickets for the 2016 walk will go on sale from June 2016. For more information, visit ℰ www.magnalonga.co.uk.

To learn more about the social history of the castle and its inhabitants you can hire an audio guide from the ticket desk or buy the excellent glossy guide written by historian and Ludlovian David Lloyd MBE. A children's guide is available too. The grounds can get muddy so bring wellies or waterproof shoes during wet spells. **Castle Tea Room**, with its warm glazed courtyard and garden terrace, is run separately, so you can visit for a cuppa without going into the castle grounds.

Castle Lodge (Castle Sq ⊙ daily; just turn up and knock on the door) is a Tudor mansion to the left of the castle entrance (not affiliated with the castle itself), with exquisite carved oak panelling from floor to ceiling on the ground floor, said to have come from a lost Surrey palace built by Henry VIII. The rest of the house feels bare and sad, though. For a few pounds you'll be admitted by owner Bill Pearson and allowed to wander freely, but it won't take long because the rooms are largely unfurnished and no interpretive information exists.

The Parish Church of St Laurence
College St ⊙ daily; Sun services at 08.00, 09.30, 11.30 & 15.30

Tucked away behind Ludlow's thoroughfares, St Laurence's is often referred to as the 'Cathedral of the Marches', a soubriquet acknowledged by Simon Jenkins in *England's Thousand Best Churches* in which he awards Ludlow's parish church five stars. For good reason: this mainly 15th-century masterpiece, built by wealthy cloth merchants, is packed from nave to chancel with treasures and topped with a 135-foot tower which, for £3 and a 200-step circular climb, turns Ludlow into a living model village and you its giant witness.

Amid the awe-inspiring perpendicular architecture, illuminated by light shining through a wealth of stained glass, you will find monuments, effigies, a thousand-year-old font (rescued from a degrading stint as a watering trough) and 28 misericords with intricate carvings conveying 15th-century concerns and cautionary tales. In the north side choir stalls, look for the ass in preacher's clothing, and the dishonest alewife being flung into the gaping maw of Hell.

Prince Arthur's heart is interred somewhere in the chancel (with 'heart' probably a euphemism for entrails): he died aged 15 in 1502 of a sweating sickness while in Ludlow with his bride Catherine of Aragon. A two-day funeral service was held here, after which the young prince's body was carried in procession to Worcester Cathedral.

A memorial plaque to **A E Housman** (page 40) is fixed to the north wall of the exterior of the church and his ashes are interred nearby. The poet made many references to this region in *A Shropshire Lad* and evoked the church in particular in 'The Recruit':

Or come you home of Monday
When Ludlow market hums
And Ludlow chimes are playing
'The conquering hero comes'.

Ludlow market does indeed still hum (in a good way) on Monday (and most other days: see page 28) and the church's modern carillon, electronically controlled, plays 'See the Conquering Hero' on Monday at 08.00, 12.00, 16.00 and 20.00. There are different chimes for the other days of the week.

The striking black-and-white **Reader's House** on Church Walk just outside dates to the 1300s and has been a grammar school, private museum and residence of assistant clergy, known as the reader.

Whitcliffe Common

Cross the river via Dinham Bridge behind Ludlow Castle and you'll find yourself with 52 tranquil acres of Whitcliffe Common to explore – the remains of a much larger medieval common used for gathering hay, firewood, brushwood and stone, and for grazing livestock. Like the rest of geologically blessed Shropshire, Whitcliffe's story is millions of years older, having once lain under a shallow tropical sea.

If your visit falls in autumn, you may see migrating salmon leaping upstream over the weirs of Mill Street and Dinham Mill. You might spot dippers, grey wagtails or kingfishers in the river too, alongside the occasional wild swimmer.

It was in 1800 from this woodland, rich with hornbeam and fern on banks rising steeply from the River Teme, that the watercolour landscape artist William Turner took his view of Ludlow Castle. The upper woodland edge is now stitched with memorial benches to local people; a peaceful, shaded place to remember or be remembered.

You'll find several routes through Whitcliffe Common, outlined on interpretive boards. My favourite is the riverside **Breadwalk** to Ludford Bridge, so called because the labourers hired to lay out the path in the 1850s were paid (at least in part) in bread rather than coins to ensure their families benefited, and not the nearby hostelries. You can also pick up the **Mortimer Trail** through the woods, a 30-mile waymarked footpath running from Ludlow to Kington in Herefordshire.

SHOPPING

Look for **Only in Ludlow** shop window stickers for a taste of the truly independent. If you're self-catering or sourcing a picnic, visit **DW Wall & Son** butchers (14 High St), **Harp Lane Deli** (4 Church St), **The Mousetrap Cheese Shop** (6 Church St) and **Price's** bakery (7 Castle St) for delicious local food. I could list a dozen more shops but for want of space; I hope these four will lead you to your own favourites.

The Bindery Shop 5 Bull Ring ✆ 01584 876003 ⌂ www.thebinderyshop.co.uk. Old-fashioned hand-printed letterpress cards and posters, hand-bound diaries and notebooks, gorgeous printed wrapping paper and bookbinding kits.

Dinham House Dinham (just behind the castle) ✆ 01584 878100 ☺ closed Thu & Sun. Housing the aspirational showrooms for Clearview Stoves, Dinham House is worth visiting for the building alone, the largest Georgian house in Ludlow. Distinguished former residents include Lucien Bonaparte, brother of Napoleon, who stayed here for six months in 1811 as a prisoner on parole.

Myriad Organics 22 Corve St ✆ 01584 872665. A long-established organic vegetable and grocery store which aims to make organic products affordable and accessible to everyone. Sharing its shop (and its sustainable ethos) is the Rural Skills Centre, displaying and selling locally made wool-related products plus tools and yarn.

Silk Top Hat Gallery 4 Quality Sq ✆ 01584 875363. As you wander towards Castle Square from Bull Ring it's easy to miss Quality Square, accessed through an alleyway on your right. Some of the brickwork in this handsome courtyard dates to the late 16th century. Silk Top Hat Gallery houses two floors of original art plus a ground-floor shop selling unusual gifts and artists' materials.

FOOD & DRINK

Charlton Arms Ludford Bridge ✆ 01584 872813. A warmly welcoming pub on the medieval Ludford Bridge and a great place for a Sunday roast, with all meat sourced from Shropshire and the Welsh Marches. Also offers B&B accommodation, with nine en-suite rooms.

Cicchetti 10 Broad St ✆ 07890 412873 ☺ 08.00–18.00 Mon–Thu, 08.00–20.00 Fri, 10.00–16.00 Sun. This tiny deli, bar and restaurant pays homage to the Venetian *bàcaro*, a cosy, cave-like establishment you'd be chuffed to stumble across on a chic Italian city break. The vibe is stylishly informal: menus are scribbled on brown paper bags and there's a refectory-style dining table at the back as well as intimate tables for two alongside the deli counter. Pronounced *chi-ket-ti*, Cicchetti refers to the delicious, bite-size pieces of food you can sample, in this case much of which is sourced from owner/chef Martyn Emsen's other business, Ludlow Traditional Smokehouse. Try the tapas-style 'Aperitivo' on Friday evenings.

Fishmore Hall Fishmore Rd, SY8 3DP (about a mile outside Ludlow off the A49) ✆ 01584 875148. In Forelles, Fishmore Hall's restaurant – with its vista of green fields to the Clee Hills – head chef Andrew Birch serves imaginative fine-dining dishes using ingredients sourced from within 30 miles of Ludlow (with the exception of seafood which comes from Brixham and the Isle of Skye). Try the tasting menu for maximum excitement (and value). Fishmore is also a hotel, with every room individually styled.

The French Pantry 15 Tower St ✆ 01584 879133. Like Cicchetti, this épicerie, café and bistro is one of those special little places I'd secretly like to keep to myself – but it's too good not to share. Authentic French cooking and excellent value for money.

The Green Café Linney, Mill on the Green (a couple of minutes' walk downhill from behind the castle) ✆ 01584 879872. Oh, to be seated on The Green Café's Teme-side patio on a sunny afternoon, sipping homemade strawberry and rhubarb cordial and looking forward to lunch. This tiny, lovely place has a stellar list of local suppliers, unusual and frequently changing menu (one summer saw saltbeef in sourdough, gently spiced dhal, gnocchi with pork) and a friendly outlook. It's licensed, using only independent, family-run vineyards and sourcing beer, cider and perry from within 30 miles of Ludlow. If you find yourself wolfing down the boca negra as fast as I invariably do, you can always walk off a few calories in nearby Whitcliffe Common. Booking strongly advised.

Ludlow Brewing Co. The Railway Shed, Station Drive ✆ 01584 873291 ⬙ www. theludlowbrewingcompany.co.uk. Located in a converted Victorian railway shed near Ludlow's train station, Ludlow Brewing Co. produces five excellent beers, with eco-friendly methods that include reclaiming heat during the brewing process. The brewery has a bar and visitor centre with info on former railway lines in the area (at which I can't help but sigh and wish they were still open). Tours are available to book in advance. You can also get your chops around a Scotch egg or pork pie made by local butcher Andrew Francis.

Mortimers 17 Corve St ✆ 01584 872325. Ludlow has high hopes for Mortimers, located in the former premises of Michelin-starred La Bécasse. It opened in late 2015, not long before another bright light of the town's fine-dining scene, Mr Underhill's, closed forever. Head chef Wayne Smith is tipped to fill the void with impeccable British/French cuisine.

The Olive Branch 2/4 Old St ✆ 01584 874314. Established in the 1960s and famous for big, oven-baked scones and creative veggie, vegan and gluten-free options, The Olive Branch is deserving of its longevity. Don't be fooled into thinking this is a vegetarian place, though: the sausages are delicious – and local, of course (from DW Wall & Son). It's licensed too. Bill Bryson endowed The Olive Branch with literary fame in *Notes From A Small Island*, referring to it as a 'pleasant little salad bar'.

2 BROMFIELD

🏠 **Bromfield Priory Gatehouse** (page 247), **The Clive** (page 247)

Two miles north of Ludlow (that's if you walk, partly following the Shropshire Way from the Dinham Bridge end of town) is Bromfield, which H Thornhill Timmins in 1899 called 'as picturesque a spot as one could wish to see, situated in a pleasant, fertile vale, close to the place where Onny and Teme unite'.

The 435 bus from Shrewsbury to Ludlow stops outside The Clive in Bromfield, as do the 738 and 740 Knighton to Ludlow services. In summer, Bromfield is a stop on the Castle Connect service (page 22).

Ludlow Food Centre

SY8 2JR ✆ 01584 856000 🖉 www.ludlowfoodcentre.co.uk

You can't miss Ludlow Food Centre as you pass through Bromfield on the A49. Located on the Earl of Plymouth's Oakly Park Estate, it's a dream of a farm shop, employing dozens of talented people, preserving artisan skills and sourcing 80% of its stock from Shropshire and surrounding counties. Food mileage barely applies in some cases: the beef, lamb and Gloucester Old Spot pork originate at Oakly Park itself, while eight production kitchens host bakers, cheesemakers, butchers and chefs whom you can see at work. Occasionally you can buy fruits and vegetables grown in Lady Windsor's walled garden, less than a mile away.

To sample the delicacies on offer before you've even gone home, **Ludlow Kitchen** just over the car park is a café almost exclusively supplied by the production kitchens: think handmade savoury tarts, burgers made from estate-reared beef, seasonal veg, handcut fries and locally brewed beer. The site is also home to a village shop and post office, The Clive restaurant with rooms and an independent plant centre.

It's worth crossing the road to see the village church of **St Mary the Virgin**. Aside from being a handsome grade I-listed building, which started life as a Benedictine Priory, the church boasts a plaster chancel ceiling, painted in 1672, depicting clouds, angels and ribbons of text. It is much quoted as being 'the best specimen of the worst period of ecclesiastical art', although I haven't been able to find the originator of that line. Nay matter: to put it even less kindly, you will be hard pushed to find uglier cherubs anywhere in Shropshire, possibly even Britain.

Henry Hickman, a pioneer of anaesthetic, although not recognised in his lifetime, was baptised at St Mary's in 1800.

3 ASHFORD BOWDLER

🏠 **Orchard House** (page 246)

Three miles south of Ludlow on the A49, the **Farm Shop** (SY8 4AQ ✆ 01584 831232) at Ashford Bowdler is a rewarding place to stop, with tea, coffee and cakes, vintage goods, upcycled furniture and other trinkets. The produce and rare-breed pork for sale are raised on the site.

CRAVEN ARMS TO THE CLUN VALLEY

> Clunton and Clunbury
> Clungunford and Clun
> Are the quietest places
> Under the sun.
> From A E Housman's *A Shropshire Lad* (1896)

Naturally Salopians over the years have inserted alternative superlative adjectives in place of 'quietest' – sometimes rude ones. This most southerly patch of southwest Shropshire, close to the Herefordshire and Powys borders, *is* quiet, however, and you'll find many places to stop, catch your breath and drink in the views. On **Clunbury Hill**, for example, you can look east to the Clee Hills across the valleys of Clun, Onny and Teme.

4 CRAVEN ARMS

The name of this modern-for-Shropshire market town comes from the 17th-century inn on Shrewsbury Road which in turn honours the Earl of Craven who owned nearby Stokesay Castle. It grew up in the age of railway, after the Shrewsbury & Hereford Railway Company built a line from the north in 1852. The **station** is still operational, on the junction between the Heart of Wales and Welsh Marches lines, giving us convenient access from Shrewsbury, Swansea, Hereford and Cardiff.

While Craven Arms is not the prettiest place, somewhat linear and dominated by Tuffins supermarket and a petrol station, it's far more than a pub, with a couple of special places to visit. The main bus service number 435 connects Craven Arms with Ludlow, Church Stretton and Shrewsbury. The town is also served by Castle Connect (see page 22).

Land of Lost Content

Market St ✆ 01588 676176 ⌖ www.lolc.org.uk ⊙ daily except Wed, closed in Dec & Jan

There are two things about the Land of Lost Content museum of British popular culture that I find moving. Firstly, the floor-to-ceiling memorabilia from ordinary British life over the past 100 years is a wistful reminder that time ticks on. Distilled in a broken doll; a packet for a discontinued sweet; the mocked-up trousseaus of pre- and post-war brides (seemingly filled with equal parts hope and nylon) is the powerful sense that the world changes, tastes change, children grow out of their toys, grow up and grow old. Curator Stella Mitchell borrowed the museum's name from A E Housman's elegy to the past. Secondly, it's Stella's passion. She and her husband Dave have built the collection from scratch without funding, and kept the museum going on 'a web of shoestrings'. I love Stella's handwritten museum notes which manage to be simultaneously literary, reflective and cynical. A music licence means your journey through the decades always has an appropriate soundtrack.

ICONS café on the mezzanine floor is run independently, so you can access it separately free of charge. It's almost as crammed with nostalgic goodness as the rest of the building and worth visiting for a bargain-price cuppa and homemade cake.

Shropshire Hills Discovery Centre

School Rd, SY7 9RS ✆ 01588 676060 ⌖ www.shropshirehillsdiscoverycentre.co.uk ⊙ daily; free entry, parking & Wi-Fi ♿ fully accessible for visitors using wheelchairs; inclusive cycle trail for specialist adaptive cycles

A hop and a skip from the high street, accessible from the A49, Shropshire Hills Discovery Centre is an excellent starting point for exploring south Shropshire. Run by social enterprise **Grow Cook Learn**, the quirky grass-roofed centre incorporates visitor information, a gift shop, gallery space, activity rooms, and comfy seating. The **licensed café** serves cooked-from-scratch lunches made wherever possible from Shropshire-sourced ingredients.

While admission to the main centre is free, the **Secret Hills Exhibition** commands a small charge and offers an engaging overview of the geology, ecology, history and people of this special part of the world. Exhibition highlights include a full-size replica of the mammoth skeleton discovered near Condover, and a panoramic film taking the form of a hot-air balloon ride over the hills. The commentary for the

FLOUNDERS' FOLLY

A waymarked walk you can take from Shropshire Hills Discovery Centre is to Flounders' Folly on Callow Hill. This stone tower was built in 1838 by an industrial entrepreneur from Yorkshire named Benjamin Flounders. Standing 80 feet high the folly is visible for miles around – particularly from the A49 between Church Stretton and Craven Arms. No-one is sure of Flounders's intention in commissioning the folly. Some say he wished to create work for unemployed labourers, while others subscribe to the rather farfetched notion that he wanted a viewpoint for his ships on the Mersey and the Bristol Channel. The folly was built in the year of Flounders's 70th birthday, however; I like the idea that he was celebrating by leaving a mark on the Shropshire landscape.

In the folly's heyday people could climb to the viewing platform on the castellated top via a wooden staircase. But around the time of World War II it began falling into disrepair. The land changed hands several times (the film star Julie Christie, who had a house nearby, was an owner for a while) and by the late 1980s it was deemed unsafe. The stones from the top were placed on the ground and Flounders' Folly was fenced off. In 2001 The Flounders Folly Trust bought the freehold of the tower and the land it stands on for £1 and secured funds to restore it.

On days when the St George's flag is flying, the folly is open from 11.00 to 15.00, giving you the opportunity to ascend the 78 stairs for a 360-degree view over south Shropshire and beyond.

latter was recorded by the late Oscar-winning actor Pete Postlethwaite, whose wish for the virtual balloon ride was 'May it soar forever'.

The centre is a gateway to **30 acres of meadowland** around the River Onny, offering gentle and level surface conditions for walking and playing. There are **four waymarked trails** of varying length and difficulty, taking you into the surrounding countryside, and countless other walks (with leaflets available to buy in the shop). It's always worth looking up forthcoming events on the website – you'll often find activities geared towards even the youngest visitors, from marshmallow toasting to den building.

Craven Arms' farmers' market takes place in the car park on the first Saturday of every month, from 09.00 to 13.30.

FOOD & DRINK

Shropshire Hills Discovery Centre café School Rd ✆ 01588 676060 ⊙ during centre hours; main lunch service ends at 14.00. If only all visitors' centres could take a leaf out of the Shropshire Hills Discovery Centre's canteen-style café, where most food is made on site (produce will soon be grown here too). Three different hot meals are always on offer, such as creamy fish pie, warming bean casserole or jacket potatoes baked properly in the oven. It's licensed, in case you fancy a glass of wine or locally brewed beer. Sundays are a special occasion when the café brings out linen, napkins and crystal for a roast lunch: book ahead.

Stokesay Inn School Rd ✐ 01588 672304. This former coaching inn with eye-catching stained-glass windows is a family-run pub serving simple but good and reasonably priced homemade food, with local veggies (often 'picked at 9 and in the pot for lunch') and meat including the famous Ludlow Sausage from DW Wall & Son.

The Plough Wistanstow SY7 8DG ✐ 01588 673251 ⊝ closed Tue. A mile north of Craven Arms is the village of Wistanstow, home of **Woods Brewery** which makes traditionally brewed beers including perennial favourite A Shropshire Lad. Next door is its tap house, the Plough, with a sun-filled dining room that's perfect for a relaxing pub grub lunch (fish and chips, roast dinner, steaks), all homemade from local ingredients.

5 STOKESAY CASTLE

🏠 **Castle View B&B** (page 246)

SY7 9AL ✐ 01588 672544 ⊝ summer 10.00–18.00 daily; winter 10.00–16.00 w/ends only; admission fee includes free audio guide (with hearing loop); parking £1 ♿ accessible toilet & hard core path from car park; be aware there are many steps around the site; Minsterley Motors' 435 service is the closest bus route; English Heritage

'Castle' is a misnomer here since Stokesay is actually a fortified medieval manor house, albeit the best preserved and probably most magnificent example of its kind of England, having never been remodelled – only conserved – by later generations. It's largely unfurnished and small in scale so you won't need hours to view it, but the castle has the power to capture imaginations and its setting is stunning. Stokesay village is less than a mile south of Craven Arms in the valley of the River Onny and cradled by wooded slopes.

The castle was built in the late 13th century by a wool merchant, Laurence of Ludlow, one of the wealthiest men in England. Its fortified appearance wasn't merely for show: while it couldn't have withstood a serious attack, Laurence had riches that needed protecting. Thanks to this Stokesay Castle has a moat (now dry and perfect for a toddler-friendly scamper). Other notable features include a cavernous hall with cruck-timbered roof. The gatehouse featured on the cover of this guide was built by Lord Craven in 1640–41, and is similar in design to many Ludlow houses of its era. The **tea room** (cash only; open to paying visitors only) serves soup, toasties, cake, tea and good coffee.

A SHROPSHIRE LAD?

You'll find references to the poet A E Housman (1859-1936) and his work all over Shropshire. Indeed, I've scattered extracts from his poems throughout this book. Wistful and beautiful, they're not only evocative of the Shropshire Hills and wider English countryside, but convey many human truths – underpinned by a nagging reminder of mortality.

However, the 'Shropshire Lad' who earned his nickname from his most famous cycle of poems wasn't a Shropshire lad at all. Alfred Edward Housman was born in Bromsgrove and wrote most of the volume in London. Rather than reflecting a profound knowledge of the county, Housman's Shropshire is a mindscape, a distant recollection of 'moonlit heath and lonesome bank' fused with immediate emotions.

Critics sometimes point to the lines 'The vane on Hughley steeple / Veers bright, a far-known sign' as evidence of this, for the church of St John the Baptist at Hughley doesn't have, and never did have, a steeple. Housman later wrote in a letter:

> I am Worcestershire by birth: Shropshire was our western horizon, which made me feel romantic about it. I do not know the county well, except in parts, and some of my topographical details are wrong and imaginary.

But for the tiny mistakes he made, Housman is easily forgiven. Not only has he given us endlessly quotable portraits of Shropshire, he has given words to our universal longing for the 'blue remembered hills' and 'happy highways' of our pasts, to which we can never return.

6 STOKESAY COURT

Onibury SY7 9BD ✆ 01584 856238 ⌂ www.stokesaycourt.com ⊙ pre-booked tours only (see website)

Stokesay Court's appeal is threefold. The late-Victorian mansion in Onibury, two miles south of Stokesay Castle, is vast and exquisite, built by the glove maker John Derby Allcroft in an earlier style (late Elizabethan/ early Jacobean) but to the latest specifications of its time. It was one of the first houses in England to have electric lighting, and the Great Hall was equipped with underfloor heating. Derby Allcroft, who was also instrumental in the conservation of Stokesay Castle, had waited years to see his dream fulfilled, but died only six months after the house's completion.

Then there's the passion of Caroline Magnus, who inherited Stokesay Court – a house she had found daunting as a child – from her aunt in 1992. Not wishing to sell to hotel developers, she decided to leave London and make a new life in Shropshire. 'I must have been bonkers!'

she laughed when I asked about her decision to preserve the house. It was in a seriously bad state, leaking everywhere, and to pay for its repair and daily upkeep (as well as settle their inheritance tax), Caroline and her brother Laurence were forced to auction its entire contents.

And then comes the third part, the Hollywood dream. In 2006 the production designer for *Atonement* – the movie adaptation of Ian McEwan's powerful novel – read an article about Stokesay Court in *Country Life*. The house was chosen as the location for the Tallis family home (although, with more than 90 rooms, deemed far too big: the Ladies' Wing would be digitally erased) and in moved an entire film crew and cast, including Keira Knightley, James McAvoy and Vanessa Redgrave. Not only did the production design team make over much of the interior, breathing life into the house, but the resulting interest in Stokesay Court brought much-needed funds. The prestigious wallpaper company Watts of Westminster launched a Stokesay Court collection, which Caroline said was a dream come true for a home owner, 'especially a cash-strapped one like me.'

If you can, go on the tour: see the bedrooms of the characters and the library where that memorable scene took place, and meet the polystyrene Triton who was fixed to the fountain from which Keira Knightley emerged in a wet slip. Caroline still has a long wish list for the house and her determination to save it is inspiring. The tour includes generous amounts of tea and cake, and the chance to wander the private grounds.

7 ASTON ON CLUN

You'll know you're in Aston on Clun – three miles west of Craven Arms – when you see a tree flanked with larch poles and decorated with flags and bunting. This bedecked black poplar is the village's **arbor tree**. The custom of tree dressing is ancient, bound up with the worship of Brigit, the Celtic goddess of fertility. In 1660 King Charles II, a man with every reason to show gratitude to trees (page 104), marked his return to the throne by proclaiming 29 May a tree-dressing holiday, known as Oak Apple Day or Arbor Day. The custom was already dying in England in the following century, although not in Aston on Clun. On 29 May 1786, a local landowner named Squire John Marston brought home his new bride, Mary Carter, where she caught sight of the village poplar dressed with flags. So delighted was Mary by the custom that she took steps to preserve it, paying for the tree dressing every year.

Her successors continued with the tradition until 1954 when the tree was entrusted to Hopesay Parish Council. The old tree blew down during a storm in 1995, but the current tree was taken from a cutting of the original in 1975.

Aston on Clun is thought to be the only village in Britain where Arbor Day is still celebrated. Visit on the last Sunday in May to find a pageant commemorating John and Mary's wedding, a fete on the Arbor Field, morris dancing and a tug of war.

Nearby **Broome station** is a halt, serving Aston on Clun as well as the village of Broome.

FOOD & DRINK

Hopesay Glebe Farm Hopesay SY7 8HD ✆ 01588 660737. This working organic smallholding is a mile north of Aston on Clun – and a lovely place to make a detour for homemade cake and organic fairtrade tea, coffee or chocolate.

8 HOPTON CASTLE

🏠 **The Baron at Bucknell** (page 247), **Hopton House** (page 246)
Hopton SY7 0QF ⌂ www.hoptoncastle.org.uk ◷ daily during daylight hours; free entry & parking but no toilets; the ruins are approximately one mile from Hopton Heath station; the Arriva bus service 740 from Ludlow to Knighton stops at Hopton Heath

The backdrop to the ruins of Hopton Castle is as perfect as if painted on canvas for a play: gentle wooded hills, big skies and a smattering of black-and-white half-timbered houses. Intense research and conservation work (including a contribution from Channel 4's *Time Team*) helped piece together the violent history of this medieval tower house: during a five-week siege in 1644, 31 Parliamentarians held out against an army of Royalist soldiers, only to be murdered once they had surrendered. The storybook-style signage will tell you more.

Nearby **Hopton Wood** (SY7 0QF ♀ SO355784; managed by the Forestry Commission) has a warm-up loop and several downhill tracks for mountain bikers.

FOOD & DRINK

The Baron at Bucknell Bucknell SY7 0AH ✆ 01547 530549. Also known as the Baron of Beef, this warm and comfortable inn is five minutes from Bucknell station. Expect generous portions of well-cooked pub food, with many ingredients sourced from Shropshire, Herefordshire and Powys. The Baron's website outlines ten walks that start and finish at the pub:

⏂ www.baronatbucknell.co.uk/walking-in-shropshire. There are also five luxurious rooms plus camping facilities.

9 CLUNTON

If, like me, your idea of a happy Sunday means a big walk followed by a hearty lunch and pint in a country pub, then Clunton – between Aston on Clun and Clun – is a destination I recommend for you. The upland oak woodland of **Clunton Coppice** is accessed from the centre of the village (take the road alongside the Crown Inn) and rich with birdlife (wood warblers, pied flycatchers and great spotted woodpeckers in particular), moss, ferns and a rare species of fungi.

"Follow the forest road to a wooden bench and a view that could make philosophers of us all."

If you're driving (which is likely: the bus, the 860 running between Lydbury North and Telford, only runs on alternate Tuesdays), **Bury Ditches** (SY7 8BD ⚲ SO335839) is accessible from Clunton: look for the brown sign and follow the narrow road uphill to the Forestry Commission car park. Dating from around 500BC, this is one of England's best-preserved Iron Age hillforts, elliptical in shape, fortified by four concentric banks, and offering open views in all directions over pine plantations and beyond. **Two circular trails** – Druid's Walk (1.8 miles) and Chieftain's Walk (1.3 miles) – have sharpish ascents but are worth the climb. For an easier time you could follow the forest road around to a wooden bench and a view that could make philosophers of us all. **Bruce Chatwin** was one of many writers inspired by this part of Shropshire; he is thought to have written *On The Black Hill* while staying at nearby Cwm Hall (although the book features an amalgam of various places in the Welsh borders, including perhaps another Black Hill in the Black Mountains, further south). The woodland around Bury Ditches is important for the endangered wood white butterfly, which the Forestry Commission is taking steps to nurture.

⁉ FOOD & DRINK

The Crown Inn ⏂ 01588 660265. A cosy pub where very capable and friendly people serve traditional pub grub. The Crown is highly regarded by the West Shropshire branch of CAMRA: regular ales are from Hobsons and there's a new guest ale on Wednesdays. The Crown's beer festival takes place in the first weekend of October.

10 CLUN

🏠 **Buckshead Eco-cottage** (page 247), **Criggin Cottage,** Llanfair Waterdine (page 247), **The Dick Turpin Cottage** (page 247), **Pooh Hall Cottages** (page 248), **The Quarry House** (page 246), **YHA Clun Mill** (page 247)

A E Housman was right: Clun, tucked away in the countryside 14 miles south of Bishop's Castle, *is* quiet. More so now than in days of yore when marcher lords staked out their borders with strongholds and moats, or even into the mid-20th century when it was an important market town. Clun's officially a village now, but don't tell that to residents.

Cross the wooden footbridge from the main car park to find the riverside ruins of **Clun Castle** (⊝ free public open access), high on a natural spur. The original motte-and-bailey structure was probably established by Picot de Say, a follower of William the Conqueror, in the years after the Norman Conquest. The stone successor you see today was built by the Fitzalan family, better known as the Earls of Arundel. Owned by the Duke of Norfolk and managed by English Heritage, the site is an atmospheric place for dog walking and picnics. The remains of the four-storey keep, unusual for being set into the side of its mound rather than perched on top, overlook the Clun Forest and into the Kerry Hills of Wales. Clun Castle is thought to have inspired Sir Walter Scott's *The Betrothed*.

Back by the car park, the uneven stone arches of Clun's 15th-century **packhorse bridge** are mostly original, although the bridge's position on a modern-day through road means the parapet has been knocked off and replaced more times than most people would care to remember. Tradition has it that crossing the narrow bridge sharpens one's wits

GREEN MAN FESTIVAL

The May Day weekend is when the **Green Man Festival** (⊘ www.clungreenman. org.uk) comes to Clun. This three-day celebration reaches its climax at noon on bank holiday Monday with a fight on the packhorse bridge between the Green Man and the Frost Queen. Legend has it that if the Frost Queen triumphs, there will be no summer in the Clun Valley. If the Green Man wins, he and his May Queen will proceed to the castle grounds where a May fair awaits, with craft stalls, games, music and dancing. It's an uplifting springtime celebration and my favourite day of the year to be in Clun. Another good time to visit is during the **Clun Valley Beer Festival** in October (⊘ www. cvbf.co.uk) when a bus usually runs between participating pubs.

(although presumably knocking the top off precludes you from making such a boast). On a quiet day you might see brown trout and kingfishers in this stretch of water and, if you're extra lucky, otters. Look for the alder trees along the riverbank: these were once prolific in this area and used by the many clog makers who lived in Clun (there are old clog patterns in the **Museum of Clun** (The Square ☉ Easter–Oct, Tue & Sun), alongside other local artefacts.

South of the bridge on a steep rise, **St George's Church** has Saxon foundations and a squat, partially Norman tower typical of borderland churches which had defensive as well as religious purposes. The playwright **John Osborne**, author of *Look Back in Anger*, made Clun his home in the last years of his life – and the churchyard of St George's is his final resting place. He's buried next to his fifth wife Helen Osborne (nee Dawson), with whom it is said he shared the happiest of his many romantic relationships. Their house, **The Hurst** in nearby Clunton, is now a writing retreat managed by the Arvon Foundation.

Still in the churchyard, look also for Clun's oldest living inhabitant: a 2,000-year-old yew tree in front of the church. Nearby you'll find a touching tomb memorial to the Hamar family, from which seven brothers and sisters were in 1811 carried off by a 'Putrid Fever with awful rapidity in the short space of Three Weeks – a sad instance of the uncertainty of human life'. The churchyard, almost circular, has areas of conservation managed under **Caring For God's Acre** (a national programme which started in Shropshire: ⊘ www.caringforgodsacre.org. uk) and, as such, is rich in plant and insect diversity.

ᵞᴵ FOOD & DRINK

The Maltings High St ⊘ 01588 640539. A tea room with home-cooked, home-style food and a peaceful ambience. It's also home to Cary's Cakes which are delicious (takeout boxes are available if you're too full up at the time of visiting). Walking for Health walks (⊘ www.walkingforhealth. org.uk) leave from here at 10.30 on the second and fourth Tuesday of the month.

The Sun Inn High St ⊘ 01588 640559. The Sun's owned by the Three Tuns Brewery so you're guaranteed a great pint. The plain-rendered exterior belies the fact that this is a cruck-truss building dating from the 16th century. In the bar is a set of three old Molly Lane 'signal box' handpumps, reputed to have come from Ye Olde Cock Tavern in London's Fleet Street, serving the likes of Charles Dickens.

The White Horse Inn The Square ⊘ 01588 640305. A welcoming pub with its own microbrewery. The traditional food is sourced from an impressive roll call of local suppliers.

11 BISHOP'S CASTLE

⌂ Castle Hotel (page 247), **Middle Woodbatch Farm** (page 246), **The Poppy House** (page 246), **The Porch House** (page 246) **▲ Foxholes Castle Camping** (page 247)

The very name Bishop's Castle conjures images of the turbulent history of the Welsh Marches. The town was founded by the Norman Bishops of Hereford in their capacity as marcher lords, who governed from the castle. The town still follows a medieval layout – a main street and two back lanes (with evidence of burgage plots and passageways called 'shuts') – but it's nevertheless hard to imagine warring lords staking out this peaceful municipality where, in recent times, a 'yarn-bombing' exercise by a local knitters' group left lampposts and iron railings swathed in multi-coloured knitwear. Even if the wool has unravelled by the time you visit, I think the memory is reflective of Bishop's Castle's creative, community-minded vibe. It's not a big town, but boasts **two breweries** – one of which, the **Three Tuns**, is the oldest working brewery in Britain.

You won't find much of a castle in Bishop's Castle today. In the 16th century John Leland described the motte-and-bailey construction as 'well maintained and set on a strong rokke, though not very hy'. Now you have to slip through a wooden gate on Castle Street to see only the mound and sorry remains of a wall. Much of the old castle site lies under the car park and gardens of Castle Hotel, while stone from the keep was used as the hard core for the hotel's bowling green.

Monday and Thursday are **market days** in Bishop's Castle, although some shops are shut on Monday. Much of the town observes early closing hours on Wednesday too. Saturday sees either the farmers' market, flea market or another specialist market. Bishop's Castle's annual calendar features an **arts festival** in February, packed with dancing, literary events, food demonstrations and, yes, knitting; a **walking festival** in May and (probably) the world's only **tandem triathlon** in early July (⊘ www. tandemtriathlon.org). Mid July sees another highlight: a **beer festival**, celebrating in particular the town's two breweries and excellent pubs.

To find out what's happening when you visit, call into the recently refurbished **Town Hall** (High St ✆ 01588 630023 ⊘ www. bishopscastletownhall.co.uk ☉ visitor information 10.00–16.00 Mon–Sat). The original building was probably the work of William Baker who also designed The Buttercross in Ludlow.

✋ For **long-distance walk** ideas from Bishop's Castle, see ⊘ www. bradtguides.com/bishopscastle.

Bishop's Castle's museums

To learn about the social and agricultural history of the town, visit the **House on Crutches Museum** (Church St ✆ 01588 630556 🖉 www. hocmuseum.org.uk ☉ Easter–Sep 14.00–17.00, Sat, Sun & bank holiday Mon; free ♿ limited access due to the age & layout of the building). One of the best town museums in Shropshire, it's housed in a picturebook-perfect Elizabethan timber-framed building – with wooden posts propping up a 17th-century upstairs extension, which feels wonderfully crooked inside.

On School Lane you'll find a veritable shed housing **Bishop's Castle Railway Society Museum** (✆ 01588 660708 🖉 www.bcrailway.co.uk ☉ Easter–Oct 14.00–17.00 Sat, Sun & bank holiday Mon) with its touching dedication to 'The memory of Bishop's Castle Railway 1865–1935'. It sometimes suffers from a lack of volunteers, so may not always be open when expected.

The church of St John the Baptist

High Street has a one-in-six gradient and becomes Church Street, leading to the church of St John the Baptist at the foot of the hill. Look for the one-handed church clock.

The churchyard holds a mystery: that of the **grave of I.D.**, an unknown 'Native of Africa', who died in 1801. No-one knows how I.D. came to be in Bishop's Castle during that that century, but the mossy inscription, while hard to make out, is elegant and includes the line from Acts 17:26: 'God hath made of one blood all Nations of men'. The idea that the grave might have been paid for by an abolitionist is a heartwarming one. English Heritage cited this grade II-listed grave among 11 others in a special project on the abolition of slavery.

🛍 SHOPPING

AJ Pugh Butchers 46 Church St ✆ 01588 638584. An exemplary butcher's shop, selling locally reared meat with farms of origin listed on boards behind the counter. The homemade sausages are excellent.

The New Deli 35 High St ✆ 01588 638190. An inviting deli selling a brilliant array of British cheeses, fine foods, booze and cookware.

Old Time Chairs 29 High St ✆ 01588 638467. Bishop's Castle and Clun were once centres of artisan chair making. Stuart and Jane Carroll have revived this traditional art, handcrafting beautiful chairs from green ash that grows abundantly in south Shropshire.

Rural Retro (The Gallery) 32 High St 🖉 01588 630555. An attractive ensemble of the 'collected' (retro and vintage items), 'crafted' (handmade, contemporary homeware and upcycled goods) and 'created' (original artwork by British artists).

🍴 FOOD & DRINK

Castle Hotel Market Sq 🖉 01588 638403. In 1899 artist H. Thornhill Timmins described this Georgian hotel as 'one of those large, roomy caravansarys'. It's just as inviting today with a secluded garden and daily changing menu upon which I'm always glad to see local ingredients, especially cheese, featuring prominently. Walkers and cyclists are made very welcome.

The Chai Shop High St 🖉 07790 194782. This café and takeaway selling Indian curries, snacks, cakes and sweets is snuggled into the foot of the Porch House, a distinguished Elizabethan building at one with the sloping high street. Don't try to resist the enticing aroma of homemade curry and samosas: step inside and let Tahira, the Chai Shop's arty and interesting owner, host you in her home-from-home kitchen diner.

The Poppy House 20 Market Sq 🖉 01588 638443 🖱 www.poppyhouse.co.uk. A light and sunny licensed tea room and restaurant with B&B rooms serving well-presented café fare (sandwiches, jacket potatoes, salads) and hearty English breakfasts. A dedicated drying room takes care of cyclists' and walkers' wet clothing.

The Six Bells Pub & Brewery Church St 🖉 01588 638930. Part of life in Bishop's Castle since 1670. As well as serving its own beer (with cheerfully vernacular names such as Ow Do and Noggin'), the pub offers home-cooked food, with meat sourced from Battlefield near Shrewsbury and veggies from the farmers' market.

The Three Tuns Inn Salop St 🖉 01588 638 797. The Three Tuns Inn shares a building with Three Tuns Brewery, an esteemed craft brewery established in 1642 when granted a licence by King Charles I. Ownership of the pub and brewery are separate but the two work harmoniously together. Refreshingly absent of piped music and fruit machines, this atmospheric 17th-century inn is the perfect place to while away an afternoon with newspapers, board games and a pint or two of Cleric's Cure. The local sourcing of the menu is excellent; the food is pub fare tweaked up a notch. Every second Wednesday at 20.00 the pub hosts the **Bishop's Castle Film Society**, screening a film in the function room (🖱 www.bishopscastlefilmsociety).

12 LYDBURY NORTH

⛺ **Walcot Hall** (page 248)

This village and large rolling parish is 3½ miles southeast of Bishop's Castle. **Lydbury North Community Shop** on its outskirts is run by a rota of volunteer villagers; you can often buy produce grown in nearby residents' gardens, as well as eggs, milk, meat, pies and cakes from local suppliers.

The grand Georgian **Walcot Hall** at the south end of the village was once owned by Clive of India (page 237). It's now in the hands of the Parish family, who open their estate for the National Gardens Scheme over the spring bank holiday weekend. Another way to see Walcot Hall's grounds is to stay there in the painted gypsy caravan, cosy converted fire truck, dipping shed or fairytale tin chapel.

FROM THE STIPERSTONES TO THE WELSH BORDER

Spreading west from the Stiperstones National Nature Reserve to the border with Wales is one of the wilder, more remote-feeling parts of Shropshire. Little wonder that legends abound in this hinterland – of Wild Edric, the Devil's Chair, and the magical dun cow of Mitchell's Fold.

13 STIPERSTONES NATIONAL NATURE RESERVE

The Stiperstones is a six-mile ridge which, at its highest, towers nearly 1,760 feet above sea level. To walk the Stiperstones on a clear day is uplifting and invigorating, while chill winds and bleak skies will inevitably cast a forbidding mood over the range. Suddenly, perhaps with a shiver as you find yourself in the shadow of a low-hanging cloud, you understand why one of the hulking quartzite rock tors is called the 'Devil's Chair'; why DH Lawrence described the ridge in his novella *St Mawr* as 'one of those places where the spirit of aboriginal England still lingers, the old savage England, whose last blood flows still in a few Englishmen, Welshmen, Cornishmen.' This, alongside the Long Mynd, is the land of Malcolm Saville's *Lone Pine Club* stories, a place to take a knapsack packed with 'eggs to hard boil, several lettuces and plenty of bread', and embark on an adventure …

Much of the Stiperstones is a National Nature Reserve (NNR), managed by Natural England who – alongside other organisations – has been responsible for restoring the purple heather heathland in which flora and fauna can thrive. The emperor moth caterpillar is making a return, while ground-nesting skylarks and stonechats are increasingly setting up home in the heather.

In August cowberries, crowberries and bilberries grow in abundance here too, the latter known locally as **whinberries** (sometimes wimberries) which feel and taste like diminutive, sharp blueberries.

Smaller reserves exist along the ridge of the Stiperstones including the Hollies just off the main footpath, where rowan trees thrive as fascinating 'cuckoos' (or 'bonded trees') in the gnarled trunk shells of old holly trees.

The Long Mynd & Stiperstones route of the Shropshire Hills Shuttle Buses (page 22) makes stops at the entrance to the NNR and at The Bog (see opposite) on Saturday, Sunday and bank holiday Monday in the summer. If driving you can park at the NNR car park.

Walking the Stiperstones

Birds are said to haunt the Stiperstones: six whistlers circle the skies over the ridge and the appearance of their seventh will herald the end of the world. Spooky whistlers aside, there is great opportunity to see real birdlife up here, from wheeling red kites, soaring buzzards and somersaulting ravens to speckled brown meadow pipits who dart skittishly among the heather. From the top you can see Wales to the west (Corndon Hill is over the border in Powys); the Long Mynd to the east and The Wrekin to the northeast. Waymarked paths will keep you

WILD EDRIC

Amy Douglas, storyteller & www.amydouglas.com

Beneath the Devil's Chair, in the quiet dark heart of the hill, a man lies sleeping. He lies waiting, to guard and defend.

Wild Edric was a real man, a Saxon noble. He held manors throughout south Shropshire and Herefordshire. When William the Conqueror invaded, Edric refused to submit and harried the conqueror up and down the borderlands. Edric was a man of the old ways, who loved the land and his people.

One day Edric was out hunting. It was spring, the woods hazy with bluebells. Edric startled a white hart and followed it deep into the forest. At last, as dusk gathered, the stag took a great leap over a bramble thicket and Edric could follow no further. He slowed

his horse and realised he could hear music. In a trance he followed it to a clearing where beautiful women danced. Edric had eyes only for the woman in the centre. Forgetting all else, he plunged forward and grabbed hold of her. The music stopped and her companions turned on Edric, who, taking the woman with him, scrambled on to his horse and galloped into the night.

The woman he claimed from the forest, Lady Godda, was one of the Fair Folk. She agreed to marry Edric, on condition that he never hinder her coming or going or reproach her for her fairy blood.

For a while, all went well. Lady Godda brought good luck. Edric made a truce from getting lost: there's a short (545-yard) **all-ability trail** and also the **Stiperstones Stomp** which takes you five miles over to Habberley. From there you can walk back or catch a Shropshire Hills Shuttle Bus when they're running.

At the northern end of the Stiperstones are **Blakemoorgate Cottages** (✆ 01743 792294 ⊙ Apr–Sep 11.00–15.00 second Sun of the month), a cluster of recently restored miners' dwellings. The stone cottages were built in the late 1800s when the general idea – although not set out in English law – was that if you could construct a home in one night and have smoke in the chimney by morning, it could stay.

14 The Bog Visitor Centre

SY5 0NG ✆ 01743 792484 ⊗ www.bogcentre.co.uk ⊙ Apr–end Oct 10.00–17.00

Miles more pleasant than its name, The Bog Visitor Centre is a gas-lit former Victorian schoolhouse 1,300 feet up in the Stiperstones National Nature Reserve – and your gateway to the mysterious ridge. Run by volunteers, The Bog is a brilliant place to fuel yourself with tea and a wedge of cake (a gluten-free option is always available) before

with William and they lived in peace and prosperity. But Godda did not behave like other women. She came and went as she pleased and tongues wagged when she spent whole nights in the forest. One day, Edric's pride and temper got the better of him. When Godda returned the forbidden words flew from Edric's tongue. Godda vanished. With Godda, all Edric's luck left too. Edric, repentant and heartsore, combed the forest looking for her, day after day. William's messengers came and went unanswered and all Edric's duties were forgotten. William declared Edric an outlaw and seized his lands. Still Edric searched, until one day he didn't return.

Now Edric is part of both this world and the Otherworld. He has gone into the hill, sleeping away the years until needed. Whenever Britain is under attack he rides out across the land, pointing the way to the enemy, the dogs ahead of him showing the years of war to come. When the Wild Hunt rides, the ground shakes in warning. The air trembles with the trampling of hooves, dogs baying, men calling. At the head of the hunt rides a proud man in green, his hair tousled and as black as his stallion. But somewhere along the way, he must have been forgiven, for only a step behind rides a woman, her golden hair streaming out behind her, her white palfrey's tail like a banner.

a mooch along the Stiperstones. The Bog is walker-friendly: muddy boots, wet clothes and dogs are welcome, and you can even eat your own packed lunch here. There are local-interest books and crafts for sale, plus displays on the geology and lead mining heritage of the area. The latter was significant: before mining ceased here, the Stiperstones area produced 10% of Britain's lead ore. There are few remnants of this chapter in history now, apart from The Bog's schoolhouse building, which served the mining community, and the entrance to the 'Somme' tunnel, now gated to protect resident bats.

Many routes start from The Bog, including the gentle Flenny Bank and Mucklewick walks; you'll find plenty of leaflets and information inside. The Shropshire Way passes by here too.

15 SNAILBEACH LEAD MINE

🏠 **Long Mountain Centre** (page 246)

Park at Snailbeach Village Hall SY5 0NX (donations for car park into honesty box) 🕾 01952 405105 🖉 www.shropshiremines.org.uk 🕒 Jun–Oct, most Sundays & bank holidays (when staffed by volunteers; check website for tours) 🕭 a specially built wheeled truck allows visitors with mobility needs to access the Day level mine (phone ahead to ask about accessibility; Minsterley Motors' bus service 552 from Shrewsbury stops by Snailbeach Village Hall, a short walk from the mines

Once upon a time, a mine in Shropshire was reputed to have yielded the greatest volume of lead per acre of any mine in all of Europe. There's evidence – a Roman lead ingot among other clues – to suggest the site at Snailbeach, a couple of miles west of the Stiperstones, may have been worked by Romans, but the 'modern' mine's heyday was in the 1840s and 50s when miners produced more than 3,000 tons of ore and up to 2,700 tons of lead per year.

"Once upon a time, a mine in Shropshire was reputed to have yielded the greatest volume of lead of any mine in Europe."

In 1895 a tragic accident at the mine made the national news. A steel winding rope snapped at the pithead and a cage of seven men plummeted half a mile, instantly crushing them.

The Snailbeach Barite Company ceased working underground in 1955. Now the mine and preserved surface buildings are in the capable hands of the Shropshire Mines Trust, a group of volunteers who manage the site for Shropshire Council. Several are also members of the **Shropshire Bat Group** who discovered a population of lesser horseshoe bats in the mine; a finding that was key to preventing the shafts being infilled in the early 1990s.

The workings go down hundreds of feet but only two levels are accessible to visitors. This is more than enough, I find, to absorb the dark, close atmosphere and begin to imagine the tough working conditions of miners. The Day level is open whenever the site is attended, offering a straightforward walk along a rail track bed and, at the end, a view 336 feet down into the engine shaft and up to daylight where the Cornish engine house (so called because the engine design was developed in Cornwall) stands. The Roberts/Perkins level is more intense (no children under five allowed): on this tour you'll cross bridges, enter a great stope, see mineral veins and look deep down into the mine.

"On the Roberts/Perkins tour you'll cross bridges, enter a great stope, see mineral veins and look deep into the mine."

You'll be given a helmet and high-powered light but the water and mud underfoot mean you'll need to bring your own wellies. Be prepared to stoop as well as splash a little: this probably isn't a place for bad backs. If the mines are closed or you don't fancy going in, you can also make a **self-guided surface tour** of the site: see the website for details.

16 MITCHELL'S FOLD STONE CIRCLE

Near Priest Weston, SY15 6DE. Head towards Montgomery: the site is signed & accessed via an unclassified road just off the A488 where you'll find a small car park; free entry
☉ daylight hours

High on the moorland of Stapeley Hill an enigmatic circle of dolerite stones has stood for over 3,000 years. It's impossible to know for what rituals or beliefs our Bronze Age ancestors hauled the stones to this spot and arranged them in a roughly circular formation; perhaps they served a calendrical or funerary purpose. No-one is even sure of the origin of the name. One local legend concerns a good fairy who bestowed the villagers with a magical dun cow. She promised that the cow's milk would never run dry, as long as everyone took only one bucket of milk each day. Naturally a wicked witch ruined everything by pumping the cow's milk into a sieve. When the cow realised the witch's trick she ran away, never to be seen again. As punishment, the fairy turned the witch to stone and made the stone circle in which to imprison her forever.

In the late 19th century Reverend Waldegrave Brewster at nearby **Holy Trinity Church** in Middleton-in-Chirbury carved the figures from the story into a stone pillar in the north transept: you can still see it today, and his other much-admired carved pew ends and stone corbels (SY15 6BY ☉ daylight hours).

17 KERRY VALE VINEYARD

Pentreheyling (just off the A489 towards Newtown) SY15 6HU ✆ 01588 620627 ☝ www. kerryvalevineyard.co.uk ☉ Jun–Sep, scheduled tours on Wed, Sat, Sun & bank holiday Mon (book in advance); café & shop 10.00–16.00 Tue–Sun ♿ accessible

As if growing a vineyard from scratch didn't feel enough like hard work, June and Geoff Ferguson unwittingly chose part of the Roman site of Pentreheyling Fort to nurture their grapes. Since the 1950s the land – overlooked by the moody hill of Corndon to the east and the flat-backed Kerry Ridgeway to the west – had been used as a smithy and smallholding, but the buildings were so dilapidated by the time it came into the Fergusons' hands in 2009, they had no choice but to start again. That was when they realised the ancient history they'd acquired. 'It's a scheduled ancient monument so any work we carried out was subjected to a Watching Brief and supervised by archaeologists,' June explained.

Aside from the well-known link between Romans and wine, the past and present are woven together beautifully at Kerry Vale thanks to stories told by the Ferguson family. Hares (thought to have been introduced to Britain by the Romans) are often found gambolling on the site and, during excavations the overseeing archaeologist discovered a fragment of Roman samian ware depicting a symbol of a hare. And so Kerry Vale has called its

"Past and present are woven together beautifully at Kerry Vale Vineyard."

UK Vineyard Association bronze award-winning rosé The Rare Hare.

You'll find the hare pottery and other unearthed objects upstairs in Kerry Vale's tasting room and art gallery, where vineyard tours end with a light-hearted presentation and the all-important tasting session.

For a vineyard that only yielded its first proper harvest in 2013, Kerry Vale is amazingly successful. Summer Days, the medium-dry white wine created from Solaris vines, also has a bronze award from the UKVA, while the dry white, Shropshire Lady, earned silver. All are made at Halfpenny Green Vineyards (page 92) and all are vegetarian.

Light and delicious lunches are available in the **café/shop**: mezze, cheeseboards and June's famous homemade cheese and onion tart. Afternoon tea may be booked in advance and enjoyed with a glass of sparkling wine. If you get the paranoid sensation of every second visitor peering at your feet while you're eating, it's because you've chosen the table by the dry-stone Roman well. Don't worry, it's covered with impenetrable glass.

AROUND CHURCH STRETTON & THE LONG MYND

In Welsh *myndd* means 'bare mountain', which is misleading here as Shropshire's Long Mynd is officially moorland: a wild, sweeping moorland plateau running for around ten miles, covering almost 6,000 heather-tufted acres and rising up to 1,700 feet above sea level. Little wonder then, that stories abound about its perils.

> … lives not a few have been lost in attempting to traverse its trackless wastes, and places here and there bear ominous names such as Deadman's Hollow, Devil's Mouth, Deadman's Beach, and the like. Moreover, the last fair of the year, held at Church Stretton on St. Andrew's Day, has acquired the title of 'Deadman's Fair', as men returning from it have been known to perish while endeavouring to reach their homes through the wild, mid-winter night.
> H Thornhill Timmins, *Nooks and Corners of Shropshire* (1899)

The Long Mynd is clearly waymarked and not half as dangerous as it sounds, as long as you tackle it in fair weather – unlike **Reverend Carr** whose story is on page 61. The ridge is flat with pleasant walking conditions: you'll see ponies and sheep grazing in the heather and bracken as you make your way over the grit and shale upland. The Long Mynd is easily accessible from **Carding Mill Valley** and **Church Stretton**. You can also drive over it via the single-track Burway, but with a gradient of one in five at times and a sheer drop at your side, it's safer and more fun on foot, horseback or bike.

This region has plenty of cosy inns serving good food to keep your energy up – and just south of Church Stretton is a **Victorian farm**, made famous by a BBC show.

🖐 Take a look at ✍ www.bradtguides.com/longmynd for some suggestions of places to stargaze.

18 CHURCH STRETTON

✿ **Middle Farm Cottages**, Betchcott (page 248), **The Pottery**, All Stretton (page 248), **Victoria House** (page 246), ▲ **Shropshire Hills Mountain Bike & Outdoor Pursuit Centre** (page 247)

> This happy place draws people to it like a seaside town, for health is in its air and a thousand delights in the little streams and green hollows of its sheltering hills.
> Arthur Mee, *The King's England: Shropshire* (1939)

In the late Victorian era Church Stretton was a fashionable retreat for the upwardly mobile. Ladies and gents would flock to the town for its fresh air and mountain-like setting, sheltered from the west by the Long Mynd and from the east by hills that include the Lawley, Caer Caradoc, Hazler and Ragleth. H Thornhill Timmins (1899) called it 'one of the healthiest places imaginable' and in 1901 the Long Mynd Hotel on Cunnery Road was opened as the Hydropathic Hotel, sealing Church Stretton's reputation as a spa town. In *Blue Remembered Hills* Shropshire historian Keith Pybus quotes a Victorian slogan that called Church Stretton 'Switzerland without the avalanches and wolves'.

In 2008 Church Stretton became Shropshire's first Walkers are Welcome town – unsurprisingly given the limitless routes rolling out from its doorstep. Independent eateries and comfortable accommodation combine to give us an excellent walking base, especially for taking on the Long Mynd and surrounding Stretton Hills.

The town's **train station** is at the foot of Sandford Avenue, with direct rail links to Shrewsbury and Ludlow (also connected by the bus service 435). Church Stretton is a popular stop on the Long Mynd & Stiperstones Shuttle Bus service at weekends from May to September (see page 22).

The library building (a former Victorian school) hosts Church Stretton's small but invaluable **visitor information centre** – although the location of the library was, at the time of writing, under judicial review. Thursday is market day and most shops are closed on Sundays.

The Norman **St Laurence's Parish Church** behind the high street was built on an older Saxon site: the open stone coffin by the front church wall probably dates from that period. Look for the rare **sheela-na-gig** above the north door: a caricature carving of a naked lady with exaggerated private parts, thought to be positioned to ward off death and evil, or as a remnant of pre-Christianity fertility symbols.

Highlights inside include a plaque memorial to a Wellington-born author. Although not well known today, **Hesba Stretton** was a contemporary and friend of Charles Dickens, regularly contributing to *All The Year Round* and *Household Words* under his editorship. Her 1886 story *Jessica's First Prayer* sold at least a million and a half copies, making her one of the first 'best-selling' novelists. The stained-glass window in St Laurence's south transept depicts the character of Jessica. In 1894 Hesba Stretton co-founded the London Society for the Prevention of Cruelty to Children which, five years later, would join with similar societies in other cities to become the NSPCC.

With the church on your left, you can cross the road and take a stroll into **Rectory Wood**. In around 1775 the owner James Mainwaring designed a woodland garden here. He was a close friend of Lancelot 'Capability' Brown and it is believed that the famous landscape gardener (or 'place maker', as he preferred to call himself) influenced Mainwaring's design. Managed as a traditional hay meadow, the wood is a rich habitat for birds, bats and butterflies. In the spring you'll find bluebells, daffodils, snowdrops and white wood anemones; on colder winter days the wood looks enchanted with a layer of frost. Three **circular waymarked walking trails** begin at Rectory Wood.

SHOPPING

Burway Books 18 Beaumont Rd ✆ 01694 723388 ⌚ www.burwaybooks.co.uk. A proudly independent bookshop which has been open more than 40 years, Burway Books is renowned for its quick and efficient ordering system.

Entertaining Elephants 43 High St ✆ 01694 723922. Tucked inside Old Barn, a 17th-century timber-framed building, this attractive shop (which took its name from a Maurice Sendak picture book) stocks wholesome food and ethical clothing. Its light and aspirational layout makes it rather more chic than chickpea.

Van Doesburg's 3 High St ✆ 01694 722867. A gourmet delicatessen with an impressive line-up of local produce, staffed by smiley people.

FOOD & DRINK

Berry's Coffee House 17 High St ✆ 01694 724452 ⌚ www.berryscoffeehouse.co.uk. Berry's is a licensed coffee house and informal eatery, intended to emulate Britain's earliest coffee houses where people gathered to hear the day's news, talk, share and learn. Inside the Queen Anne townhouse, the décor achieves thrown-together elegance with mismatched furniture and incidental flowers. Berry's long list of local suppliers tells you all you need to

Walk to Pole Bank,
the highest point on the Long Mynd

Kindly shared by Church Stretton Walkers are Welcome

❄ OS Explorer map 217; start at Church Stretton station ♀ SO455936; 6 miles, following blue waymarks. Moderate (generally easy underfoot but with some scrambling over small rocky outcrops, so you'll need a reasonable head for heights); allow 2–3 hours

Just a few minutes' walk out of Church Stretton and you'll find yourself in a timeless landscape of secretive valleys and bracken-clad moors, seemingly untouched by human hands. Keep going for big views over Wales and then a pleasing diversion into Carding Mill Valley with its National Trust tea room.

1 Leave the station by the Platform 1 exit. At the main road, bear left along Sandford Avenue and take the first turning left into Easthope Road. Pass the public toilets and turn right into Lion Meadow in front of the Co-op store. The top of the road faces the Bucks Head.

   Take the narrow passage to the left of the pub and go through the iron gate into the churchyard. Bear right to the side of St Laurence's Church and then bear left around to the main entrance before emerging through double iron gates on to Church Street.

2 Turn right and then shortly left between two tall gate pillars and enter Rectory Field through the wooden kissing-gate.

   Ignoring the steps at the edge of the wood on the right, climb up to the centre of the field, keeping the wood on your right. Where the wood swings to the right, keep close to it and make the steep climb towards a red-banded post and a kissing-gate at the top of the hill through which you should pass into Rectory Wood.

   Follow the path in front of you as it leads down to another red-banded post. From this veer leftwards and keep to the left at the path's next junction. This path borders a steep drop from which it is separated by a wooden guardrail fence. At the bottom of the descending path, cross the stream by way of the bridge (a recycled gravestone) and climb the path ahead to a kissing-gate.

3 Pass through a gate and at the Victorian reservoir, which once stored the water supply for Church Stretton, go straight ahead with the railings on your left. The reservoir is served by the aptly named Town Brook, a stream that will be your gurgling companion as you leave the railings behind and begin to follow the brook's gentle upward course.

   Gradually, as you climb higher, the brook falls away to your left. Where the head of the valley comes clearly into view, and you can see a marker post on the top, take extra care as the path leads over small rocky outcrops.

4 For the final approach to the summit, the path follows a zigzag route, generally leftwards, to reach a pink-banded post. Although you are now only a quarter of the way around the walk, the most physically demanding section has been completed.

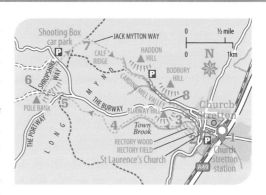

Turn right and follow the waymarked posts across the moorland for about a mile until you reach a tarmac road.

5 Turn left along the road for about 100 yards until it swings sharply to the left, exposing a rough track leading ahead and upwards.

6 Climb the track to the junction with the Medlicott path (signed on a wooden post), turn sharp left and follow the path up to Pole Bank. At 1,700 feet this is the highest point on the Long Mynd. From here, on a clear day, you can see Cader Idris, the Clee Hills and the Brecon Beacons.

Retrace your steps to the junction with the Medlicott path. Ignore the path to the right, along which you came, and walk straight ahead, eventually crossing the road at Shooting Box.

7 A post marked Carding Mill indicates the path straight ahead which eventually joins a broader track coming in from the right. Continue forward for about 300 yards to a major path junction. Here, bear to the right following the waymarked posts and, 20 yards further on, bear right again on to a loose stone surfaced track. From here the route is clear. You are now on Motts Road which leads downhill eventually to a stream at a junction with a major path coming in from the right.

Cross the stream and continue downwards into Carding Mill Valley with its National Trust shop and café.

8 Shortly after the café, take the track on the right that climbs diagonally up the hillside. At the top, turn left across the cattle grid and descend the Burway. Past the post box, bear left on to the grassy track. Then bear right just after a couple of large trees and pass a seat to reach a war memorial. Continue straight ahead down a grassy slope and a little narrow rocky path down to the road, bearing left to the crossroads.

Cross straight ahead into Sandford Avenue and continue down to the train station entrance.

know about the owners' dedication to provenance and goodness. Make mine a Border Kir, with Lyonshall cassis and white wine from Wroxeter. Plenty of gluten-free and veggie options.

Jemima's Kitchen Victoria House, 48 High St ✆ 01694 723823. Owner Diane Chadwick named this popular café after her Scottish mum, who inspired her to cook. Fruit, cheese and plain scones are freshly baked – and what isn't made in-house is sourced locally. An excellent place to fuel up with breakfast before a walk on the Long Mynd. Guest rooms are available at Victoria House.

Green Dragon Little Stretton SY6 6RE ✆ 01694 722925. Two miles south of Church Stretton is Little Stretton, with pretty black-and-white cottages and an unusual thatched-roof church. I love the Green Dragon pub – with thanks in no small part to the potent cider from its microbrewery. This is an excellent place for Sunday lunch, with meat sourced from Bert Butler Butchers of Condover. Look for the collection of Broseley clay pipes in the bar.

19 CARDING MILL VALLEY

SY6 6JG ☺ tea room closed in Jan

Carding Mill Valley, northwest of Church Stretton and within strolling distance of the town, is a steep-sided batch in the side of the Long Mynd with plenty of opportunities for walking and exploring. A stream runs down it, so don't forget your wellies for paddling or damming. The National Trust, which manages the area, gives you a wonderful (and all too rare) sense that most activities are possible here: even the reservoir is open for **wild swimming**. This is also a great spot for cycling and horseriding.

From the car park there are three waymarked trails plus an adventure trail for children with bridges, a rope pull, bird hide, fort and den building. The **Chalet Pavilion** has a tea room, gift shop (you can buy a net for fishing), toilets, small secondhand bookshop and Discovery Room detailing the history and geology of the Long Mynd.

20 ACTON SCOTT HISTORIC WORKING FARM

🏠 **Eaton Manor Country Estate** (page 247), **Henley Cottage** (page 247) ▲ **Feather Down Farm** (page 247)

Acton Scott SY6 6QN ✆ 01694 781307 ⟐ www.actonscott.com ☺ Apr–Nov

'When I see the words "You can pet the animals at Acton Scott Historic Working Farm", I always change it to "*pat* the animals,"' Suzy Gibson, project manager, told me one rainy May morning. 'Our farm is about education and staying as close as possible to Victorian farming techniques – although we also love people to enjoy our animals, of course'.

A NIGHT IN THE SNOW

*Suddenly my feet flew from under me, and I found myself shooting
at a fearful pace down the side of one of the steep ravines …*
Reverend E Donald Carr

One foul-weathered Sunday in January 1865 the Reverend E Donald Carr finished a sermon at Ratlinghope and attempted to cross the Long Mynd to his usual parish of Wolstaston 'exactly on the opposite side of the mountain' – a journey he had undertaken nearly 2,500 times before 'in all weathers, and at all hours of the day and night'. His morning journey had not been easy, a crawl through deep drifts of snow, but Reverend Carr did not expect any greater difficulties on his return and was, as he explained, 'anxious to get back to Wolstaston in time for my six o'clock evening service'. However this time, 'the aspect of the weather had completely changed' and a 'furious gale had come in from E.S.E.', driving 'clouds of snow and icy sleet' before the open moorland. It knocked him flat, time and again, the sleet stinging

his eyes so that he was unable to lift his head. When he made a 'tremendous glissade' down a ravine, he felt the pace he was travelling 'must have been very great, yet it seemed to me to occupy a marvellous space of time, long enough for the events of my whole previous life to pass in review before me'. And there began a terrible night of endurance as, numb with cold, he fought and scratched his way back home, talking to himself, fighting the temptation to 'give in and lie down in the snow', turning snow blind, unable to feel that he'd lost his boots.

Against the odds, Reverend Carr made it back to Carding Mill to tell the tale, which he was persuaded to recount in a short book, *A Night in the Snow or A Struggle for Life*. You can download it for free at *&* www.gutenberg.org/ebooks/20287.

The Actons are one of those fabled Shropshire families who have held the same estate for years. In their case, close to 900 years. Tom Acton established Acton Scott Historic Working Farm in his family's home-farm buildings in the 1970s, with the intention of preserving 19th-century farming practices increasingly lost to modern machinery. This 23-acre upland farm, about four miles south of Church Stretton, is now a popular visitor attraction (featured on BBC2's *Victorian Farm* and Ben Fogle's *Escape in Time*) where heavy horses work the land and you can pat Tamworth pigs, Shropshire sheep and Longhorn and Shorthorn cows – the 'traditional' livestock that someone farming in south Shropshire between around 1870–1920 would recognise. Acton Scott also nurtures the skills of yesteryears: a blacksmith, wheelwright and farrier make daily visits and demonstrations during open season.

And if you fancy learning a new skill yourself, look for hands-on rural trade and craft courses in disciplines as varied as ploughing, coracle-making, stick-carving and whittling, baking and loom-weaving.

The gift shop contains an admirable collection of locally produced items, including handmade lace, eggs, beeswax products and honey. If you think you might return soon, a day ticket can be converted into a season pass for a small additional charge.

FOOD & DRINK

Acton Scott Historic Working Farm has thoughtfully provided covered areas to eat your picnic on rainy days, but also consider lunch in the **Old Schoolhouse**, a smart black-and-white building added to the estate by Frances Stackhouse Acton (a celebrated horticulturalist and historian) in 1866. The café is run by chef Mat Poulton (who trained under John Burton Race) whose team performs wizardry with foraged food, local produce (think Ludlow Vineyard cider and apple juice, Coopers Gourmet Sausage Rolls) and enormous slices of homemade cake.

21 WENTNOR

The Crown Inn (page 247), **The Green Caravan Park** (page 247)

Set upon a hilltop plateau to the west of the Long Mynd, the pretty village of Wentnor was described by John Betjeman in 1951 as 'Shropshire as the tourist imagines it from the railway posters before he goes there'. **St Michael and All Angels** is largely a late Victorian reconstruction of a much earlier church: the foundations are early medieval and the west wall is Norman. I love the weather-boarded tower, which gives the impression the village is bracing itself for a battering storm. One family for whom this is poignant were the Pirkinses, remembered by what's known as the **hurricane tomb** inside the church. On 2 February 1772, seven members of the same family were killed by a storm. Don't miss their poetic epitaph.

FOOD & DRINK

The Crown Inn SY9 5EE ⊘ 01588 650613 Wentnor's 16th-century inn is homely and welcoming, all low beams, exposed brick inglenook fireplaces and hanging horse tack. Local breweries (including Hobsons) are well represented and the pub fare is satisfying, using meat sourced from Church Stretton and vegetables grown locally. I bought homemade strawberry jam from the pub one summer and delicious it was too. The pub doubles as a B&B.

22 RATLINGHOPE & BRIDGES

🏠 **The Bridges** (page 247), **YHA Bridges** (page 247), ⛺ **Brow Farm Campsite** (page 246)

On the west flank of the Long Mynd, **Bridges**, a hamlet within the civil parish of Ratlinghope, is a stop on the Stiperstones & Long Mynd Shuttle bus route (page 23) and worth a visit for a wonderful pub called the **Horseshoe Inn**, also known as the Bridges.

Two circular walks start from here: you can download the directions for Adstone (5½ miles) and the gentler Darnford (6½ miles) from 🖳 www.shropshirewalking.co.uk/activity-walks/stiperstones.php.

The churchyard of **St Margaret's** at nearby **Ratlinghope** contains the grave of the last known **sin eater** in England, Richard Munslow (d1906). Sin eating was a custom peculiar to the Welsh Marches and north Wales wherein a willing person was paid to eat bread and drink ale or wine over the corpse of a person who had died suddenly without the chance to confess their sins. Believers thought the sin eater would take on the sins of the deceased, allowing their purified soul to enter heaven. While sin eaters were usually very poor, Richard Munslow was a farmer with 70–75 acres of land at nearby Upper Darnford. The grave may give a clue as to why Mr Munslow decided to revive the custom of sin eating: he lost four infant children in his lifetime; three in the space of one week in 1870. Mary Webb (pages 98–9), who explored the practice of sin eating in *Precious Bane,* reimagined Ratlinghope as 'Slepe' in her first novel *The Golden Arrow,* such is the village's quietude.

The churchyard is a haven for plant diversity and the inventory of species found there (pinned up by the door) reads like a witch's spell: hairy lady's mantle, smooth hawk's beard, cat's ear, nipplewort, devil's bit scabious …

Nearby at Gatten Farm, **Farmer Phil's Festival** takes place in mid-August, a three-day family-friendly event with eclectic music and free camping (🖳 www.farmerphilsfestival.com).

🍴 FOOD & DRINK

Horseshoe Inn Bridges SY5 0ST 🕾 01588 650260, Also known as the Bridges, located at the foot of the Long Mynd where the River East Onny meets Darnford Brook, this former coaching stop between Shrewsbury and Bishop's Castle attracts walkers (including dog walkers, whose pets are welcome in the bar), cyclists and people who appreciate good beer. It's a tap house for the Three Tuns Brewery. The food is traditional pub fare inspired by the Shropshire Hills; I can still feel hungry at the memory of a bowl of smoky cauliflower and Shropshire Blue cheese soup, the perfect overture to Sunday lunch.

THE CLEE HILLS & CORVEDALE TO CLEOBURY MORTIMER

In this easterly part of south Shropshire, the River Corve (a tributary of the River Teme, which it joins in Ludlow) runs through a broad, alder-lined valley known as the Corvedale (or sometimes Corve Dale). Nearby are the Clee Hills, rich with walking opportunities and your chance to scale the highest point in Shropshire: Abdon Burf, one of the twin peaks of **Brown Clee Hill**.

23 WESTHOPE COLLEGE

⌂ **The Crown Country Inn**, Munslow (page 247), **Westhope College** (page 247)
SY7 9JL ✆ 01584 861293 ⌂ www.westhope.org.uk ♿ specially adapted downstairs rooms available for residential guests with accessibility needs

Just above the Corvedale, shaded beneath the banks and coppices of Wenlock Edge, is Westhope College. Predominantly a craft college, offering a dazzling variety of one-off sessions, longer courses and full-board residential programmes, this is a place for nurturing mind and soul as well as acquiring new skills and preserving old ones: embroidery, patchwork, felting, basketry and willow weaving, copper foiling, glasswork, sewing and needlework, dyeing, batik, applique, tapestry, woodcarving, enamelling …

If even your fingers are in need of a break, philosophy and meditation courses now also feature in the brochure, which you can download from the college website.

In 1981 Anne Dyer MBE founded the college with Elizabeth Rumble in the handsome gabled house, originally a pair of cottages, which has been owned and extended by her distinguished family for several generations. The college grounds, stretching over ten acres (open for wandering at weekends for a small fee), are particularly distinctive: Anne told me she is applying to have the garden registered as a Site of Special Scientific Interest, not least because of a profusion of common spotted orchids thriving in the meadow. The walled garden provides sustenance to college residents and nearby in the valley Anne owns castlemilk moorit sheep, longhorn cattle and kunekune pigs which also make their way to the dining room in various forms.

If you're craft-minded, get ready to swoon at the **Friends' Shop**, stocking yarns, fabrics, buttons and accessories, and the libraries of craft-related books. **The Tea Shed** is open (☉ w/ends in summer, 10.30–15.30 & other times by arrangement) to anyone in need of homemade cake, good coffee or a long cool drink.

Half a mile down a country lane on orchard land also owned by Anne is **Westhope Green Burial Ground,** a hidden, peaceful spot with a pretty Victorian chapel, spectacular with snowdrops and daffodils in early spring.

⊺⊺ FOOD & DRINK

The Crown Country Inn Munslow SY7 9ET ✆ 01584 841205. Once a Shropshire hundred house, then licensed as an inn in 1790, the Crown Country Inn – with its inglenook fireplaces, flagstone floors and inviting wood beams – is one of those places I dream of retreating to on a chilly autumn evening. Especially as I know the food in the two AA-rosette Corvedale Restaurant (which was a courtroom in the 17th century, sometimes presided over by 'the hanging' Judge Jeffreys) will be excellent: chef-patron Richard Arnold serves the best of the region's ingredients in generous portions and always with an exciting twist. It's about five miles from Westhope, on the B4368. After dinner and wine, you can stumble up to a comfortable timber-beamed bedroom: the Georgian stable block behind the inn houses three B&B rooms.

24 BROWN CLEE HILL

A E Housman wrote about the 'high-reared head of Clee' and actually Brown Clee Hill, northeast of Ludlow, has twin summits, **Clee Burf** and **Abdon Burf**. The latter, at 1,772 feet above sea level, is the highest point in Shropshire. This land was worked from the Neolithic period and served as a burial ground in the Bronze Age. From the 1900s it was intensively mined; you can still see the scars of bell pits and spoil tips although, as with so many places in Shropshire, nature has reclaimed the earth, replanting the upland commons with beech trees and bracken. Walking up one July I saw white fluffy bolls from cotton plants, looking for all the world like the snagged remains of walkers' socks.

> *"From the 1900s Brown Clee Hill was intensively mined: you can still see scars of bell pits and spoil tips although, as with so many places in Shropshire, nature has reclaimed the earth."*

Being so lofty, the Clee Hills were a hazard to planes; as you approach Clee Burf look for the **memorial** to 23 British, Canadian and German airmen who crashed here during World War II.

An ideal place to start your walk is at the hamlet of Abdon where you can follow the seven-mile **Brown Clee Circular** section of the Shropshire Way (a route leaflet is available to download from ✎ www. shropshirewalking.co.uk). It takes in **Nordy Bank**, an Iron Age hillfort and the camping location for the children in Sheena Porter's 1964 novel of the same name.

The **toposcope** on Abdon Burf is useful for naming the beauty over which you tower, over Wenlock Edge to the Long Mynd and further to Cader Idris. What it doesn't tell you is that, looking east, there are no higher hills until the Urals of Russia.

25 HEATH CHAPEL

🏠 **Upper Heath Farm** (page 248)

Nearly 787 feet up in the Clee Hills is a hamlet called Heath with an unusual feature: a **grade I-listed Norman chapel** standing isolated in a field of grass and buttercups riding rough over ridge and furrow. Apart from updates to the roof over the centuries and some 16th or 17th-century whitewashing (from beneath which traces of medieval murals have since resurfaced), the chapel is largely unchanged since the 12th century. While Heath is considered an abandoned town, with villagers over the centuries scattering to more distant farmsteads, the chapel is still consecrated. A church service takes place here on the second Sunday of the month at 18.30. At other times, you'll find the hefty iron key to the door behind the noticeboard at the entrance to the field (♀ SO557856) – a tiny adventure in itself.

26 TITTERSTONE CLEE HILL

🏠 **Timberstone Bed & Breakfast**, Clee Stanton (page 246)

Five miles south of Brown Clee Hill, and sometimes called locally – confusingly – Clee Hill, is the table-topped Titterstone Clee Hill. At 1,749 feet it's the third highest hill in Shropshire and the only named hill in Britain ('Mons Clece') to be included in the Mappa Mundi (c1300), a medieval map on vellum (now displayed in Hereford Cathedral) which gives us unique insight into how scholars of the time viewed the world, spiritually as well as geographically.

Much of the land at the top of Titterstone Clee Hill is a Site of Special Scientific Interest, including a 70-acre enclosure thought to be an Iron Age hillfort. More recent human imprints are old bell pits created by coal mining and the scars left from quarrying the dolerite dhustone (*dhu* is Gaelic for black), one of the hardest stones found in Britain. (It's still quarried today, behind Cleehill village.) The radar station on top is run by the National Air Traffic Service.

While I'd always recommend walking, you can drive up to the old quarry buildings by following the single-track road signposted 'Titterstone Clee Summit' from Cleehill village. Then you can walk to the summit, rewarded with almost 360-degree views which, on a clear day, stretch over Shropshire into Wales, Herefordshire, Worcestershire and the West Midlands.

27 HOPE BAGOT

🏠 **Annie's Cabin**, Caynham Mill (page 247), **Redford Farm Barns**, Nash (page 248)

The hilly civil parish and hamlet of Hope Bagot, two miles south of Cleehill village and six miles east of Ludlow, is blessed with the delightful and predominantly Norman **church of St John the Baptist**, one of the smallest churches in Shropshire. Through the lychgate and along a tiny path to the right you'll find a 'holy well' and, nurtured by its waters (said to help sore eyes), a gnarled and drooping yew tree, over 1,600 years old.

Look for the millstones in the base of the tower … and then consult the church guidebook on Valentine the miller who drowned in the 13th century. It's a fascinating story. On the north wall of the chancel is a 1795 memorial to Benjamin Giles, an unfortunate young man who met the 'irresistible summons of the King of Terrors'.

If you approach Hope Bagot from Ludlow you'll pass the turning for **Mahorall Farm Cider** (✆ 01584 890296 ⬧ www.farmcider.co.uk ◷ 12.00–17.00 daily). It's run by the King-Turner family: one-time dairy farmers who, in 1998, decided to turn their hands to the magic of apple pressing. You can buy their cider on draught or by the bottle in the small farm shop (cash only). Their 150 acres include open pasture and woodland as well as orchards, a varied landscape they've used to effect with an hour-long **nature trail**.

🍴 FOOD & DRINK

Bennetts End Inn Knowbury SY8 3LL ✆ 01584 890220. An inn since 1640, Bennetts End is a cracking country pub a mile from Hope Bagot (and just over four miles east of Ludlow). Early diners (18.00–19.00) can enjoy the three-course '15-mile' menu for £15, with ingredients sourced wherever possible from within 15 miles of the inn.

28 CLEOBURY MORTIMER

🏠 **Broome Park Farm** (page 246)

On the road from Ludlow to Bewdley in Worcestershire is this well-heeled town which, in John Betjeman's words in 1951, has 'a long airy curving street of brick Georgian houses and shops interspersed with genuine half-timber'. It still looks like that today. The French suffix to Cleobury (often pronounced locally as 'Clibree') comes from the Mortimer dynasty of marcher lords.

The pale green wooden steeple of **St Mary's Church** is twisted – that's 20 degrees of wonkiness, in fact – because of the warping of unseasoned timber beneath the stone. A sneering piece of folklore has it that a virgin was getting married in the church and the spire, bending over to have a look, got stuck; it will only straighten itself should such an unusual occurrence happen again. St Mary's is part of *L'Association des Clochers Torts d'Europe* – the European Association of Twisted Spires – with St Mary's & All Saints at Chesterfield in Derbyshire its only other English member. **William Langland**, the conjectured 14th-century poet author of *Piers Plowman*, may have been born in Cleobury Mortimer – although Ledbury and Great Malvern also claim him as their son. Never mind: the stained glass in the east window of St Mary's depicts the vision of Piers Plowman anyway.

Hobsons Brewery Sustainable Tasting Room

Newhouse Farm (on the southwest side of Cleobury Mortimer), Tenbury Rd, DY14 8RD
🖉 01299 270837 ⌀ www.hobsons-brewery.co.uk ◌ 09.00–17.00 Mon–Fri for collections

Hobsons, established in 1993, has a vision to become the UK's leading sustainable brewery. The family firm is well on its way, sourcing primary ingredients from supply chains created with hop and barley farmers from within 30 miles of Cleobury Mortimer. Hobsons also shows innovative use of green technologies: a wind turbine, rainwater harvesting, photovoltaic panels and a ground source heat pump system the team developed themselves to simultaneously heat their bottle conditioning room while cooling their barrel store (and warming their offices into the bargain). Meanwhile, lightweight beer bottles help to reduce packaging waste.

For me Hobsons is extra special for the local stories it tells through the names of its beers: Postman's Knock remembers Simon Evans (👜 see ⌀ www.bradtguides.com/postmanpoet for details), Old Prickly

JUST OVER THE BORDER

- **Aardvark Books**, a vast secondhand bookshop and tea room in Brampton Bryan, just into Herefordshire ◊ www.aardvark-books.com
- **Berrington Hall**, National Trust-owned country house by architect Henry Holland.
- **Knighton** in Powys, including **Offa's Dyke Centre** ◊ www.offasdyke.demon.co.uk/odc.htm
- **Montgomery**, mid-Welsh market town with Michelin-starred The Checkers.
- **Mortimer Forest**, with walking and cycling trails.
- **The Sun at Leintwardine**, a classic parlour pub with real ale. Order fish and chips from The Fiddler's Elbow in the village and they'll bring it to your table in The Sun.
- **Tenbury Wells**, a Worcestershire market town and home to **Burford House & Gardens**.
- **Welshpool & Llanfair Light Railway**, giving you a 16-mile return narrow gauge railway ride through the Banwy Valley in mid Wales.

commemorates the Shropshire-founded British Hedgehog Preservation Society and Twisted Spire is named in homage to the flawed steeple of nearby St Mary's Church.

In spring 2014 Hobsons Brewery opened its sustainable tasting room, an airy bar and kitchen for hosting brewery trips and special events. The highly insulated, low-energy building was crafted by local tradespeople using locally sourced materials. As well as regular brewery nights (incorporating a 'beer infused hot buffet'; I can't think of many things I'd enjoy more), look out for Hobsons' hugely popular foodie evenings with visiting producers and chefs (including the boys from Shrewsbury's CSONS). You'll need to book early.

If you're more of a cider drinker, don't miss the crisply delicious **Oldfields Orchard cider** by Hobsons' sister company in Worcestershire.

FOLLOW BRADT

For the latest news, special offers and competitions, subscribe to the Bradt newsletter via the website ◊ www.bradtguides.com and follow Bradt on:

- www.facebook.com/BradtTravelGuides
- @BradtGuides
- @bradtguides
- www.pinterest.com/bradtguides

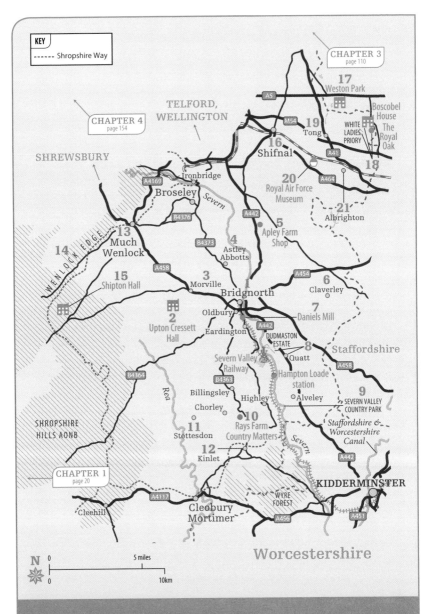

CHAPTER 3
page 110

17
Weston Park

Boscobel
House

WHITE
LADIES
PRIORY

The
Royal
Oak

18

TELFORD,
WELLINGTON

CHAPTER 4
page 154

A5

M54

19
Tong

A41

A464

SHREWSBURY

16
Shifnal

20
Royal Air Force
Museum

21
Albrighton

A4169

Ironbridge

Broseley

Severn

B4376

A442

5
Apley Farm
Shop

13
Much
Wenlock

14

B4373

4
Astley
Abbotts

6
Claverley

A454

WENLOCK EDGE

A458

15
Shipton Hall

3
Morville

1
Bridgnorth

7
Daniels Mill

2
Upton Cressett
Hall

Oldbury

Eardington

A442

DUDMASTON
ESTATE

8
Quatt

Staffordshire

A458

Severn Valley
Railway

Hampton Loade
station

9

B4364

Rea

B4363

Billingsley

Highley

Alveley

SEVERN VALLEY
COUNTRY PARK

SHROPSHIRE
HILLS AONB

Chorley

10
Rays Farm
Country Matters

Staffordshire &
Worcestershire
Canal

11
Stottesdon

Severn

CHAPTER 1
page 20

12
Kinlet

A442

KIDDERMINSTER

A4117

Cleobury
Mortimer

WYRE
FOREST

A451

Cleehill

A456

Worcestershire

N

0   5 miles

0   10km

SOUTHEAST SHROPSHIRE

2

SOUTHEAST SHROPSHIRE

Displayed in Bridgnorth's Northgate Museum is a 340-year-old faceless turret clock. In its glory days the clock sat high in a manor house called Larden Hall, now demolished, chiming out the hours for labourers in the fields. Well, perhaps not exact hours but as close to hours as its 17th-century foliot – an early kind of pendulum – could keep. I think it's only right to take inspiration from the turret clock's vague timekeeping while exploring this fascinating region.

We don't have the dreaming hills of the south to unite the scenery or even the flattish rurality of the north. Nor do we have the turbulent history and romance of Welsh borders; Shropshire's southeastern edges mingle with Staffordshire and Worcestershire, reaching into the Midlands' industrial past. What we do have are many individual treasures to discover, brought together before a backdrop of twisty lanes, sleepy villages, characterful pubs. There are the spectacular highs and Bassa Villa lows of **Bridgnorth**; quietly important **Much Wenlock**; the **Severn Valley Railway heritage line** and the site of the **Royal Oak** which sheltered the future King Charles II as he bolted from Cromwell's patrols. You'll find English country mansions and rolling landscapes at **Dudmaston** and **Weston Park**; an Elizabethan manor house living out its latest chapter at **Upton Cressett**. And all around are tangible echoes of British history: the age of steam, the English Civil War, the Norman Conquest.

Going beyond the more obvious attractions will lead you to a quiet church in **Astley Abbotts**, where an 18th-century funeral garland tells the tragic tale of a bride who never saw her wedding day. It may take you in the footsteps of Charles Dickens as he wrote *The Old Curiosity Shop*, to the churchyard in **Tong** where Victorian tourists reputedly wept over a fictitious grave. It could show you the old railway town of **Shifnal**, birthplace of a maid named Hannah Cullwick, whose adult life would play out as one of Shropshire's most intriguing love stories.

The more closely you look, the more secrets southeast Shropshire yields. This is a perfect reason to slow down and be guided simply by your appetite for eating and daylight for walking. Like the turret clock, a mere grasp of the hours is all the timekeeping you'll need …

It's not easy to divide southeast Shropshire into natural regions, so I've used Bridgnorth as a focal point and located most other places in relation to the town. Broseley is absent from this chapter; I've listed it in *Chapter 3* instead, due to its geographical and historical proximity to Ironbridge Gorge.

GETTING THERE & AROUND

Embrace Slow travel at its finest and catch the **Severn Valley Railway** heritage line from Kidderminster to Highley, Hampton Loade or Bridgnorth. The more conventional London Midland **train** line runs directly from Birmingham New Street (through Wolverhampton) and stops at Shifnal, Cosford and Albrighton before continuing to Telford Central, Oakengates, Wellington and Shrewsbury. Bridgnorth and Much Wenlock are well served with **buses** (except on Sundays) but unfortunately that isn't the case for every place listed in this chapter. I have given details throughout. On Saturdays, Sundays and bank holiday Mondays from May to the end of October you can take advantage of Regional Transport's 'hop on hop off' service between Shrewsbury and Ironbridge, which stops in Much Wenlock (⬧ www.cityxplora.com).

WALKING

This region lacks the dramatic hills and forests of south Shropshire and the diversity of scenery afforded by the meres and mosses in the north of the county. But the even terrain of southeast Shropshire makes for gentle expeditions, from village to farmland to woodland, and there are pleasant routes south of Bridgnorth following the line of the Severn Valley Railway and the river. Many excellent circular walks are outlined at ⬧ www.visitbridgnorth.co.uk/walkingsearch.php.

Try the **Severn Valley Country Park** for a shorter stroll combined with industrial history, or seek out the **Wyre Forest** spilling into Worcestershire where you'll find children's trails as well as longer waymarked routes. Some of the best walks take you into south Shropshire: the southeast has ideal entry points to **Wenlock Edge**, or you could approach **Brown Clee**

TOURIST INFORMATION

Bridgnorth The Library, Listley St, WV16 4AW ✆ 01746 763257 ◷ 09.30–17.00 Mon–Fri, 09.00–17.00 Sat
Much Wenlock Much Wenlock Museum, High St, TF13 6HR ✆ 01952 727679 ◷ Apr–Oct 10.30–13.00 & 13.30–16.00 Tue–Sun

Hill from Ditton Priors, at the parking area next to the road that runs from Cleobury North to Abdon (♥ SO607872).

The **Severn Way** is a long-distance waymarked trail following the River Severn from mid Wales to England's West Country. Starting in Bridgnorth, head south towards Bewdley in Worcestershire or north towards Ironbridge; the waymark depicts a cargo boat (trow) in blue. The **Mercian Way** (see below) and the **Jack Mytton Way** (see page 74) are also suitable for walkers, although the latter can get muddy in places. The 109-mile **Geopark Way** starts in Bridgnorth and travels south through the Wyre Forest into Worcestershire (⊘ www.geopark.org.uk).

The central part of this region is covered by ✻ OS Explorer map 218.

CYCLING

For traffic-free cycling, you can pick up the section of the National Cycle Network's route 45 which passes through Shropshire (including Bridgnorth): it's known as the **Mercian Way**. Part of this includes a ten-mile Bridgnorth to Ironbridge ride which follows a disused section of the Severn Valley Railway. For young families with bikes and a bike rack Kay Dartnell of Wheely Wonderful Cycling (which provides cycling holidays in Shropshire ⊘ www.wheely wonderfulcycling.co.uk) recommends the Mercian Way section accessed from the **Severn Valley Country Park**: 'It's great fun for kids and you'll get to see the trains as well as enjoying the cycling,' she said. Kay also offers an important safety tip: 'Generally the area along the Severn Valley is characterised by some steep climbs out of the valley and traffic pinch points,' she says. 'We all have to cross the river sometime so take care when negotiating these points.'

BIKE HIRE

Live the Adventure The Old Vicarage Centre, The Bullring, Stottesdon DY14 8UH ✆ 01746 718436 ⊘ www.livetheadventure.co. Formerly called the Old Vicarage Adventure Centre,

Live the Adventure offers mountain bike hire (including a drop-off and collection service) and guided rides, as well as many other outdoor pursuits.

BIKE SALES & REPAIRS

Paul's Pedals 58 Whitburn St, Bridgnorth WV16 4QP ℘ 01746 768792 ⟡ www. paulspedals.co.uk. Free pick-up and drop-off service in the Bridgnorth area.

HORSERIDING

Starting near Rays Farm Country Matters in Billingsley, the **Jack Mytton Way** is a waymarked trail of over 100 miles of bridleways and quiet country lanes. It's named after the 18th-century Shropshire squire John 'Mad Jack' Mytton, famous for his horsemanship and infamous for other reasons (page 218). The original Jack Mytton Way is marked on OS Explorer maps but for the latest information (including the development of a southern loop, which allows you to make circular rides), visit ⟡ www.shropshire.gov.uk/outdoor-recreation/the-jack-mytton-way.

If you're out on a hack southeast of Bridgnorth, **Stables Tea Room** at Broad Acre Stables in Broad Lanes (WV15 6EG ℘ 01746 781019 ☉ closed Sun & Mon) is a warmly welcoming place to tether your horse while you enjoy tea and cake. It's run by Mark and Lisa Welling on the six-acre site of their former racehorse training yard.

HORSE HIRE & RIDING LESSONS

Country Treks, part of Live the Adventure The Old Vicarage Centre, Stottesdon DY14 8UH ℘ 01746 718436 ⟡ www.horsetreks.co.uk. Horse or pony hire, as well as guided treks from short instructional rides to four-day trails.

WET-WEATHER ACTIVITIES

Afternoon tea at the David Austin Plant Centre (page 108)
House at Dudmaston Estate (pages 88–9)
Pigg's Playbarn at Apley Farm Shop (for children; pages 85–6)
RAF Museum at Cosford (page 107)
Weston Park house tour (page 102)

BRIDGNORTH & AROUND

Bridgnorth gives us two towns for the price of one: lofty High Town and, a hundred feet below on the banks of the River Severn, Low Town.

Or as it was known in the medieval period, Bassa Villa (Latin for 'basin of the town'). The two are connected by steps and road, as well as a quirky funicular railway. Nearby are the once-moated Elizabethan manor house Upton Cressett Hall; a garden of many stories at Morville; the leafy village of Astley Abbotts with its fascinating church; and the pretty village of Claverley.

1 BRIDGNORTH

🏠 **The Down Inn** (page 248)

Besieged by Henry I and ravaged during the Civil War, Bridgnorth's violent past is belied today by hanging baskets and Britain in Bloom awards. Maybe it's the cheery influence of the river which in summer is covered with the dainty white flowers of water crowfoot, but on a sunny day I find Bridgnorth feels like a seaside town without the sea. There are plenty of picnic spots (try **Castle Gardens** or Severn Park), bars for

"Bridgnorth feels like a seaside town without the sea."

alfresco drinking and dining, and views over the Severn Valley that Charles I is reputed to have declared the finest in all his kingdom. In the soft red sandstone at several locations around the town is evidence of former cave houses, dwellings of the poor. **Guided tours** of Bridgnorth are available on Friday and Saturday from April to October, leaving from the visitor information centre (Listley Street) at 14.15 (☏ 01746 767147).

The most scenic way to arrive in Bridgnorth is on the **Severn Valley Railway** from Kidderminster. Otherwise the Arriva **bus** service numbers 88a, 99 and 99a run to Bridgnorth from Telford bus station (via Ironbridge and Broseley) from Monday to Saturday. You can also catch the Arriva bus number 890 from Wolverhampton. **Parking** isn't always easy, especially at weekends: there's a pay and display car park opposite the library building on Listley Street (WV16 4AW) or you could try the larger private car park opposite Sainsbury's on Whitburn Street: pull over by the kiosk and pay a flat all-day fee (currently £2) to the owner. A park and ride scheme was recently being trialled on Saturdays, from an auction site in Tasley (WV16 4QR).

A memorable way of arriving **on foot** is to walk along the Severn – either from Ironbridge to the north (then catch the bus back), or from the south from any of several stations on the Severn Valley Railway (then return by train).

High Town

With its head up in heaven, its toes in the Severn.
Anon

Most of Bridgnorth's attractions are 'up in heaven', in High Town, where you'll find two important churches, the crooked remains of a castle and a healthy dose of independent shops. In 2003 Bridgnorth became Shropshire's first Fairtrade town, with an active community group working as part of Shropshire's Fairtrade Coalition. Reach High Town by ascending one of seven different flights of steps (choose the donkey-friendly Stoneway Steps to pass an 18th-century congregational chapel which is now **Theatre on the Steps** ✆ www.theatreonthesteps.co.uk), the **Cartway**, the road snaking up from Low Town (rock-cut cave dwellings here were inhabited by families until 1856) or – most people's favourite – the **funicular railway**.

The oak-framed black-and-white building dominating Bridgnorth's High Street, forcing traffic around its stone pillar stilts like a marvellously stubborn time traveller, is the old **Town Hall**. In an early version of upcycling, it was constructed in 1652 partly from a redundant tithe barn from Much Wenlock. Underneath is a covered market area: you'll find traders there on Friday, Saturday and Sunday or, if you visit on a non-market day, it's easier to see the 'Millennium boards' charting Bridgnorth's lively history from 895 to the late 1990s. You can go inside the Town Hall (☉ summer 10.00–15.00 daily, except Thu; winter 11.00–15.00 Fri–Sun) and see the old council chamber,

THE GIPSY DIVORCE

On your way up the Town Hall stairs to the tea room, pause for a moment by the oil painting of Hubert Smith, who was town clerk of Bridgnorth from 1873 to 1887. He looks unexceptional, but wait: Smith married a vivacious gipsy girl named Esmeralda Locke when he was in his 50s; she just 19. He was infatuated with her (in his book *Tent Life with English Gypsies in Norway* he described her 'dark hair, and eyes full of fathomless fire') but young Esmeralda did not return his feelings. After more than one attempt to escape the marriage she ran away with a scholar named Francis Hind Groome. In 1876 the 'gipsy divorce' was sensationalised by the Victorian press, with newspapers dubbing the case EXTRAORDINARY, REMARKABLE and, bafflingly, given that their unhappy story included duplicity and violence, ROMANTIC.

court room and waiting room; the latter is now a comfortable **tea room**. The striking stained glass depicting English monarchs was installed to commemorate Queen Victoria's golden jubilee.

Like the Town Hall, **North Gate** cuts a striking figure across Bridgnorth's High Street. It's the only one remaining of the town's five medieval fortifications and even this has been rebuilt, remodelled, patched and propped. The outside steps lead to **Northgate Museum** (⊙ w/ends from Easter to Oct & in school holidays) which has been run by volunteers from the Bridgnorth & District Historical Society since 1951. It contains over 4,000 local-interest objects, including a coracle (page 126–7) used in the 1930s. Admission is free, but donations are of course welcome and help to keep the museum running.

Bridgnorth's two main churches, both in High Town, are remarkable in different ways. Tucked behind High Street in a cathedral-like close, **St Leonard's** is a Victorian restoration of a gothic church, its tower soaring into the Bridgnorth skyline, its spirelet a cocked little finger. The original church was almost entirely destroyed during the Civil War, catching fire and partially exploding (perhaps unsurprisingly given its use as an ammunition store) after being hit by cannon shot fired from the castle by Royalists. The dark red sandstone of the exterior hides an airiness inside, although it never seems to be open when I want to go in. St Leonard's is redundant as a place of worship but is the main venue for **English Haydn Festival** concerts in early June (⊘ www.haydn.org.uk).

Entirely different yet equally impressive, the **church of St Mary Magdalene** at the end of handsome East Castle Street is a Thomas Telford design, built between 1792 and 1795. Six great windows flood the interior with light. Unusually, St Mary's is built to a north–south orientation, ensuring its grand square tower with four clock faces and green dome casts a benevolent gaze over the Severn Valley.

St Mary's shares grounds with the remains of **Bridgnorth Castle**. A Royalist stronghold during the Civil War, this once-great building was besieged for four weeks before the king's men surrendered. Parliamentarians pulled down the castle's walls and attempted to blow up the keep; their botched job means the ruin leans at 17 degrees – three times more than the Leaning Tower of Pisa. The surrounding **Castle Gardens** are a peaceful place to sit and listen for SVR engines chuffing through the valley – and don't miss the views down from **Castle Walk**.

Bridgnorth Cliff Railway

6A Castle Terrace ✆ 01746 762052 ⌨ www.bridgnorthcliffrailway.co.uk ⊝ daily ♿ not accessible; help can be given with folding wheelchairs & buggies

> If you approach the High Town by the railway you feel you are being lifted up to heaven.
> John Betjeman & John Piper's *Shell Guide to Shropshire* (1951)

For the definitive Bridgnorth experience – and a neat way to avoid the steps between High Town and Low Town – take a ride in 'England's oldest and steepest inland electric funicular railway'. Built in 1892, Bridgnorth Cliff Railway operates two cars on parallel tracks which counterbalance each other via steel ropes. The original design used a water ballast system and wooden cars but the model you'll ride today has aluminium cars (from 1955, so still agreeably vintage) powered by an electric winding engine. It's an inexpensive ride (a return ticket currently costs £1.20), and because it makes at least 150 trips every day, you'll never have to wait for long.

Low Town

In pre-rail times Bridgnorth was a busy port, the River Severn a vital passage to Bristol and beyond. From High Town you can follow the steep **Cartway** on foot to see where goods were hauled from barges and trows to the markets above. Towards the bottom of Cartway, look for the striking black-and-white building with a cobblestone front. The late-Elizabethan manor is known as **Bishop Percy's House** after a former owner, the author and reverend Thomas Percy, later Bishop of Dromore. Dated 1580 it's a rare survivor of medieval Bridgnorth, as much of the town was destroyed by fire during the Civil War. At the time of writing its owners had received planning permission to turn it into a tea room and holiday lets.

In Low Town, besides inspiring views back up to High Town, you'll find **Severn Park**, with children's playground and picnic area. The **Hermitage Caves** on the brow over Low Town (over the Wolverhampton Road) were once dwellings, dating to Saxon times and occupied until 1939. One, 33 feet in length, was used as a chapel. Several generations of children played in the empty caves until, tragically in 2009, a teenage boy was killed when a sandstone roof partially collapsed. The caves were permanently fenced off the following year; there are no plans to reopen them.

OLD MOORE

One of the stranger publications sold in UK newsagents (ignoring any specialist magazines lurking on the top shelves) is the horoscope and astral diary *Old Moore's Almanack*. Its story began in Bridgnorth. Francis Moore was born here in 1657 to the poorest of homes: his family dwelling was hewn from soft sandstone in the side of a cliff. He taught himself to read and, by his mid-twenties, had a physician's licence. Besides medicine he practised astrology, and served at the court of King Charles II. He brought out his first almanac primarily as an advertising ploy, to sell his own pills. Curiosity nudged me into buying the latest edition of *Old*

Moore's Almanack (not to be confused with the Irish version, spelled *Almanac*). I was amazed to see that being born in the 17th century is no barrier to Old Moore's ability to dish out world and sporting predictions even today. In fact he now has a 'massive new computer' through which (for 60p per minute) you can access 'enlightened insights into how best to exploit the day and the *moment*'. Other highlights are the ads: I now know where to procure Magickal Oils, Spell Kits and Life After Death DVD's [sic], or how to contact, via a premium-rate number, a Native American Shaman (based conveniently in south London).

The soft red sandstone from which the caves were carved is so much a part of Bridgnorth's story. In the landscaped gardens by Underhill Street you can see **Lavington's Hole**, a partial tunnel dug on the orders of Colonel Lavington during the Civil War. It was meant to reach beneath Castle Hill to allow Parliamentarian soldiers to blow up St Mary's Church, which housed munitions. But the Royalists surrendered before the tunnel was finished.

The clock tower on the bridge has a plaque commemorating the 1808 building of the world's first passenger locomotive at a nearby foundry.

SHOPPING

Bridgnorth Delicatessen 45 High St, High Town ✆ 01746 769001. Charcuterie, artisan bread and local cheeses, served from a cheeringly old-fashioned deli counter.

Tania Holland Gallery 7a Castle Terrace, High Town ✆ 07879 452807 ⊙ closed Thu & sometimes Tue & Sun. Contemporary fine art, craft and design gallery, with upcycled items up the creaky stairs on the first floor. Tania Holland's mixed-media depictions of Shropshire landmarks make lovely gifts.

Tanners Wines 36 High St, High Town ✆ 01746 763148 ⏚ www.tanners-wines.co.uk. A specialist Shropshire business (see page 173) acclaimed 'the best wine merchant in central England' by *The Observer*.

🍴 FOOD & DRINK

BamBoo with The Pie Room 15 Bridge St, Low Town ✐ 01746 765333. A cosy, friendly wine bar (closely associated with Tanners) located by the bridge in Low Town. From 17.30 they serve tasty, filling pies made by the local butcher.

Bec's 68A St Mary's St, High Town ✐ 01746 761850. I was first enticed to Bec's coffee shop by the chalkboard that is sometimes planted between St Mary's St and High St: 'Good Books, Great Coffee (Staff are OK)'. If that's not typical of the British sense of humour, I don't know what is. Upstairs is a comfy sofa area with books.

The Black Boy Inn 58 Cartway ✐ 01746 766497. An ale house since 1790 and named after King Charles II who was lovingly nicknamed the Black Boy, this pub has been restored and reopened recently to great acclaim. Landlord Stephen Illedge and his team truly know how to source, keep and serve top-quality beer.

The White Lion 3 West Castle St, High Town ✐ 01746 763962. Home to the Hop & Stagger Brewery and host to guest ales plus regular storytelling and folk music nights. The menu is small but includes homemade Scotch eggs.

The Winding House 6 Castle Terrace, High Town ✐ 01746 761962. This tea room shares a building with the Bridgnorth Cliff Railway kiosk so on a sunny day take a seat in the garden terrace and watch the funicular fun unfold. There are light lunches and afternoon tea (as well as coffee from Wolverhampton-based Shropshire coffee), and homemade jams to take away.

SEVERN VALLEY RAILWAY

Hollybush Rd, WV16 5DT (address for Bridgnorth Station) ✐ 01562 757900 (ticketing & general enquiries) ⛭ www.svr.co.uk ♿ good provision is made for wheelchair users

Bridgnorth is the northern terminus for the Severn Valley Railway, a heritage line on which full-size, mainly steam-hauled passenger trains run for 16 rumbling miles through the rural Severn Valley. You can reach the station by crossing the modern footbridge from High Town. Some of the restored period carriages date back a hundred years, their fine condition evidence of the care and work of the Severn Valley Railway Preservation Society, which was established in 1965 (just two years after the mass closure of lines and stations following the Beeching reports).

A ride on the SVR is ideal when you need to please several generations of the same family, offering as gentle or action-packed an adventure as you choose. Most families have at least one train enthusiast, I've discovered, but even without a penchant for rail it's easy to get swept up in the atmosphere: the slam-door carriages, the heady scent of steam, the wheezy whistle evoking a golden age of travel. Then there's verdant scenery, and the excitement of being plunged into darkness through the

A GUIDE TO SVR STATION STOPS

It's good to know that the Severn Valley Railway stations all link in with the river path, making station-to-station walking with the river as your guide (and the occasional puffing train to wave at) a real joy. To alight at either of the request stops, tell the guard before you join the train. To embark, signal to the driver by extending your arm horizontally as the train approaches the platform.

In Shropshire

Bridgnorth The station site is adjacent to the scheduled ancient monument Panpudding Hill, the earthworks of a medieval ringwork and bailey castle. Wander around the engine sheds and you may see trains being restored. The **Railwayman's Arms** on the platform opened in 1861 and holds the proud boast of being the station refreshment room that never closed, even when the trains stopped running in the 1960s. It serves plenty of regular and guest real ales. And in case only a cuppa will do, you'll find a tea room at Bridgnorth station, too.

Hampton Loade A picnic spot, with a steam model railway on Sundays. The name is misleading. The station is on the Hampton side of the river and the only way across to Hampton Loade (to venture into the woodland and parkland of Dudmaston Estate, for example) is to use the current-powered foot ferry ('lode' is an old word for ferry). River levels permitting, it operates from the end of March to mid-July on weekends and bank holidays, from 10.30 to 18.00. Ring the bell to summon the ferryman. You can also make a peaceful and meandering six-mile walk to Bridgnorth on the Hampton side of the river, following it upstream along the Severn Way footpath.

Country Park Halt (request stop) An unstaffed station leading to Severn Valley Country Park.

Highley Gift shop, children's play area, The Engine House museum and visitor centre (free entry for 'Freedom of the Line' ticketholders) including a reserve collection of locomotives and balcony views across the Severn Valley. Licensed Flag & Whistle Food Stop. Access to the Highley side of Severn Valley Country Park.

Into Worcestershire

Arley Arley Arboretum, ten minutes' walk from the station.

Northwood Halt (request stop) A tiny unstaffed station with replica Great Western Railway pagoda.

Bewdley A pretty Georgian riverside town, ten minutes' walk from the station.

Kidderminster Gift shop, restaurant and bar, Kidderminster Railway Museum (free entry), and Coalyard miniature railway running at weekends.

Bewdley Tunnel. You can also have bottled ales from Bewdley Brewery brought to your seat. Finally, I defy anyone not to be enchanted by the elephants and rhinos you can spot from the window as your train trundles surreally past the West Midlands Safari Park. It's no wonder the volunteers are delightful: they clearly love being part of it all.

The best-value **fares** are 'Freedom of the Line', a day pass allowing you to make unlimited stops, or 'Flexi-Rover', suitable for more than one consecutive day of travel. With the former you can save a little by purchasing online in advance; tickets are open-ended so you don't need to name your date. To enhance your knowledge of the route, pick up a free *From the Window* guide when you collect your tickets. The SVR runs a Sunday dining service, annual gala days and special events (including murder mysteries, fish and chip evenings and the highly popular Santa Steam Specials) which must all be booked in advance. Would-be drivers of both diesel and steam locomotives can have their dreams fulfilled thanks to footplate experience days.

"Would-be drivers of both diesels and steamies can have their dreams fulfilled thanks to footplate experience days."

If arriving by car you may wish to embark at the Kidderminster end, which is more geared up for parking than Bridgnorth. For those travelling with small children: there are toilets on board and at all stations except the halts.

2 UPTON CRESSETT HALL

Upton Cressett WV16 6UH ℰ 01746 714616 ⏲ www.uptoncressetthall.co.uk ☺ May–Sep, usually Sat & Sun afternoons

John Betjeman's 1951 *Shropshire* guide for Shell was a celebration of the freedom afforded by motoring, but even he suggested Upton Cressett is 'best approached on foot, horse or bicycle; only so can its peace and various landscape be appreciated'. I'd like to add that today Upton Cressett is not served by any bus route and navigating the narrow dust-track lanes with few passing places in the car is not my idea of fun. In case you want to arrive on your own two feet: the Jack Mytton Way passes about half a mile away (♀ SO655924).

Depending on your attitude, visiting Upton Cressett Hall is an opportunity either to see one of England's finest Elizabethan moated manor houses, or to peep inside the intriguing world of England's landed gentry. William Cash, son of Tory MP Bill Cash and current heritage spokesperson for UKIP, resides here with his third wife Lady Laura Cathcart – a celebrated society milliner – and it's likely that one·

or the other will lead your guided tour. A quick Google search should tell you that anything could happen while you're there; Cash admits on his blog that every weekend at Upton Cressett brings an 'abundance of episodes, mostly darkly comic': lost pugs, disastrous WI tours, a semi-naked Bill Cash sunbathing in the next-door garden (or perhaps not now the two have famously fallen out).

On the day of my visit we were rushed around the stately gatehouse (which can be hired, should you wish to follow in the pillow-dents of Margaret Thatcher) and manor by William Cash himself, who periodically barked 'Come on!' while tour-goers scrambled to keep up, a chocolate labrador whipping in and out of our calves. After less than half an hour he strode away, leaving us unsure as to whether the tour had ended: should we follow? (No.) For me, the tiny Norman church, rare white peacocks and **Lady Laura's Millinery Tea Room** nearly made up for the expensive tour fee and uncomfortable notion that I was indirectly funding UKIP. But not quite.

3 MORVILLE

Here is a scattered village set against the wooded slopes of Meadowley Bank, three miles northwest of Bridgnorth. You can reach it on the 436 bus that runs between Bridgnorth and Shrewsbury (also stopping at Much Wenlock), every day except Sunday.

It's hard to believe, but this tranquil spot was one of the most important settlements in Shropshire before the Norman Conquest, part of a vast Saxon manor to which Bridgnorth was of only minor importance. Past the junction into Morville from the A458, look for the remains of the village whipping post.

The rural location of the **church of St Gregory the Great** ($\odot$ daylight hours) shows how much greater this settlement would once have been. The stone building is predominantly Norman and even the door is probably original. A violent storm erupted on the day the church was consecrated by the Bishop of Hereford. The story goes that five horses and two women were killed from a lightning strike.

Built from stone and timber from the demolished Morville Priory, the Elizabethan **Morville Hall** was expanded in around 1750, giving it the appearance of a grand Georgian residence. Although managed by the National Trust, current tenanting arrangements mean the property isn't open for private tours – although you might get lucky

A ROSE FOR MORVILLE

Dr Katherine Swift

The first two volumes in Katherine Swift's Morville trilogy are *The Morville Hours* (2008) and *The Morville Year* (2010). Here she describes her inspiration for the third (*A Rose for Morville*, 2016): a Slow journey home.

A Rose for Morville was inspired by the landscapes of southwest Shropshire. I had been spending the winter in deep snow up at Shelve – the highest village in the county. When spring came, and with it the necessity to return to Morville, I decided to walk home, over the Shropshire Hills, a journey which by car would take an hour, and if walked in a straight line might take perhaps two weeks.

But this was to be a walk geological, historical, botanical; ecological, biographical, technological: from Mitchell's Fold to Buildwas, from the Welsh border to the Severn, from Stone Age to nuclear – against the grain of the land, walking in the footsteps of vanished lead miners and colliers, lime burners and quarrymen, drovers and coffin bearers, ignoring the roads – from pre-Cambrian to Coal Measures, dolerite to dhustone, limestone to new red sandstone, across the history and geology of Shropshire, and back through the layers of my own history, back to Morville.

More *paysage moralisé* than pastoral. I would search for the five wild roses of Shropshire, and find the places where the Industrial Revolution began. No need for geological maps: the stone of the churches and the soil in the fields would be my guides. Perhaps I could do without maps altogether, and plot my course from the top of one hill to the next, asking directions from the people I met. I would find people and places by accident, allowing myself to become lost. It would be less of a walk than a wander; not so much a ramble as an amble, proceeding at my own pace; my path a braid of stories, stretching eastwards over the hills into the rising sun. I decided to allow myself six weeks.

If I set off on Good Friday I could be home by Ascension Day …

during Morville Festival (page 85). You can, however, visit the **Dower House Garden** any Sunday, Wednesday or bank holiday Monday (☉ Apr–Sep, Sun, Wed & bank holiday Mon 14.00–18.00). This enchanting place is tenanted by Katherine Swift, a gifted writer and gardener who has divided her 1.5 acres into a sequence of gardens to tell the story of Morville Hall and the people who have lived here, from the arrival of Benedictine monks in 1138 through to the early 20th century. Following the structure of medieval *Books of Hours*, which guided monks through their day from Vigils to Compline, Dr Swift has woven her story – which is also the story of the garden, of Shropshire and of time itself – into *The Morville Hours*. In Shropshire it is the bestselling book ever, outselling even the *Harry Potter* titles.

When you visit, don't miss the chance to sit down for cream tea: freshly baked scones with jam made from fruits in the garden, probably served by Dr Swift herself. A great time of year to visit Morville is over the May bank holiday weekend when bunting, cream cakes and maypole dancers are out in (gentle) force for **Morville Festival** (⊘ www.morvillefestival.co.uk).

Just northwest of Morville, on the A458, is **Aldenham Park**, a former country seat of the important Actons of Acton Burnell. It's a private-hire venue now but as you pass take a peek at the wrought-iron gates: the depiction of the leg dripping blood is thought to recall a tale about an early Acton who severed his own limb and hurled it across the stream to claim ownership of the land on which it fell.

4 ASTLEY ABBOTTS

The manor at Astley once belonged to Shrewsbury Abbey, hence the Abbotts suffix to the name of this tree-shaded village and parish just north of Bridgnorth (along the B4373 and down a country lane flanked by fields and farmland). The church dedicated to **St Calixtus** (☉ daylight hours) is built on a Saxon site; relics of the latter including the sandstone-hewn font (which spent some undignified years as a cattle trough in a neighbouring field) and possibly the corbels in the hammer-beamed roof: two flying horses, a lion, phoenix, eagle and a unicorn. In the alcove next to the organ is a heart-shaped wooden frame adorned with gloves and ribbons. This is a maiden's garland (page 186), dedicated to Hannah Phillips, who drowned in May 1707 while crossing the Severn to prepare the church for her wedding day. Hannah's sister Catherine is remembered less mournfully on a benefaction board in the nave: she left a legacy for poor widows and children of the parish.

5 APLEY FARM SHOP

🏠 **The Hundred House** (page 248)

Norton TF11 9EF (a sat nav error may take you the wrong way, so look for signs) ⊘ 01952 730345 ⊘ www.apleyfarmshop.co.uk ☉ daily; the playbarn & café tend to close earlier than the shops

It's always good to see clued-up landowners opening their estates to families and fun. Lord and Lady Hamilton of the Apley Estate are a case in point, lovingly developing Apley Farm Shop in a huge diversification and restoration project that included a renewable energy programme. The Hamilton family has owned the 8,500-acre estate since 1868 – and we should feel very glad they still do. World War II experts believe Adolf Hitler had earmarked Apley Hall as his UK headquarters had the German invasion of Britain been successful. Thankfully, history conspired otherwise and alongside many other blessings brought us not Nazis but Apley Farm Shop. It's one of my favourite farm shops anywhere, with a deli stocked with local cheeses and a butchery selling

"World War II experts believe Adolf Hitler had earmarked Apley Hall as his UK headquarters had the German invasion of Britain been successful."

meat directly from the estate. But the site is much more than a farm shop now. For fair weather there is **Scotty's Animal Park**, offering close encounters of the alpaca, chicken, goose, horse, pig and sheep kind. The mile-long **Skylark Nature Trail**, beginning and ending at the car park, has periodic benches and seven information boards. When you need indoor activities, try **Pigg's Playbarn**, a soft-play centre big enough for little legs to burn up energy and small enough for adults to be able to recline on the sofas, worry-free, with coffee and homemade cake. Both Pigg's and Scotty's incur an entry fee; Skylark is free. The courtyard shops sell toys, high-end skincare and clothing.

⊺⊺ FOOD & DRINK

The Creamery Café Apley Farm Shop. Housed in the barn where Apley Cheese was once produced (there are plans to bring it back), the Creamery Café is big on flavours and small on food miles, using ingredients from the Apley Estate and local suppliers. Typical dishes are charcuterie boards, ploughman's lunches, sausage or steak baguettes and homemade soups and tarts. It's child-friendly, with a healthy children's menu, plenty of highchairs, and a basket of toys to whisk out for the bored.

The Hundred House Norton TF11 9EE ✆ 01952 580240. Half a mile north of Apley Farm is this eccentric-in-a-good-way Georgian country inn with restaurant and quirkily decadent rooms, lauded for its Secret Gardens and two AA-rosette dining. The menu is inspired by cuisines from across the world and realised using the best of local and seasonal produce. This is fine dining without fussiness (or indeed measly portions: you'll need a big appetite).

6 CLAVERLEY

Claverley means 'the clearing where the clover grows': a suitably pretty name for this pretty village five miles east of Bridgnorth, where jutting and sloping red sandstone cottages and black-and-white houses appear at one with the rolling countryside. **All Saints' Church** is medieval and Norman, with important features that include an effigy-topped tomb for Sir Robert Broke (also rendered Brook or Brooke), Speaker of the House of Commons in 1554. The churchyard nurtures one of the oldest and biggest yew trees in the country, predating the church itself.

"All Saints' Church features an effigy-topped tomb for Sir Robert Broke, and the churchyard nurtures one of the oldest yew trees in the country."

A good time to visit is during Claverley's Flower Festival, held in the church in the second weekend of July. The owners of nearby **Ludstone Hall** (former home of Sir Robert Broke) usually open their glorious gardens to the public on the Sunday of the Flower Festival weekend to raise money for the church. It's a privilege to see the Jacobean house and medieval moat up close. The family's smartly converted Coach House Museum charts the history of the house and there is also a section relating to their personal history in founding the Poundland empire.

About a mile north of Claverley, off the A454 at Rudge Heath Nurseries (so just nudging into Wolverhampton), is **Jones of Shropshire** (WV6 7EE ✆ 01746 710033 ⊙ 10.00–17.00 daily) the self-styled 'permanent vintage fair', crammed with artfully curated vintage items, crafts and antiques, including clothing and jewellery. Tea and cake is on hand thanks to the **Lovecake** vintage caravan (⊙ 11.00–16.00).

FOOD & DRINK

The Plough Inn Aston Lane, WV5 7DX ✆ 01746 710667. A real-ale pub and restaurant with oak beams, toasty fires, homemade pub grub and handcut chips that cannot fail to comfort. Booking is essential on Sundays.

SOUTH OF BRIDGNORTH & THE SEVERN VALLEY

South of Bridgnorth is the rural Severn Valley, known as much for the popular steam railway running through its scenic farmland as for the mighty river it carries, the longest in the UK. The soft sandstone around the Severn is not ideal for load-bearing bridges, so there are no public road crossings after Bridgnorth until Bewdley in Worcestershire.

7 DANIELS MILL

Eardington WV16 5JL ✆ 01746 762753 ⊘ www.danielsmill.co.uk ⊙ Easter– end Oct
11.00–16.00 Wed–Sun, & bank holiday Mon

Just under two miles south of Bridgnorth, Daniels Mill has been owned – and saved – by the same family for over 250 years. The name probably came by way of Donynges, Dunnings, Dunhills and Dunnells, and stabilised as Daniels in the mid 19th century (with the occasional appearance of an apostrophe). The water which powers the mill is from Potseething Spring, which rises about half a mile away and is said to have a mineral content that soothes sore eyes. It's remarkable to see the grand wheel in motion (at 38 feet in diameter it's the largest wheel on a working corn mill in England) and hear the mill's story told by someone living the reality of its latest chapter. Peter George told me how the industry has given rise to not only obviously mill-related expressions ('like a millpond', 'been through the mill', 'all's grist to the mill') but also less obvious phrases: 'sling your hook' and 'test your mettle'. A small museum focuses on milling, the generations who have lived at Daniels Mill, restoration projects, and the disastrous local floods of 2007. Milling experience days were new in 2015. Enjoy tea and homemade scones in the on-site **Stables Tea Room**; you can also buy freshly milled stoneground flour.

8 QUATT & DUDMASTON ESTATE

With model sandstone cottages lining the main road (the A442 from Bridgnorth to Kidderminster), neatly pretty **Quatt** is a great landing point for nearby Dudmaston Estate. The **Farm Shop & Deli** is a friendly place to call in for a coffee and locally made ice cream, or to pick up organic veg. Once the village school, the idyllic **Quatt Village Hall** is lucky to have volunteers making huge efforts to engage with the rural community: you can see a list of events at ⊘ www.quatt.info. Quatt is served, although not frequently, by the Arriva **bus** service 297 that runs between Bridgnorth and Kidderminster.

Dudmaston Estate

🏠 **Mose Cottage & Big Mose Bunkhouse** (page 248)

WV15 6QN ✆ 01746 780866 ⊙ mid-Mar–end Oct, check daily times before visiting;
National Trust

With its 17th-century hall in red sandstone so typical of this area, undulating gardens, lake (the tranquil Big Pool), parkland, dingle and farmland, Dudmaston is the perfect place to see a traditional Shropshire estate. We owe thanks to its last owner Lady Rachel Labouchere (who preferred to be known as Lady L) for bequeathing it to the National Trust for posterity. Indeed the hall's most interesting exhibition, for me, is the one celebrating Lady L's life in China, Argentina, Austria, Hungary and Belgium with her diplomat husband, Sir George Labouchere. Lady L was a direct descendant of the Abraham Darbys and instrumental in the establishment of the Ironbridge Gorge Museum Trust, serving for 14 years as its president.

Also notable at Dudmaston are Lady L's Dutch floral paintings and Sir George's eclectic modern art collection. Apparently aware that his taste was not of the mainstream, Sir George would often 'pop up' at a visitor's shoulder to ask their opinion. And if when you envisage Queen Victoria, you see a large solemn widow in black, don't miss the portrait in the inner hall of the monarch as a radiant 20 year old.

The house is now tenanted by the Hamilton Russell family and a much-loved family home, so don't be surprised if you see a pair of children's shoes peeping out from under a table.

As with most National Trust properties there are commendable efforts at Dudmaston towards sustainability: for example, waste water filtered through a reed-bed sewage system is returned to the Big Pool. The estate offers a full day out, with children's play area, gift shop and secondhand bookshop. **The Apple Store** in the Brewhouse Courtyard is the place to go for a quick pastry, sandwich, handmade cake or drink: look for apple juice pressed from Dudmaston's many orchard varieties. **The Orchard** tea room offers more substantial, seasonal hot lunches (hotpots and freshly baked bread, perhaps), with much of the produce originating from the estate's kitchen garden (⊙ opening hours as per the estate).

You can pick up walk cards at the entrance, guiding you through Dudmaston's wooded valley.

9 SEVERN VALLEY COUNTRY PARK

Alveley WV15 6NG (follow signs from Alveley instead of your sat nav) ✐ 01746 781192 (for visitor centre & tea shop) ⊙ Apr–Oct 11.00–17.00 Wed to Sun (also bank holidays & every day in school holidays), Nov–Mar 11.00–16.00 w/ends

A true beauty that belies an industrial past is Severn Valley Country Park, site of the former Alveley and Highley collieries about eight miles south of Bridgnorth. A reclamation scheme begun in the 1980s has swapped spoil heaps for footpaths and woodland: now there are 126 acres of countryside to explore, including waymarked trails, picnic areas, ponds, meadows, a permanent orienteering trail and an accessible bird hide. The children's playground is made from natural materials (sand for digging and stones for hopping over) and gets extra exciting when SVR engines trundle through the valley below with a toot and a puff of steam.

"A reclamation scheme has swapped spoil heaps for footpaths and woodland."

Dogs are welcome – you will probably find a bowl of water for them outside the **visitor centre and tea shop**, which is run by Shropshire Council. There are beanbags and crayons inside for the smallest visitors, plus toilets with baby-changing facilities. The shop sells local interest books, maps and walking leaflets.

Alveley and Highley's mining heritage has not been forgotten: at the **Station Road Site** (♀ SO746831) a huge pulley wheel stands in memory of the men who were at the core of this mining community, which was of course hit hard, economically and emotionally, by the pit closures.

To arrive at the main site by train, request the Country Park Halt from the Severn Valley Railway or, by bike, follow Route 45 (Mercian Way) from Bridgnorth or Bewdley. For drivers, there's a pay and display car park.

10 RAYS FARM COUNTRY MATTERS

Chorley, Billingsley WV16 6PF (but look for signs instead of following your sat nav as the postcode may take you the wrong way down bumpy lanes) ℰ 01299 841255 ⌂ www.raysfarm.com ♿ special thought is given to visitors with accessibility needs: see website

About six miles south of Bridgnorth (on the west side of the Severn), Rays Farm Country Matters is a pleasing place to spend a sunny day with your favourite small people. Donkeys, sheep, alpaca and rabbits are always popular with my lot but the magic of Rays Farm lies, for us, with the Fairytale Forest walk. Around fifty wooden sculptures – gnomes, dragons, characters from nursery rhymes – make a stroll in the glades more fun. The bumpy route isn't suitable for buggies or wheelchairs, although the rest of the farm shows special thought for people with accessibility needs. A soft play area makes Rays Farm an all-weather possibility for families with small children. I found the **café** disappointing and wished I'd taken a picnic to enjoy away from the busy courtyard.

For horseriders, walkers and cyclists, the **Jack Mytton Way** starts here.

11 STOTTESDON

🏠 **Live the Adventure House** (page 248), **The Old Rectory** (page 248)

In Saxon times Stottesdon (about four miles by road east of Billingsley; nine miles south of Bridgnorth) – which probably means 'the hill of the herd of horses' – encompassed a huge manor and seven villages. Consequently the substantial size of **St Mary's Church** (☉ usually open during the day; if not, a list of keyholders is displayed in the porch), built before the Norman Conquest (although only parts of the original building remain), is disproportionate now to Stottesdon's modern-day population of just over 700 people. Of special note inside are the medieval tiles in the north side of the chancel floor and the Norman font (c1138) with intricate carvings of creatures that include cockatrices, centaurs and griffins. Over the west door beneath the tower (you can reach it through the door at the back of the organ) is a tympanum, thought to be more than 900 years old, with simple animal carvings and mysterious symbols presided over by an elongated, bearded and rather spooky face.

> *"Over the west door is a tympanum, with simple animal carvings and mysterious symbols presided over by an elongated, bearded and spooky face."*

The Old Vicarage is the headquarters of **Live the Adventure** (⬠ www.livetheadventure.co), offering training, residential courses and a huge range of outdoor activities including climbing, raft building, paintballing, archery and orienteering.

This area is somewhat bereft of **bus** routes but you'll find inspiring rambles and ambles to follow at ⬠ www.stottystrollers.org.uk, or you could follow the **Simon Evans Way** from Cleobury Mortimer (🖐 for more on Simon Evans, go to www.bradtguides.com/postmanpoet).

🍴 FOOD & DRINK

The Fighting Cocks (☎ 01746 718270) is the very model of a pub's ability to service what could easily become an isolated community (see ⬠ www.pubisthehub.org.uk). Proprietor Sandra Jefferies has converted a stone outbuilding to become **Shop at the Cocks**, supporting local suppliers and giving the people of Stottesdon a place to buy essentials and stop for a chat. For this Sandra has been personally congratulated by Prince Charles. For her homemade pies, seasonal produce (which is very local: the sausages come from Sandra's own pigs) and roaring fire, Sandra is personally congratulated – perhaps not as impressively but every bit as heartily – by me.

12 KINLET

This large parish on the northern edge of the Wyre Forest incorporates the hamlets of Kinlet village, Button Bridge and Button Oak. I've mentioned it because of the special **church of St John the Baptist** (♀ SO711810) which stands lonely on the side of a hill. Simon Jenkins in *England's Thousand Best Churches* describes how the 'village has gone, the only locals being the ghosts in the churchyard and rooks in the high trees'. Inside are some astonishing monuments, most notably the two-tier tomb of Sir George Blount (d1581), with cadaver chest beneath and intricate marble carvings of Blount, his wife Constantia, daughter Dorothy and son John above. John Blount died young, having reputedly choked on an apple 'skork', his early demise symbolised here by a terrifying, teeth-baring skull in his right hand. An intriguing tale about the bottled ghost of Sir George Blount is recounted in full in the church's glossy pamphlet. Be sure to flip back through the visitors' book: with entries starting in the 1940s, even this tells its own tales, of changing handwriting, pen types and sentiment.

The Stourbridge to Bridgnorth **bus** service number 125 stops outside the **Eagle & Serpent** (which, incidentally, always has at least two guest ales on draught). To reach the church cross the road and follow the wide country track by the sign for Moffatts School (a private day and boarding school in what was formerly Kinlet Hall) for about a mile.

Kinlet would once have had dense tree cover, part of the ancient woodland of the **Wyre Forest**. The remaining forest stretches into Worcestershire and is therefore beyond the scope of this book, but the best access point is at nearby **Callow Hill** (DY14 9XQ ♀ SO750740) where you'll find a visitors' centre and café, Go Ape! high-ropes course, wooden playground, waymarked cycle and walking trails, and children's trails (often themed with Julia Donaldson's popular stories).

JUST OVER THE BORDER

- **Bewdley** A handsome Georgian riverside town.
- **Chillington Hall** ⬧ www.chillingtonhall.co.uk
- **Halfpenny Green Vineyards** ⬧ www.halfpenny-green-vineyards.co.uk
- **Kinver Edge** National Trust-managed sandstone ridge with rock houses.
- **West Midlands Safari Park** ⬧ www.wmsp.co.uk

13 MUCH WENLOCK

🏠 **End Barn** (page 248), **Raven Hotel** (page 248), **Wenlock Pottery** (page 248)

If you think the charm of the prettiest English towns lies in uniformity of architecture, please visit Much Wenlock where medieval, Georgian and Victorian buildings loll shoulder to shoulder in sleepy companionship. Somnolent it is, although by design not dereliction. 'Somewhere in the Middle Ages it had fallen asleep,' said the early 20th-century Shropshire writer Mary Webb in her short story 'Many Mansions' – a quote that many towns would shy away from celebrating but which often appears in Much Wenlock's tourism literature. One sunny June when I was in town, a minor road accident occurred on Sheinton Street (notice, by the way, how this road turns into Shineton Street by the other end); more of a nudge than a crash, causing nothing worse than a twisted wheel and perhaps dented pride. The one person involved, I'm happy to report, popped into a tea room to await breakdown rescue. As I shopped for picnic goods I followed the breaking news as it spread breathlessly from the convenience store to the butcher's to the deli. It was clearly the biggest thing to happen all week and, for that reason (as well as many others), I adore Much Wenlock and its friendly residents.

The town grew up around Wenlock Priory, founded by the 7th-century King Merewalh of Mercia and flourishing in the hands of his daughter Milburga. Retaining a medieval street pattern and passageways called 'shuts', the town was extended during the early 19th century to accommodate a growing population of railway and quarry workers.

On the subject of quarrying: the rough pale grey stone found in abundance here is Wenlock limestone, extracted from Wenlock Edge. Peer at coarser specimens (such as the stone used for Jubilee Fountain in the town square) and you'll see crystals, fossil corals and crinoids: miniscule messengers from 400 million years ago reminding us that this region was once a coral reef in a tropical sea (see *Geology* by Dr Peter Toghill on pages 12–13).

Getting here by public transport is easy, six days a week anyway. The Arriva **bus** service number 88 runs to Much Wenlock from Telford bus station (via Ironbridge and Broseley) about every two hours (Monday to Saturday only), taking just under an hour. Also Arriva bus service 436 from Shrewsbury (Raven Meadows bus station; just over half an hour) or Bridgnorth (by the Falcon Hotel in Low Town; just under half an hour). Buses don't run on Sundays. If you're **driving**, you'll find the main car parks are off St Marys Road (TF13 6HD will take you to the vicinity). There are usually spaces in the pay and display car park by Wenlock Priory too and the proceeds go to English Heritage. If you need inspiration for nearby walks, the post office sells OS maps and locally produced walking guides.

MUCH WENLOCK'S HISTORIC CENTRE

To imagine Much Wenlock's importance in the 16th century we need only look to Wilmore Street and the **Guildhall**, the grand magpie building with open market space beneath (called the **Buttermarket** – where you'll find food and drink stalls most days). From 1540 the Guildhall was the judicial and administrative heart of the borough, updated regularly in the centuries that followed, including in 1624 with 'Lattinge and plastering the Comon gaol overhead To Keep the Smoake and Nesty Smell' out of the council chamber. By the gates you can see hand irons, the remains of the town whipping posts. Upstairs is a **museum** (☉ Apr–Oct Fri–Mon; free entry) set among 17th-century and Victorian wood panelling, documenting life in the courtroom. It contains displays on A E Housman and Dr William Penny Brookes

THE BIRTHPLACE OF THE MODERN OLYMPICS

One of the mascots for the London 2012 Olympic Games was Wenlock, named in honour of this market town's place in modern Olympic history. Much Wenlock was home to a Victorian doctor and social reformer called William Penny Brookes, who founded the Much Wenlock Olympian Society to 'promote the Moral and Physical benefits of Exercise' and later helped establish the National Olympian Association. Inspired by a visit to the town in 1889, when the Wenlock Olympian Games were staged for his benefit, the French aristocrat Baron Pierre de Coubertin took on Dr Brookes's dream of reviving the ancient games on an international level. Sadly, Dr Brookes died, aged 86, four months before the 1896 Summer Olympics in Athens, but his legacy is kept very much alive in this quiet Shropshire town. The Wenlock Olympian Games are held every July on the Gaskell Field and Much Wenlock's 1⅓-mile **Olympian Trail** takes you, by way of bronze pavement markers, past landmarks that include Dr Brookes's childhood home at 4 Wilmore Street and to his family resting place, surrounded by wrought-iron Olympian wreaths, in the gardenlike grounds of Holy Trinity Church. The Olympian Trail starts and ends at Much Wenlock Museum, where you can pick up a free trail leaflet.

(who made substantial contributions to updating the Guildhall during his lifetime).

Also remembered in the museum is **Mary Webb**, a memorial to whom nestles in flowerbeds behind the Guildhall, facing the churchyard. Discovering her work – ablaze with sumptuous nature writing and wry human observations – has been one of my greatest joys in researching this book. In 1949 Much Wenlock was abuzz with the filming of *Gone To Earth* (a movie adaptation of Mary Webb's most famous novel), starring Jennifer Jones as the half-gipsy heroine Hazel Woodus. Over 300 local people had parts as extras: the film company paid 30s per day and more for those who came on horseback. Mary Palmer, a Much Wenlock resident and member of the Mary Webb Society, was in a maypole dancing scene. 'I was only five years old, but I do remember we were taken up in a bus to the village hall at Minsterley where we were so excited to be fitted out with dresses,' she told me. 'Mine was a longish red spotted dress and my pigtails were taken loose and brushed. I also remember a group of us singing to Jennifer Jones outside her caravan.'

"In 1949 Much Wenlock was abuzz with the filming of Gone to Earth, *starring Jennifer Jones as half-gipsy heroine Hazel."*

The nave of the gracefully aged **Holy Trinity** parish church dates to the 12th century, although St Milburga founded a nuns' church here as early as AD680. On the rear wall are memorials to Dr William Penny Brookes: a Victorian plaque with a relief of his likeness, and a poignant 2012 addition. Look to the Jacobean pulpit to see curious two-tailed mer-men.

WENLOCK PRIORY
5 Sheinton St, TF13 6HS ✆ 01952 727466 ◷ daily in summer; Nov–mid-Feb w/ends only (see website for up-to-date times); parking £1 all day; English Heritage

Before power was given over to the Guildhall, life in medieval Much Wenlock revolved around the Cluniac Priory. Here stand their imagination-inspiring ruins on the site of a Saxon predecessor. St Milburga's relics turned up conveniently in 1101, bringing pilgrims and prosperity to the area. (You'll also find Milburga's Well just off Barrow Street in Much Wenlock; the water was thought to be a cure for eye diseases.) Visit today for tranquillity and topiary: Wenlock Priory is a fine place to picnic on a summer's day, with hedges shaped like animals in the cloister garden. There's an interesting monks' washing fountain (lavabo) with 12th-century carvings, and the humbling ruins of an extravagant chapter house, dating from c1140. Modern visitors have the added bonus of a small gift shop and toilets with baby-changing facilities.

"Lady Catherine Milnes Gaskell was an author who entertained the likes of Henry James and Thomas Hardy in Much Wenlock."

The kissing-gate on the left as you head up Bull Ring toward Wenlock Priory takes you along a public footpath between fields. Choose the left fork to cut through to Station Road. Wenlock station has been converted into a private dwelling: the last passenger train chugged out of town on 21 July 1962 – a victim of Dr Beeching's axe. Choose the right fork for a slightly longer walk to the **Linden Field** (also known as the **Gaskell Field**, after Lady Catherine Milnes Gaskell, an author who entertained the likes of Henry James and Thomas Hardy in Much Wenlock). The Linden Field, named after the lime trees planted by Dr Penny Brookes, is where the **Wenlock Olympian Games** are held. Turn left along the row of lime trees to reach Station Road.

MUCH WENLOCK MUSEUM & VISITOR CENTRE & HIGH STREET

High St ✒ 01952 727679 ◷ Apr–Oct 10.30–13.00 & 13.30–16.00 Tue–Sun; free entry & free Wi-Fi ♿ fully accessible

The welcoming and well-curated Much Wenlock Museum and visitor centre underwent a major refurbishment with Heritage Lottery Fund

MUCH FUN

It might have been called 'Sleepy Hollow' in an 1860 travelogue by Walter White (the writer, not the *Breaking Bad* character) but Much Wenlock sure knows how to host a gathering. The three-day **Wenlock Poetry Festival** (⌘ www.wenlockpoetryfestival. org) is held towards the end of April at **The Edge** (an arts centre attached to William Brookes School) and other venues around town, attracting performers of international renown. Its patron is Poet Laureate Carol

Ann Duffy who described Much Wenlock as 'the perfect place for poetry'. The **Much Wenlock Festival** (⌘ www. muchwenlockfestival.co.uk) in early June has a programme of literary events, concerts, plays, walks and open gardens. In July there are the **Wenlock Olympian Games** (⌘ www.wenlock-olympian-society.org.uk) and **Festival at the Edge** (⌘ www. festivalattheedge.org) – a weekend of storytelling at nearby Stokes Barn.

support and reopened in 2012 to coincide with the London Olympic Games. It focuses mainly on the Olympic and geological legacy of Much Wenlock and beyond, with displays also on Mary Webb and local archaeology. The shop sells walking maps and guidebooks.

A brook runs beneath **High Street**. **Ashfield Hall** was once Blue Bridge Inn, taking its name from a blue stone footbridge that crossed the stream. This site has seen rags and riches: Charles I is thought to have stayed at Ashfield Hall *en route* from Shrewsbury to Oxford in 1642, while its 13th-century incarnation as St John's Hospital provided shelter to 'lost and naked beggars'. Hence High Street used to be called Spittle Street – its name derived from 'hospital'. Also on High Street is the **Corn Exchange**, built in 1852 thanks in part to Dr William Penny Brookes who raised funds from public subscription. A plaque commemorates the passing of the Olympic torch through Much Wenlock in 2012 and the 'small spark of imagination that inspired the world'. Markets are held here most days.

 SHOPPING

I can cheerfully lose hours pottering around Much Wenlock's shops. These include two indie bookshops on the High Street: the forgivably ungrammatically named **Much More Books** (a secondhand, rare, antiquarian and out-of-print specialist) and shiny red-fronted **Wenlock Books** in a 15th-century building that naturally lends itself to cosy reading nooks and lost (in-a-novel) spouses. Owner Anna Dreda also founded Wenlock Poetry Festival. If you see people queuing in the High Street it's probably for **A. Ryan & Sons**, the butchers' shop, which has been established more than 30 years. The homemade pies, pasties and quiches are, to quote my husband, 'legendary'. **Wenlock Deli** opposite sells plenty of local produce, too.

CRAFTS

Twenty Twenty Gallery 3–4 High St ✆ 01952 727952 ⏁ www.twenty-twenty.co.uk. Champions British contemporary art and crafts.

Wenlock Pottery & Craft Centre Shineton St ✆ 01952 727600 ⏁ www.wenlockpottery. co.uk. As well as housing a popular B&B this former Methodist chapel is now *the* place in Shropshire to throw pots. Enjoy a drink in the licensed bar or buy some handmade stoneware. Pre-booked tours are available (including evening tours), as well as a 'ceramic café' for visitors who wish to paint their own plates and mugs. It's best to contact the owners in advance if you're coming from any great distance: they get busy with commissions and occasionally have to close.

🍴 FOOD & DRINK

You can't go far wrong when eating out in Much Wenlock, with tea rooms, pubs and hotels to suit all budgets and occasions, and almost every establishment paying due attention to seasonality and locality. A special mention goes to the two AA-rosette restaurant with rooms the **Raven Hotel** on Barrow St (✆ 01952 727251) which has a special place in Much Wenlock's Olympic history. In 1890 it hosted a pivotal dinner meeting between Dr William Penny Brookes and Baron Pierre de Coubertin following the Wenlock Olympian Games. (Look for a copy of the menu from that night in the Brookes Bar which is housed in the original 17th-century coaching inn.) Of course history alone is not enough to recommend a place: thankfully now the Raven has understated elegance, and a bright young chef in Jason Hodnett who works super-local produce into a frequently changing, fine-dining British menu. For a treat representing excellent value look for the five- or seven-course surprise tasting menu with optional wine flight.

MARY WEBB'S SHROPSHIRE

Dr Gladys Mary Coles is the world authority on Mary Webb, and president of the Mary Webb Society. Her latest book, *Mary Webb and her Shropshire World, with a Guide to the Mary Webb Country*, will be published by Headland in autumn 2016.

Mary Webb was born at Leighton near The Wrekin in 1881, the first child of George Edward Meredith (an Oxford MA proud of his Welsh descent) and wealthy Sarah Alice Scott (proud of her claimed kinship with Sir Walter Scott). Before Mary was two, the Merediths moved to Much Wenlock where she spent most of her childhood, educated in her father's boarding school and later by a governess. The two greatest influences on Mary were the Shropshire countryside and her beloved father, a poet who loved nature and Shropshire's legends and folklore. Mary lived most of her 46 years in her home county and, like Emily Brontë, felt unhappy when away from the country of her heart. Shropshire was the source of her inspiration, whether in novels, short stories and nature essays, or in her poetry. She was writing from an early age, and it was her six novels, all set in the south Shropshire border landscape, and all bestsellers throughout the 1930s, which put Shropshire firmly on the literary map of Britain. Within a few years of her death in 1927, pilgrims were visiting what had become known as 'Mary Webb Country'. GK Chesterton called her 'the Shropshire Lass' and in a 1928 speech to the Royal Literary Society, Prime Minister Stanley Baldwin praised her 'first class' writing (his favourite novel was *Precious Bane*).

Mary Webb's fictional Shropshire recalls the Wessex of Thomas Hardy's novels, and her locations, like his, are based on real places in the countryside, although renamed. Shrewsbury, for instance, becomes 'Silverton', Church Stretton 'Shepwardine', Craven Arms 'The Junction', Bishop's Castle support and reopened in 2012 to coincide with the London Olympic Games. It focuses mainly on the Olympic and geological legacy of Much Wenlock and beyond, with displays also on Mary Webb and local archaeology. The shop sells walking maps and guidebooks.

A brook runs beneath **High Street. Ashfield Hall** was once Blue Bridge Inn, taking its name from a blue stone footbridge that crossed the stream. This site has seen rags and riches: Charles I is thought to have stayed at Ashfield Hall *en route* from Shrewsbury to Oxford in 1642, while its 13th-century incarnation as St John's Hospital provided shelter to 'lost and naked beggars'. Hence High Street used to be called Spittle Street – its name derived from 'hospital'. Also on High Street is the **Corn Exchange**, built in 1852 thanks in part to Dr William Penny Brookes who raised funds from public subscription. A plaque commemorates the passing of the Olympic torch through Much Wenlock in 2012 and the 'small spark of imagination that inspired the world'. Markets are held here most days.

SHOPPING

I can cheerfully lose hours pottering around Much Wenlock's shops. These include two indie bookshops on the High Street: the forgivably ungrammatically named **Much More Books** (a secondhand, rare, antiquarian and out-of-print specialist) and shiny red-fronted **Wenlock Books** in a 15th-century building that naturally lends itself to cosy reading nooks and lost (in-a-novel) spouses. Owner Anna Dreda also founded Wenlock Poetry Festival. If you see people queuing in the High Street it's probably for **A. Ryan & Sons**, the butchers' shop, which has been established more than 30 years. The homemade pies, pasties and quiches are, to quote my husband, 'legendary'. **Wenlock Deli** opposite sells plenty of local produce, too.

CRAFTS

Twenty Twenty Gallery 3–4 High St ℘ 01952 727952 ♦ www.twenty-twenty.co.uk. Champions British contemporary art and crafts.

Wenlock Pottery & Craft Centre Shineton St ℘ 01952 727600 ♦ www.wenlockpottery. co.uk. As well as housing a popular B&B this former Methodist chapel is now *the* place in Shropshire to throw pots. Enjoy a drink in the licensed bar or buy some handmade stoneware. Pre-booked tours are available (including evening tours), as well as a 'ceramic café' for visitors who wish to paint their own plates and mugs. It's best to contact the owners in advance if you're coming from any great distance: they get busy with commissions and occasionally have to close.

🍴 FOOD & DRINK

You can't go far wrong when eating out in Much Wenlock, with tea rooms, pubs and hotels to suit all budgets and occasions, and almost every establishment paying due attention to seasonality and locality. A special mention goes to the two AA-rosette restaurant with rooms the **Raven Hotel** on Barrow St (✆ 01952 727251) which has a special place in Much Wenlock's Olympic history. In 1890 it hosted a pivotal dinner meeting between Dr William Penny Brookes and Baron Pierre de Coubertin following the Wenlock Olympian Games. (Look for a copy of the menu from that night in the Brookes Bar which is housed in the original 17th-century coaching inn.) Of course history alone is not enough to recommend a place: thankfully now the Raven has understated elegance, and a bright young chef in Jason Hodnett who works super-local produce into a frequently changing, fine-dining British menu. For a treat representing excellent value look for the five- or seven-course surprise tasting menu with optional wine flight.

MARY WEBB'S SHROPSHIRE

Dr Gladys Mary Coles is the world authority on Mary Webb, and president of the Mary Webb Society. Her latest book, *Mary Webb and her Shropshire World, with a Guide to the Mary Webb Country*, will be published by Headland in autumn 2016.

Mary Webb was born at Leighton near The Wrekin in 1881, the first child of George Edward Meredith (an Oxford MA proud of his Welsh descent) and wealthy Sarah Alice Scott (proud of her claimed kinship with Sir Walter Scott). Before Mary was two, the Merediths moved to Much Wenlock where she spent most of her childhood, educated in her father's boarding school and later by a governess. The two greatest influences on Mary were the Shropshire countryside and her beloved father, a poet who loved nature and Shropshire's legends and folklore. Mary lived most of her 46 years in her home county and, like Emily Brontë, felt unhappy when away from the country of her heart. Shropshire was the source of her inspiration, whether in novels, short stories and nature essays, or in her poetry. She was writing from an early age, and it was her six novels, all set in the south Shropshire border landscape, and all bestsellers throughout the 1930s, which put Shropshire firmly on the literary map of Britain. Within a few years of her death in 1927, pilgrims were visiting what had become known as 'Mary Webb Country'. GK Chesterton called her 'the Shropshire Lass' and in a 1928 speech to the Royal Literary Society, Prime Minister Stanley Baldwin praised her 'first class' writing (his favourite novel was *Precious Bane*).

Mary Webb's fictional Shropshire recalls the Wessex of Thomas Hardy's novels, and her locations, like his, are based on real places in the countryside, although renamed. Shrewsbury, for instance, becomes 'Silverton', Church Stretton 'Shepwardine', Craven Arms 'The Junction', Bishop's Castle

14 WENLOCK EDGE
☗ YHA Wilderhope Manor, Longville (page 248)

> Even now the scenery about Wenlock Edge is wild and romantic;
> but in early times its thickly timbered dales afforded harbourage to
> robbers and outlaws who, issuing from the tangled thickets, preyed
> upon passing travellers as they wandered through its devious,
> unfrequented trackways.
>
> H Thornhill Timmins, *Nooks and Corners of Shropshire* (1899)

You'd be unlucky to encounter outlaws in the woods along Wenlock Edge
today; more likely bees, small skipper butterflies, red clover and yellow
rattle. This limestone escarpment, densely wooded with beech, oak and
ash, runs for 15 miles from near Ironbridge to Craven Arms, bringing us

'Mallard's Keep', Ludlow 'Lullingford', the Stiperstones 'Diafol Mountain', Long Mynd 'Wilderhope', Lordshill 'God's Little Mountain'. Bomere Pool and Colemere are fused as 'Sarn Mere', and the Clun Forest is 'Dysgwlfas-on-the-wild-moors'.

There have been many dramatisations of Webb's novels for stage, screen and radio. The best-known are *Gone to Earth* (1917), declared a 'Book of the Year' by Rebecca West, made into a major Hollywood film (1950); and *Precious Bane* (1924), considered to be her masterpiece, set in the early 19th century, winner of the Prix Femina, in which the central character Prudence Sarn wins love in spite of facial deformity. BBC TV's adaptation (1989) was a huge success.

All of Mary Webb's novels resonate with rich descriptions, the landscape as important as the well-drawn characters. They are powerful in human drama, timeless and universal in their themes: the tensions between love and lust, givers and takers, selflessness and self-interest, good and evil. Local legends, superstitions and folklore are woven in brilliantly, enhancing atmosphere, influencing plot and character.

Mary Webb's life held much of joy and pain. From the age of 20 she suffered from Graves' disease, an incurable thyroid disorder, one of the causes of her early death. A vegetarian, she hated cruelty of any kind, and was ahead of her time in her views on sexuality, love, the need for self-development, and the importance of the natural environment. She married Henry Webb in 1912. While living at Pontesbury she wrote her first novel *The Golden Arrow* (1916) and began *Gone to Earth*, completed at Lyth Hill, her favourite place, where her home Spring Cottage overlooks the Shropshire plain and all the hills significant in her life. Mary Webb is buried in Shrewsbury Cemetery.

rewarding walks in a rich natural habitat and views along the way to the Long Mynd and Stretton Hills. Almost every aspect of Wenlock Edge – its shape, trees, flora and fauna – is influenced by the underlying fossil-rich rock, formed in shallow tropical seas during the Silurian period, 400 million years ago. The rock is so important in geological terms that it has its own name, Wenlock limestone. Of course over time humans have laid down their own stories and legends upon this natural wonder: for example an outcrop near Easthope called Ippikin's Rock (📍 SO569964) is named after a 13th-century robber knight. His malevolent spirit should leave you alone unless you dare to utter, 'Ippikin, Ippikin, keep away with your long chin', in which case he'll push you over the cliff edge. A Civil War story with a smidgeon more substance and just as much intrigue is that of Major Smallman of Wilderhope Manor, a Royalist who rode his horse over the precipice of Wenlock Edge to avoid being captured by Roundheads. The horse was killed but Major Smallman lived to see the Restoration. It is thought his jump, commemorated at Major's Leap (📍 SO600991), inspired the ending of Mary Webb's *Gone to Earth*.

"Humans have laid down their own stories and legends upon this natural wonder: beware of Ippikin the robber knight."

Eight miles of Wenlock Edge is in the hands of the National Trust, which has been acquiring sections since 1982. Hence the main entry points are free National Trust car parks near Much Wenlock (TF13 6DH), at Wilderhope Manor (TF13 6EG) and at Presthope (SY5 6NX). Route 12 of the Shropshire Way runs from Much Wenlock to Wilderhope Manor, as do sections of the Jack Mytton Way. Wildlife sites include Harton Hollow, Edge Wood, Easthope Wood and Longville Coppice. The nearest bus routes are those that stop in Much Wenlock.

15 SHIPTON HALL

Shipton TF13 6JZ ✆ 01746 785225 ⊖ Easter–end Sep 14.30–17.30 Thu & Sun & Mon during bank holiday w/ends

It's not open often due to being a family home, but the fine Elizabethan manor house of Shipton Hall and its traditional gardens (seven miles southwest of Much Wenlock) are worth a look if you're passing by on a Thursday or bank holiday afternoon in summer. The rococo interiors are by Thomas Farnolls Pritchard, who designed the pioneering iron bridge (page 128).

STAFFORDSHIRE BORDERS

Where Shropshire meets Staffordshire you'll find smart villages and leafy lanes; a rural, generally well-heeled place for commuters who enjoy easy access to Wolverhampton and the wider West Midlands. My temptation to claim that these eastern fringes are not quintessential Shropshire is tempered by the knowledge that this is a county of contrasts, and the fact that its fertile soil nurtures Shropshire's most fragrant export, **David Austin Roses**.

16 SHIFNAL

It's not a tourist hotspot, Shifnal. But that's not to say it's unattractive or lacking in interest. The market town eleven miles north of Bridgnorth developed as a coaching stop on the London to Holyhead road and was

THE LOVE STORY OF HANNAH CULLWICK & ARTHUR MUNBY

Shifnal was the birthplace of a Victorian domestic servant named Hannah Cullwick, the heroine of one of Shropshire's most intriguing love stories. In 1854 Hannah was 21 and readying her employers' house in London for 'the Season' when she met Arthur Munby, a solicitor working for the Ecclesiastical Commission. Their mutual physical attraction was overpowering and they began a furtive relationship that would last the rest of their lives. They were made for each other: Arthur had a penchant for strong, dirty working women, while Hannah enjoyed being grimy and subservient. They married in secret in 1873 but Hannah never felt comfortable in the role of a lady, preferring instead to call Arthur 'Massa' (master) and be his 'drudge and slave'. She enjoyed licking his boots, cradling him in her arms, and climbing naked up chimney flues to cover herself in filth. If you're interested in learning more Diane Atkinson has written an excellent biography called *Love & Dirt,* drawing directly from Hannah and Arthur's letters, photographs and diaries. Not only does their story transcend class and upset our notions of Victorian prudishness, it reveals many glimpses of rural Shropshire too, as Hannah returned home regularly for work and to visit family. After carrying out further research of my own, I went in search of Hannah's grave at **St Andrew's Church** in Shifnal – paid for by Arthur upon her death in 1909. It wasn't easy to find (on the eastern side, beneath a towering Wellingtonia) and rather unkempt, the epigraph hard to read:

She was for 56 years of pure and unbroken love the wedded wife of Arthur Munby.

divided by a viaduct when rail arrived in 1849. I think the existence of Shifnal's modern-day train station, independent shops and very decent pubs make it a worthwhile stopping point.

¶¶ FOOD & DRINK

Blue Market Pl ✆ 01952 462626 ⌖ www.blue-shifnal.co.uk. Jan Park has combined a florist shop, a vintage-style tea room (China Blue Café offering premium coffee, a huge selection of teas, panini, soup and freshly made cakes) and a boutique selling women's ethical fashion (The Thread) and made the whole thing flow. I feel anything but Blue after a visit.

Fennels Market Pl ✆ 01952 463020. A perennial favourite with locals, with owner-chef Richard Brooks serving a small but perfectly executed menu of European cuisine. His cheese soufflé is a hit with veggies. Fennels is an intimate venue, so booking is advisable.

Plough Inn 26 Broadway ✆ 01952 463118. A good drinking pub. Take your pick from the 'hymnboard of ales' or fill a carton if you're driving.

White Hart High St ✆ 01952 461161. Plenty of real ales and guest ales here, also available for taking away. The menu doesn't deviate far from standard pub fare, but it's done well and mostly homemade. Cash only, but there's an ATM across the road at the Co-op.

17 WESTON PARK

🏠 **Temple of Diana** (page 248)

Weston-under-Lizard TF11 8LE ✆ 01952 852100 ⌖ www.weston-park.com ☺ see website; the Granary including art gallery are open all year round

Five miles northeast of Shifnal, just off the A5, the Weston Park estate straddles Staffordshire and Shropshire. Visit in summer for 1,000 acres of Capability Brown parkland and a magnificent 17th-century stately home, the ancestral seat of the Earls of Bradford. You can wander freely on Friday, Sunday and Monday when the house is open, but the guided tours (Tuesday to Thursday) bring the estate's many riches and stories to life. Exhibits include paintings by Constable, Gainsborough, Reynolds, van Dyck and the equestrian artist George Stubbs.

Younger visitors are well catered for, with a woodland playground including zip wire and cargo net and an indoor activity room with dressing-up boxes. On Sundays an extensive miniature railway, for a small additional charge, will chug you through Capability Brown's Temple Wood.

Once you have paid your entry fee, you can wander freely in the grounds, taking in the deer park and landscaped gardens. Head gardener Martin Gee is the latest and sadly last in a 200-year line of Gee family members who have tended to the estate.

THE SECRETS OF WESTON PARK

Every great ancestral home holds intrigues – and from its secret bookcase doors to a surprising taxidermy parrot (see *Benjamin Disraeli* box, page 164), Weston Park is packed with them. To start with the external, it's a Palladian-style mansion built in 1671 to the vision of one Lady Elizabeth Wilbrahim. Her annotated copy of *Palladio's First Book of Architecture* remains in Weston Park's collection today. The overseeing architect William Taylor also designed the church of the Holy Trinity in Minsterley.

The daughters of the second Earl of Bradford were Lady Lucy and Lady Charlotte Bridgeman, early pioneers of photography. It's sad to think what they might have achieved had the flounce of Lucy's crinoline gown not been caught by a spark from the library fire in November 1858. Rushing to her sister's side, Charlotte too became engulfed in flames. They died a few days apart, aged just 32 and 31. In her astonishing book *The Morville Hours*

Katherine Swift says their descendants refer to them, somewhat irreverently it seems to me, as the 'burnt aunts'.

There is evidence to suggest P G Wodehouse imagined Weston Park, especially its grounds, when he wrote his novels and short stories featuring Blandings, the seat of the fictional Lord Emsworth. Several other estates lay claim to this honour too, though, including Apley Hall (page 86), so it is more likely Blandings Castle was a mixture of places Wodehouse remembered from his childhood.

Weston Park is an exclusive-use venue and in 1998 hosted the leaders attending the G8 summit in Birmingham. If it's strange to think of Blair, Chirac, Clinton and Yeltsin et al gathering under Shropshire skies, then please push your imagination a little further and picture them huddled together in Weston Park's second salon watching the FA Cup Final together. Because that, apparently, is exactly what happened.

The 1767 great barn is known as the **Granary**, housing two dining venues, a deli and an upstairs art gallery, with on-loan artwork alongside selling exhibitions that change monthly. You can visit the gallery for free and, outside of the main summer season, the walled kitchen garden.

A warning: every August since 1996 Weston Park has hosted the Midlands leg of the V Festival (⊘ www.vfestival.com), a major music event held simultaneously in Chelmsford and here in Staffordshire/Shropshire. I'd suggest avoiding the area that weekend unless you're planning to attend the festival, as the roads get snarled up with traffic.

There is no easy way to get to Weston Park by **public transport** from within Shropshire: the nearest bus stop is just over ten minutes' walk away in Weston-under-Lizard, but the buses run within Staffordshire. You could take a taxi from Telford Central train station, a 12-minute drive.

🍴 FOOD & DRINK

Granary Grill is a Mediterranean-inspired bistro which makes admirable use of produce from Weston Park's walled kitchen garden. **Granary Deli & Café** is ideal for informal dining (or just coffee and cake) with an impressive deli counter of predominantly local produce.

18 BOSCOBEL HOUSE, THE ROYAL OAK & WHITE LADIES PRIORY

Brewood, Bishops Wood ST19 9AR ✆ 01902 850244; English Heritage

Brewood, seven miles east of Shifnal, just nudging into Staffordshire, is where you'll find Boscobel House. Its name, from the Italian *bosco bello*, means beautiful wood or forest. Originally a timber-framed lodge, Boscobel House was built in the early 17th century by John Giffard, a landowner from nearby Chillington in Staffordshire. Much extended over the years, undergoing spells as a farmhouse, hunting lodge and holiday home, Boscobel House is still a vision of rustic beauty. But that, of course, is not the main reason people still travel from afar to see it.

THE ROYAL OAK

Beyond the garden gate at Boscobel stands a ring-fenced oak tree with a story that has brought visitors here since the 17th century. In fact the original oak tree was denuded thanks to 17th-century souvenir hunters pocketing a twig or two. Following the beheading of Charles I in 1649 at the hands of Parliamentarians, his eldest son made a play for the throne. Charles II was defeated at the 1651 Battle of Worcester and went on the run. Blocked from crossing the River Severn by Oliver Cromwell's patrols, he sought refuge at Boscobel House, hiding in a coppiced oak tree with his officer, Colonel William Careless, before spending the night in a priest hole in the attic. Then he travelled on in disguise via other safe houses.

When he became King Charles II in 1660, the importance of this Royal Oak was not forgotten. That year, the Lord Mayor's pageant proceeding through London featured a wheeled platform recreating the scene at Boscobel Wood. Charles II's birthday, 29 May, was made a public holiday: Oak Apple Day. Even now we have many pubs named the Royal Oak: according to several sources only the Red Lion and the Crown are more ubiquitous.

The tree you'll see at Boscobel is a descendant of the original oak (another pub name, right there). An even younger replacement, planted by the Prince of Wales in 2001, grows nearby. Inside the house, usually in the oratory, is a carved oak chest, reputed to be made from the wood of the very tree that hid Charles II. Look hard: his face is depicted among the leaves, scarcely bigger than a thumbnail.

In 1651 Boscobel House played an important role in English history when it successfully hid the future King Charles II from Parliamentarians. He spent some hours concealed in an oak tree in the woods before passing what must have been an uncomfortable night in a priest hole in the attic (Charles was 6 feet 2 inches). Ever since the Reformation, people have flocked to see where this remarkable story unfolded.

In 1812 an industrialist from Derbyshire called Walter Evans bought Boscobel House, developing the farmyard and restoring the house in an antiquarian style, 'as it was when Charles was there'. The 19th-century Romantic movement had stoked interest in the story of the fleeing king.

Visit today for tours of the house and to see the famous tree. You can wander in the farmyard among tame ducks and chickens or play quoits and skittles in the Victorian garden behind the handsome red-brick wall. An education and family room has dressing-up, colouring-in and finding-out for younger guests. The site has no café or tea room but refreshments are available in the gift shop, including hot drinks from a vending machine.

White Ladies Priory

Founded in the mid 12th century, **White Ladies Priory** was an Augustinian house of canonesses, taking its name from the white religious habits of the nuns. In 1651 it was a house in the ownership of the Giffard family, and another of Charles II's hiding places. The ruins are a two-mile round walk from Boscobel House. You can access the site without paying to go in to Boscobel House, although the walk from the Royal Oak, through fields and kissing-gates, is prettier and probably safer than negotiating the country lane on foot. You can wander around in daylight hours and admission is free.

19 TONG

About 3½ miles east of Shifnal is the village of Tong; the solid spire of the church leaps into your vision from the A41. In 1868 an American consul to Birmingham declared **St Bartholomew's** a 'little Westminster'. Elihu Burritt was much enthused by its 'beautiful and costly monuments to the memory of so many noble families' and no doubt by the church's stately form, with battlemented parapets and central octagonal tower rising in three stages to a pinnacle over the village. St Bartholomew's is certainly a treasure and this has much to do with its interior collection of tombs and monuments. All the male effigies are depicted as knights, representing five of the seven categorised periods of medieval armour. All are noteworthy (you can buy a church-produced or glossy photographic guide inside and conduct your own tour), although my personal fascination lies with the Stanley monument. Effigies of Sir Thomas Stanley and his wife Margaret repose on top; their son Sir Edward Stanley (d1632) is displayed on an open stage below. The epitaph at each end of the monument is reputed to have been written by William Shakespeare. This claim is well authenticated and the Stanleys were indeed patrons of the Bard himself. Look also for the Victorian sign indicating when the church's Great Bell (the largest in Shropshire) should be tolled, including 'on the birth of a child to the Sovereign'. The Great Bell's presence makes Tong seem onomatopoeic, but the name is likely to have derived from the word meaning 'a fork in the river'.

"The epitaph on the Stanley monument is reputed to have been written by Shakespeare – a well-authenticated claim."

It is generally accepted that Charles Dickens set the final chapters of *The Old Curiosity Shop* in Tong and the 'very aged, ghostly' church in which Little Nell finds peace broadly matches the state of St Bartholomew's before its 1892 restoration. The sign outside the main south door, marked 'The Reputed Grave of Little Nell', was the work of an enterprising verger in around 1910, who even went to the trouble of recording a false entry in the church's burial records. It seems he was fairly successful in duping those inclined to be swept away by Dickens's ability to create lifelike characters. The late *Shropshire Star* journalist Wilfred Byford-Jones wrote in his 1967 *Severn Valley Stories* that 'even today Dickens fans make pilgrimages from distant places to the churchyard and weep tears over a small "grave" near the church door'.

The church narrowly escaped destruction during the Civil War: you can wander around to the north wall and see damage caused by cannonball fire. Tong Castle, a gothic country house with Capability Brown parkland, has been less enduring: it was damaged by fire in 1911 and finally demolished in 1954 when it became unstable. The best I can offer you now is a fine painting in the passageway that leads to the second salon at Weston Park.

Tong is served by the number 891 Arriva Midlands **bus** which runs between Telford town centre and Wolverhampton bus station.

20 ROYAL AIR FORCE MUSEUM

Cosford TF11 8UP ✆ 01902 376 200 ⌕ www.rafmuseum.org.uk/cosford ☉ all year; free, just pay for parking; half-mile walk from Cosford train station & well signposted; or catch the 892 bus from Wolverhampton to Wellington, alight at Cosford Garage & walk for about a mile

Located next to a working airfield, the RAF Museum at Cosford holds an internationally important collection of over 70 aircraft, including the world's oldest Spitfire and the three 'V' bombers: Vulcan, Victor and Valiant. Entry is free which feels almost too good to be true because the museum represents a substantial day out and has something to interest most people. (Even if you're not crazy about planes, there's a fascinating display on aviation mascots and lucky charms.) It's also an ideal place to spend a rainy day as most exhibits are in hangars, with a 'Fun 'n' Flight' interactive gallery to amuse younger visitors.

It's worth chatting to the volunteers for off-the-placard info: Frank Redfern, who was a radar fitter in the 1950s (and is father to bestselling author and UFO expert Nick Redfern), showed me his photo of a 'ghost pilot' in the museum's formidable-looking Black Lincoln.

Visit on a Saturday and have the chance to sit in the cockpit of a Jet Provost T.3. On Tuesdays at 10.00 'Meet our Veterans' takes place. And on any day of the week it's a dizzying experience to ascend to the high-level viewing gallery in the excellent National Cold War exhibition and view the immense Belfast Transporter from above.

In 2015 the museum signed up a new catering company for five years, promising locally sourced, homemade and seasonal menus. There are also picnic benches for temperate weather days. **Cosford Food Festival** takes place in the museum grounds in the last weekend of July.

21 ALBRIGHTON

This large village 5½ miles southeast of Shifnal is the Albrighton with a Wolverhampton postcode, as opposed to its Shrewsbury namesake. The **train** station sees London Midland trains running between Shrewsbury and Birmingham New Street. The Arriva **bus** service 891 which runs between Telford and Wolverhampton stops by the Crown pub.

Albrighton has a high street lined with lime trees and is one of the few villages in Shropshire with a green. The parish churches of Albrighton and Donington are curiously close in proximity. This quirk in village planning gave rise to an old story about two rich spinsters (not my terminology) who wanted to build a church but, unable to agree on the design, each hired a different builder. The journalist Wilfred Byford-Jones suggested it was more likely that the 12th-century St Mary's in Albrighton was built near to the earlier St Cuthbert's in Donington to offer protection from the many outlaws and highwaymen who took cover in the dense forests.

You can pick up a walking map from the post office, or consult the guide on the wall of the shoe shop next to the Red House (village hall). If you find yourself sweet on this part of Shropshire, you'll find ideas for further days out at ⊘ www.albrightontourism.co.uk.

Albrighton is hardly a metropolis but local beauty spot **Donington Pool & Albrighton Nature Reserve** offers a spot of tranquillity amidst the hum of village life, shielded by yew trees, scrub roses and alder. Birdlife spotted here includes greater spotted woodpecker, blackcap and migrating chiffchaff. Donington Pool was created in the early 17th century by a miller who dammed the nearby Humphreston Brook. His first attempt flooded the village and he was ordered to pay a fine. To find the nature reserve, cross the road from the Shrewsbury Arms and head down the hill, away from St Mary's Church. Rectory Road is the second turning on your right; just follow it round.

David Austin Plant Centre

Bowling Green Lane, WV7 3HB 🖉 01902 376341 (tea room) ⊘ www.davidaustinroses.co.uk
☺ daily except between Christmas & New Year; free entry

One of Shropshire's modern success stories, David Austin is considered the world over to produce the Rolls-Royce of English roses. They're hugely popular across Europe and even in Japan, although the company is thoroughly rooted in the county where David Austin himself grew up. Shropshire's rich history is honoured in many David Austin rose varieties: A Shropshire Lad, Boscobel, Brother Cadfael, Corvedale, Abraham Darby, Charles Darwin, Wollerton Old Hall, Wild Edric, and many others. Resident rose expert Michael Marriott told me, 'Shropshire is the perfect county for a rose garden: horticultural, rural, beautiful. The soil isn't ideal, but we get around that.'

"Shropshire's history is honoured in rose names: A Shropshire Lad, Boscobel, Brother Cadfael..."

And certainly they do. You can enjoy the feted blooms in abundance from late May at the David Austin Plant Centre just outside Albrighton village. Two fragrant acres of rose gardens, divided into smaller areas by clipped evergreen hedges, proudly display more than 700 varieties of roses, as well as sculptures by the late Mrs Pat Austin. The gardens were in 2015 included in the World Federation of Rose Society's Awards of Garden Excellence – one of only three such gardens in England.

You'll find the **Plant Centre** beautifully stocked with container, bare root (November to March) and specimen roses for sale, plus other complementary plants. An indoor section features high-quality gifts, homeware and books. Lunch and cream tea are served in the traditional-style licensed **tea room** (book in advance for Sunday lunch or afternoon tea), on delicate rose-decorated china. On warm days you can dine on the terrace.

¶¶ FOOD & DRINK

The Harp Hotel High St ✆ 01902 374381. A real ale pub (no food), which hosts Jazz Club 90 (⌒ www.jazzclub90.co.uk) on Sunday lunchtimes and Tuesday evenings. Charles Dickens is reputed to have stayed here while writing *The Old Curiosity Shop*.

Shrewsbury Arms High St ✆ 01902 373003. Parts of this half-timbered building date to the late 15th or early 16th century; recent modernisation has been sensitive and effective. Known locally as the Shrew, the pub offers an excellent and varied menu, with plenty for Vegetarians. Other points in the Shrew's favour are a good wine list, sun-trap garden, all-day Sunday roasts and live music on Friday and Saturday nights.

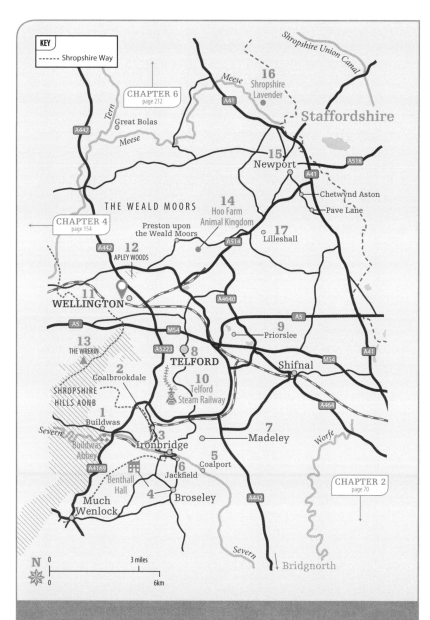

CHAPTER 6
page 212

CHAPTER 4
page 154

CHAPTER 2
page 70

KEY
----- Shropshire Way

Shropshire Union Canal

Meese

16 Shropshire Lavender

A41

Staffordshire

Tern

Great Bolas

Meese

A442

A518

15 Newport

A41

Chetwynd Aston

Pave Lane

THE WEALD MOORS

14 Hoo Farm Animal Kingdom

Preston upon the Weald Moors

A514

17 Lilleshall

12 APLEY WOODS

A442

11 WELLINGTON

A5

13 THE WREKIN

SHROPSHIRE HILLS AONB

2 Coalbrookdale

M54

A5223

8 TELFORD

10 Telford Steam Railway

A5

9 Priorslee

A4640

Shifnal

M54

A41

1 Buildwas

Severn

Buildwas Abbey

A4169

3 Ironbridge

6 Jackfield

5 Coalport

7 Madeley

Worfe

A464

4 Broseley

Benthall Hall

Much Wenlock

A442

N

0   3 miles

0   6km

Severn

Bridgnorth

IRONBRIDGE GORGE & THE WREKIN

3
IRONBRIDGE GORGE
& THE WREKIN

In Coalbrookdale, Shropshire in 1709 an entrepreneur named Abraham Darby first produced pig iron in a coke-fuelled blast furnace. He wasn't looking to set the world alight (and nor was his discovery the only spark that ignited it); rather he wanted to find an easier, cheaper and less labour-intensive way of casting 'iron bellied potts'. Nevertheless, Darby's breakthrough also set into motion the principles of mass production, contributing greatly to the **Industrial Revolution**. After the first cast iron hollowware followed the first iron barge, the first iron bridge, the first rail locomotive, all dreamed up in these few square miles. It's no exaggeration to say Ironbridge Gorge – then called Severn Gorge – was the birthplace of heavy modern industry, paving the way for much that we now take for granted.

At the peak of the Industrial Revolution, the story of the gorge was already thousands of years old. Back, back in time, during the last glacial age, thick ice sheets forged the deep valley, slicing through Wenlock Edge, forming what would become the River Severn and revealing limestone, coal, iron stone and clay. It's as though Nature, having shifted and shaped this patch of Earth, creating a perfect transport network and revealing perfect raw materials, sat back and waited 19,000 years for humans to realise their good fortune.

And when we view time in those vast, unwieldy, geological terms, it's humbling to think that an entire industrial world sprung up and declined in Shropshire in the blow of a hammer, the turn of a flywheel. A relative few frenzied years of innovation, changing human destiny forever, and then industry focus moved elsewhere: production shifted to south Wales and the Black Country. Ironbridge Gorge retained an important trade in ornamental castings and tiles, but by the mid 20th century was in slow decline. People moved away and many factories, warehouses and workshops would become dilapidated.

Luckily for us, Nature was swift to reclaim the gorge for her own, repopulating the slopes of the valley with dense woodland, returning dragonflies and damselflies to the river, bringing wildflower meadows alive once again with cowslips, daisies, orchids and vetches upon which bees and butterflies feast. The topographer Edmund Vale in 1949 wrote of the 'endless tips and spoil-banks' that proved to be 'of a nature kindly to vegetation' and that 50 years' growth, even then, meant the 'gorge is once more a beautiful place, and the nightingale sings above the toll-house of the iron bridge'. The flora and fauna became jewels in the crown of a place that, in the 1960s when 'Telford New Town' was emerging from blueprints, became a source of interest rather than dereliction and shame. In 1986 Ironbridge Gorge was designated a **World Heritage Site** and visitor attractions grew up around it: shops, tea rooms, galleries and museums.

Shropshire's industrial legacy is still evident too – and not only through books, wall plaques and the conservation efforts of **UNESCO** and the **Ironbridge Gorge Museum Trust**. In this region, we have former mining towns to explore, canals and towpaths, disused railway tracks (as well as the working sections lovingly restored by **Telford Steam Railway**). Even Telford, derided as it is by aesthetes, is a product of endeavour and ambition: the new-fangled vision that would relieve congestion in Birmingham and Wolverhampton.

And there is no greater lasting symbol of innovation than the sublime 30-metre **iron bridge**, built in 1779 to showcase the genius of the Coalbrookdale ironmasters.

Although the area covered by this chapter is roughly the same as that known as Telford & Wrekin (after the local authority overseeing it), I've taken a liberty with the boundary at the south by extending it to include the town of Broseley and village of Benthall. This reflects how entwined with Ironbridge Gorge are their history, geography and identity. I've also swiped Buildwas from the mid Shropshire region, as you can walk the gentle two miles to its cooling towers and abbey ruins along the river from Ironbridge.

GETTING THERE & AROUND

A solid bus network and three mainline train stations make public transport to this region a very practical option. Virgin Trains operates a twice-daily service between London Euston and Shrewsbury, stopping at Telford Central, Telford Oakengates and Wellington. At those three same stations you'll find Arriva Trains Wales' hourly off-peak services between Birmingham International and Shrewsbury, with alternate trains continuing to Aberystwyth or Holyhead. Also hourly, London Midland runs services between Birmingham New Street and Shrewsbury (which take around an hour), stopping at Wolverhampton (as well as other Shropshire stations: Albrighton, Cosford and Shifnal: see *Chapter 2*).

National Express runs two coaches to Telford from London a day.

Telford's main **bus** station is in the shopping centre and well signposted from Telford Central. From there you can catch buses to Ironbridge Gorge, Newport, Bridgnorth, Shifnal and Shrewsbury: it's all laid out clearly with a separate door and departures board for each service, like a small airport terminal. You may find Wellington's bus station useful for its links with services to Shrewsbury and Madeley.

Regional Transport's 'hop on hop off' service serves Ironbridge Gorge between May and the end of October: see page 72.

WALKING

This is a varied and exciting region for walking: you could head out with sturdy shoes every day for a year and always find a different path to follow. It may help to go armed with ❊ OS Explorer map 242.

One of the first walks to conquer is **The Wrekin**. It's no Ben Nevis, but the 'little mountain' symbolises home to many people who live in Shropshire. According to local tradition, you may only consider yourself a true Salopian once you've passed through the cleft in Needle's Eye, an outcrop of rock near the summit.

A dense network of footpaths, waymarked woodland trails and quiet lanes thread through and around **Ironbridge Gorge**. For inspiration, download the free walking trails from the Severn Gorge Countryside Trust (⌂ www.severngorge.org.uk) which include the 3½-mile circular **Iron Trail**.

Wellington is a **Walkers are Welcome** town, meaning it is accredited by a national scheme for its efforts in being attractive and accessible for walkers. The friendly Walkers are Welcome group runs free guided walks of between 90 and 120 minutes from outside Wellington Leisure Centre on the first and third Sunday of each month, starting at 14.00. Some of their favourite routes are at ⌂ www.wellingtonwalkersarewelcome.org.uk.

The group organises the annual (but not fixed to a particular month) **Wellington Walking Festival**, offering a diverse programme including literary walks, 'memory' walks, and routes designed for families with children. You'll also find walking and cycling trails around Wellington and The Wrekin at ⊘ www.wellingtonla21.org.uk.

Longer-distance paths include the **Silkin Way** from Telford to Ironbridge Gorge and the 12-mile **South Telford Heritage Trail** which can be broken into smaller sections (⊘ www.walktelfordheritage.co.uk).

CYCLING

Ironbridge Gorge is actually better suited to two wheels than four, due to narrow lanes, and the iron bridge itself being inaccessible to motorists. Telford Town Park is another great place to start, for cyclists of all abilities. You can hire bikes from Telford Cycle Centre and head out on waymarked trails, or pick up Sustrans' National Cycle route 55 past Newport to Stafford. It's also possible to link parts of routes 45, 55 and 81 to make a 36-mile traffic-free circuit around The Wrekin (visit ⊘ www. shropshiresgreatoutdoors.co.uk/cycling and navigate to 'National Cycle Network' to find a leaflet). The Mercian Way section of National Cycle Route 45 passes through Ironbridge, taking you north to Whitchurch or south to Bridgnorth.

The Silkin Way (see *Walking* above) follows dry canal beds and disused railway tracks and is therefore suitable for cyclists as well as walkers. The few sets of steps along the route are broad and shallow.

North of Telford, you may find the Weald Moors a rewarding place to cycle.

BIKE HIRE

The Tandem Experience John Rose Building, Coalport TF8 7HT ✆ 01952 458340 ⊘ www. tandeming.co.uk ☺ 10.00–17.00 Mon–Fri, 09.00–16.00 Sat (closed for lunch 13.00–13.30); closed Sun & bank holiday Mon. For renting bicycles made for two.

Telford Cycle Centre Visitor Centre, Telford Town Park, Telford TF3 4EP ✆ 0330 0241783
🖱 www.cycleexperience.com/telfordcyclecentre ☺ 10.00–16.30 Tue–Sun. This friendly
hub in Telford Town Park offers bike hire (including children's seats and trailers), trying-out
sessions, group guided rides, mountain bike sessions, tuition for children and family rides.

BIKE SALES & REPAIRS

Bicycles by Design John Rose Building, Coalport TF8 7HT ✆ 01952 459900 🖱 www.
bicycles-by-design.co.uk. These guys don't just sell bikes and tandems – they hand-build
them too, and can train you to do the same.
Bike Debug ✆ 07765 768619 🖱 www.bikedebug.co.uk ☺ 09.00–19.00 Mon–Sat,
11.00–15.00 Sun. Mobile mechanic named Matt, based in Telford.
Perry's Cycle Shop 33 Tan Bank, Wellington TF1 1HJ ✆ 01952 244802
For accessories, spare parts, repairs and new bike sales.
Telford Cycle Centre Visitor Centre, Telford Town Park, Telford TF3 4EP ✆ 0330 0241783
🖱 www.cycleexperience.com/telfordcyclecentre. Bike repairs and maintenance training.

HORSERIDING

While Shropshire's main bridleways are found in the south of the
county (with the exception of Humphrey Kynaston Way which heads
up to Clive), you'll still find fulfilling places to ride in this region. All the
Telford Town Park trails are suitable for horseriders as well as walkers
and cyclists, for example, giving you confidence in clearly waymarked
and well-maintained paths. Anthony Francis-Jones, chairman of the
Telford Bridleways Association, recommends Ironbridge Gorge. 'The
Severn Gorge Countryside Trust has lots of good routes in and around
Ironbridge Gorge … you can ride over the iron bridge itself and there is
good parking [for car and horsebox] in the Station Yard Car Park to the
south of the bridge,' he said. 'It's also great to ride right outside Benthall
Hall and up to the power station cooling towers at Buildwas.'

WET-WEATHER ACTIVITIES

The indoor museums of Ironbridge Gorge (page 117)
Cineworld cinema with IMAX at Southwater (🖱 www.cineworld.co.uk)
House at Sunnycroft (page 145)
Jungleland A soft play centre just outside Telford (🖱 www.junglelandtelford.com)
Snowboard and Ski Centre in Madeley (🖱 www.telfordandwrekinleisure.co.uk)
Telford Ice Rink at Saint Quentin Gate (🖱 www.telfordandwrekinleisure.co.uk)
Tenpin Telford bowling at Saint Quentin Gate (🖱 www.tenpin.co.uk)

AROUND THE IRONBRIDGE GORGE WORLD HERITAGE SITE

Ironbridge Gorge covers a three-mile stretch around the River Severn from Coalbrookdale to Coalport, taking in Ironbridge, Jackfield and part of the former mining town of Madeley. It was designated a World Heritage Site by UNESCO in 1986 in recognition of its unique contribution to the Industrial Revolution.

A few years ago the BBC ran a series of programmes telling the history of the world in 100 objects. It's significant that several of the featured objects exist in this disproportionately small area, including a replica of the Trevithick engine, the world's first steam railway locomotive (Blists Hill Victorian Town) and a cast-iron cooking pot and patent secured by Abraham Darby I (Museum of Iron). And of course nothing is more representative of the gorge's contribution to industrialised society than the first iron bridge, built in 1779 to link Broseley, Madeley and Coalbrookdale. It gave the area, originally called Severn Gorge, its name.

"I love it in the hour after a spell of rain."

While you enjoy the lush greenness of the gorge today (I love it most in the hour after a spell of rain), it's hard to imagine the smelting, the banging, the plumes of smoke that billowed up during the peak of the Industrial Revolution. Ironbridge Gorge is surrounded by accessible countryside, footpaths, meadows and walks and, because of the river, it's easier and more rewarding to navigate on foot or by bike than negotiating the twisty narrow roads by car.

Shropshire Raft Tours should be up and running in summer 2016, giving you an environmentally friendly and unique way to see the gorge from the river (www.shropshirerafttours.co.uk).

1 BUILDWAS

Morrells Wood Farm, Leighton (page 249)

Before Ironbridge Gorge and the UNESCO area, a diversion. Two miles west of Ironbridge at Buildwas is where the River Severn enters its gorge at Buildwas. The landscape is dominated by the four 1960s **cooling towers** (pink-tinted to blend with the reddish Shropshire soil) of the recently decommissioned Ironbridge Power Station. The future of the towers is currently unknown, with opinion divided on whether they should be demolished – removing a 'blight' on the landscape – or retained as an important remnant of the gorge's 20th-century industrial heritage.

The **pratt truss bridge**, where the Buildwas Abbey monks first placed their medieval toll-raising bridge (see below), was the site of an iron bridge by Thomas Telford in 1796, although it has since been rebuilt, strengthened and widened.

THE TEN MUSEUMS OF IRONBRIDGE GORGE WORLD HERITAGE SITE

The geographical, historical, industrial and social stories of Ironbridge Gorge are brought to life in ten museums run by the Ironbridge Gorge Museum Trust, an independent educational charity with a strong environmental policy and resulting Green Tourism Gold award. While each is unique in character and content, the museums are united through being housed in 'original' buildings (such as former warehouses and factories connected with the gorge's heritage). Gift shops, where present, are thoughtfully curated with an attention to handmade and locally produced goods. For super-local, high-quality souvenirs look for the 'Made in the Gorge' brand.

Don't try to squeeze all the museums into one day, or even two. The Trust's **Annual Passport Ticket** lasts a year and represents the best value for money even if you're only visiting a handful of the attractions.

When it comes to transport, most of the museums have pay and display **car parks** with only a small charge (which goes directly to the Trust), apart from the Museum of the Gorge and Ironbridge car parks where local authority charges and tighter time limits apply. I have given details under individual listings. There is a **park and ride service** (🕙 w/ends, bank holidays & in school holidays) running every 12 minutes. It's free to park and adult tickets are just £1. Follow signs to the car park just off the A1469 at Jiggers Bank or key TF4 3QE into your sat nav. Once at the Museum of the Gorge interchange you can catch the **Gorge Connect shuttle bus** (🕙 Easter–Oct) to as many museums as you can manage: this service runs at least every 30 minutes and Annual Passport Ticket holders travel for free.

Follow brown signs to Blists Hill Victorian Town for:
Blists Hill Victorian Town (page 136)
Coalport China Museum (page 132)
Tar Tunnel (page 133)

Follow brown signs to Ironbridge Museums for:
The iron bridge & Toll House (page 127)
Museum of the Gorge (page 126)
Jackfield Tile Museum (page 134)
Broseley Pipeworks (page 130)

Follow brown signs to Coalbrookdale Museums for:
Coalbrookdale Museum of Iron (page 119)
Darby Houses (page 120)
Enginuity (page 120)

Buildwas Abbey

TF8 7BW ℰ 01952 433274 ☉ end Mar–end Sep 10.00–17.00 (closed Mon & Tue)
♿ accessible toilets & handrails but no ramps; the Arriva Midlands bus service 96
between Shrewsbury & Telford stops here; free parking; English Heritage

In a peaceful woodland setting by the River Severn stand the ruins of
a Cistercian abbey. Buildwas Abbey was founded by Roger De Clinton,
Bishop of Coventry. The abbey's small community of monks from
Furness in Cumbria made their living by charging a toll to travellers
crossing their bridge. In 1342 a monk named Thomas Tong murdered
his abbot, evaded arrest and subsequently petitioned to be reinstated to
the Cistercian order. Despite the abbey's turbulent borderlands history,
the ruins are in good nick: the vaulted chapter house still has floor
tiles and the church remains relatively unaltered since its 12th-century
beginnings (lost roof notwithstanding).

A **nature trail** starting near the entrance is laid out on what was once
a system of fish ponds constructed by the monks.

2 COALBROOKDALE

⌂ **YHA Coalbrookdale** (page 248)

In 1787, when Ironbridge Gorge pulsed and heaved with industry,
fumes and noise, an aristocratic Italian diplomat named Carlo
Castone della Torre di Rezzonico Comasco described the approach to
Coalbrookdale as a 'veritable descent to the infernal regions'. Around
four years later the dramatist and writer Charles Dibdin declared that
even an atheist, 'left to awake at the mouth of one of those furnaces
[…] would infallibly tremble at the last
judgement that in imagination would
appear to him'. Just as it's hard to imagine
18th-century tourists travelling to see the
gorge, smoke-filled, red-skied and like
nowhere else they'd been, it's hard today to
picture Coalbrookdale as hellish, swathed
as it is in woodland and greenery. **Upper
Furnace Pool**, which once provided water
to power Abraham Darby's famous blast furnace, now hums with insect
activity; the various watercourses around Coalbrookdale are regularly
visited by coots, moorhens, kingfishers and dragonflies. **Dale End Park**
has a picnic-perfect riverside setting.

*"The watercourses
around Coalbrookdale
are visited by coots,
moorhens, kingfishers and
dragonflies, while Dale
End Park has a picnic-
perfect riverside setting."*

Nevertheless it's useful to keep those industrial furnaces in mind as you make your physical and educational journey through Ironbridge Gorge (perhaps starting in Coalbrookdale as Abraham Darby I did), because upon such innovation was our modern world founded. And industry does continue here, albeit in the production of exquisite teddy bears (page 123) and at the AGA-Rayburn factory where world-famous cookers and cookware are forged.

If you're driving, it's a good idea to park in the Coalbrookdale Museum of Iron car park (accessed beneath the railway viaduct): everywhere nearby is accessible from there.

Coalbrookdale Museum of Iron
TF8 7DQ ⊙ 10.00–17.00 daily

The Museum of Iron would be an excellent first stop because it tells the industrial story of the gorge: how Abraham Darby I came to the area from Bristol not to start a revolution but to find an easier, cheaper and less labour-intensive way of casting iron pots. And how subsequent generations of the Darby family – and others – built upon his success in mass-producing iron parts to secure

"Abraham Darby I came not to start a revolution but to find a cheaper way of casting iron pots."

Shropshire's place at the heart of industrialisation. Upstairs is a gallery dedicated to the Great Exhibition of 1851 and the iron pieces sent to represent Shropshire at the glittering Crystal Palace in London.

On the expansive lawn outside you'll find another of those castings: the Coalbrookdale Company's **Boy and Swan Fountain**, which would have stood at the gates dividing Hyde Park from Kensington Gardens, cascading perfume to mask the odours of the teeming crowds. Behind it, protected by a modern sloping-roofed building into which you can wander, is the **Old Furnace**, which began as a blast furnace and was later powered by coke.

True to the museum's theme, the gift shop on the ground floor stocks some attractive and useful cast iron goods, including cooking equipment. The **canteen-style café** has a market hall feeling thanks to its entranceway: decorative green and cherry red cast iron gates manufactured by the Coalbrookdale Company for Kirkgate Market in Bradford. It offers decent light meals (wraps, baguettes, salads, soup) and is open to people who are not visiting the museum.

Enginuity

TF8 7DQ ☺ 10.00–17.00 daily

In a warehouse behind the Museum of Iron, sharing its car park, is Enginuity – a science and technology museum which explains complex engineering principles in ways that are designed to be simple, fun and hands on for children and adults alike. You can learn how to generate electricity from flowing water, for example, or boost your muscle power with the aid of gears and pulleys to move a 10-ton train. The **Fab Lab** (membership and induction required) gives budding engineers of any age affordable and supported access to useful technology, software and equipment such as laser and vinyl cutters and 3D printers.

Enginuity would also be a good place to amuse little ones as there's a small soft play area for children aged under six. I'm told the museum is poised for an upgrade in the next couple of years.

The Darby Houses & more Coalbrookdale

For the Darby family's personal story, make your way by foot under the railway viaduct, turn right and head up the steep Darby Road to the Georgian **Darby Houses**, incorporating Rosehill and Dale House. (If you're going straight to the Darby Houses it's still best to park at the Museum of Iron and walk from there.) The interiors of these smart Georgian residences have been refurbished to around 1850 and contain original family furniture, letters and other mementoes. For our selfie generation, the last but one room in Rosehill offers replica Quaker and 'fashionable' period clothing to try on. If the Darby family's domestic story intrigues you, it's worth noting that Lady Rachel Labouchere of Dudmaston (page 89) transcribed the diaries of several Darbys (from whom she descended); you can buy copies both at Rosehill and in the gift shop at Coalport China Museum.

"The interiors of the Darby Houses have been refurbished to around 1850 and contain original family furniture, letters and other mementoes."

Behind the Darby Houses you'll see the workers' cottages of Tea Kettle Row and the lofty tops of fir trees above the nearby **Quaker burial ground** – the resting place of important ironmasters, including Abraham Darby III who commissioned the building of the iron bridge.

A little further up the hill is a gate leading to **three waymarked trails** managed by Severn Gorge Countryside Trust. The longest of these,

Loamhole Circular, takes only 45 minutes and leads you into **Loamhole Dingle,** an area of wet, semi-natural woodland where a rare species of cranefly thrives in the rotting wood by the stream.

Holy Trinity Church

From behind the Museum of Iron and Enginuity it's a five-minute walk up Church Road to what is nicknamed the 'Jewel of the Dale'. Holy Trinity Church was built between 1850 and 1854, endowed by Abraham Darby IV and family who had abandoned Quaker beliefs for Anglican. The church, in a heavenly position overlooking Coalbrookdale and offset by the dense green clouds of Dale Coppice, is not normally open outside times of worship but the churchyard is worth a browse: look for the iron gates, iron grave surrounds and iron grave markers. Matthew Webb and Sarah Cartwright, the parents of Captain Matthew Webb (pages 122–3) are buried behind the church where the land has been deliberately run to meadow.

If you wish to look inside the church, try phoning one of the helpful parishioners listed on the notice by the porch. Margaret Darlington showed me some highlights: a commemorative plaque for Captain Webb, stone corbel face carvings, a rare Flemish stained-glass window depicting the Last Supper (including a hit with schoolchildren: the man in yellow with six fingers) and a star-spangled chancel ceiling, commissioned in memory of Maurice Darby, killed in World War I aged just 20. Margaret grew up in the gorge. 'The funny thing was, we were never taught about the Industrial Revolution at school, even though it was all here on our doorstep,' she said. 'I couldn't have told you who Abraham Darby was or what he did. I suppose they thought we just absorbed it as we grew up.'

Green Wood Centre

Station Rd, TF8 7DR ⊝ car park closes at 17.00

Tucked away in the glades off Station Road (it was once the site of Coalbrookdale station) is the intriguing Green Wood Centre. Greeted by a herb garden and some enthusiastic wicker work, you could be forgiven for thinking at first that you'd wandered into a secret commune. The buildings include a cruck-framed barn, crafted from oak trees grown in Ironbridge Gorge, and a timber boiler room, where a burner powered by logs from locally coppiced woods provides heat and hot water for the

CAPTAIN MATTHEW WEBB

The River Severn's strong currents and sudden drops in depth at the bottleneck stretch of Ironbridge Gorge should deter even the most foolhardy swimmer. In the 1850s, however, a small boy from Dawley learned to swim in those waters. In 1875 he would emerge from the choppy sea at Calais, the first person in history to swim the English Channel.

Born to a surgeon, one of 14 children, Matthew Webb proved himself a proficient swimmer in 1863 when he saved his younger brother Henry from drowning. By then Matthew was already pursuing a maritime career, having joined the merchant navy aged 12. As second mate on the Cunard Line ship *Russia* in 1873, he dived into the Atlantic after a fellow sailor who had fallen overboard. Although the rescue attempt was unsuccessful Webb received £100 and the first Stanhope Medal from the Royal Humane Society.

In 1874 Captain Webb became a professional endurance swimmer. His first Channel attempt was aborted due to adverse weather but on 24 August 1875, smeared in porpoise oil and accompanied by a lugger named *Ann* and two small rowing boats, he dived into the sea from Dover's Admiralty pier and spent the next 21 hours and 45 minutes beating out a steady breaststroke all the way to France. He countered fatigue and a jellyfish sting with the occasional slug of brandy. According to a Press Association telegram, an exhausted Captain Webb responded to hearty greetings in Calais by saying he felt 'all right'.

And so was a national hero made. Great crowds, accompanied by rousing music from the 7th Shropshire Rifles, gathered at Wellington station to cheer him home. So jubilant were Webb's fellow Salopians, they unhitched his horses and towed his

whole site, boosted in the summer with solar panels. This lovely place is the headquarters of **SmallWoods**, an environmentally conscious organisation which promotes the benefits and produce afforded by small woodland areas. Striving to help people reconnect with the UK countryside, SmallWoods runs courses in disciplines such as woodcraft, coppicing, social forestry and coracle-making (⬧ www.smallwoods.org).

Shropshire Apple Trust (⬧ www.shropshireappletrust.co.uk) is based at the Green Wood Centre too, working hard to raise awareness of the importance of traditional orchards (including their wildlife) and preserving the diversity of apple species. On the Trust's annual **Apple Day** in October, out comes a hefty restored 19th-century twin-screw apple press to turn a community-gathered stockpile of apples into juice. The festivities are enlivened with cider, bands, morris dancing, a hog roast (including veggie option) and craft demonstrations.

carriage themselves to Ironbridge. Just like today's famous sportspeople, Webb inspired memorabilia and endorsed products, including safety matches. The Museum of the Gorge displays a commemorative milk jug.

Captain Webb took part in further swimming exhibitions, lectures and races, becoming wealthy from testimonial funds. From a circus-style stunt, which saw him floating in water for 128 hours at the Boston Horticultural Show, he pocketed £1,000.

In 1883, married with two infant children, Captain Webb answered a call to swim through the rapids at the Niagara Falls, describing them to a *New York Herald* reporter as 'the angriest bit of water in the world'. Incredulous spectators gathered to watch him: 5 feet and 8½ inches tall, moustachioed and muscular. But tragedy struck. Minutes after entering the rapids Captain Webb was caught by a huge wave and dragged down by a whirlpool. His body was recovered four days later. Some parishioners believe the reason his plaque hangs in the porch of Holy Trinity Church, Coalbrookdale rather than in the sacred nave, is because his act of derring-do was tantamount to suicide.

Captain Webb's grave is at Oakwood Cemetery near Niagara, but just south of Telford in Dawley is a memorial fountain raised in 1909. Juxtaposed against a Costcutters store and currently shut-down pub, there is something pathetic about it, in the original sense of the word, made more poignant with its exclamation mark: 'Nothing great is easy!'

In 2015 a low-budget film, *Captain Webb*, met with largely damp reviews. For another Captain Matthew Webb depiction in art form, look up Sir John Betjeman's acerbic poem, *A Shropshire Lad*.

SHOPPING

Ironbridge Antiques, Arts and Crafts Centre Merrythought Village, Dale End TF8 7NJ ✆ 01952 433124. This Victorian former factory at Dale End houses vintage and antique goods, bric-a-brac, pictures, and reasonably priced handmade items from local craftspeople. Riverside Tea Room looks out over the Severn: visit for proper tea leaves, mismatched china and knitted tea cosies (note: no toilets).

Merrythought Teddy Bear Shop Dale End Rd, TF8 7NJ ✆ 01952 433029. Merrythought has been making collectable teddy bears by hand in Ironbridge Gorge since 1930, building a fan base that spans the world. (I'm told the Punkie range in particular has a cult following in Japan.) Merrythought is an archaic word for wishbone – from which the company takes its emblem – but no-one can remember why the brand was named as such. It is the last remaining teddy bear manufacturer to make its products in Britain and takes pride in using traditional techniques and high-quality components including mohair. Merrythought bears are characterful: nearly all have fully jointed arms, legs and heads; some come with a music box or growl. The shop functions as a small museum too: I like the cabinet of vintage bears, especially the Disney-commissioned characters from the 1950s and 60s.

The factory isn't open to visitors, but you have Merrythought's blessing to peep through the windows during operating hours. Look also for the iron railings outside, topped with teddy heads.

FOOD & DRINK

Cherry's Real Food Café Woodland Hall, Green Wood Centre, Station Rd, TF8 7DR ☏ 01952 435857 ☉ 11.00–15.00 Wed–Sun. Built from local timber and with a range of ecologically sound features that include cellulose insulation and low-flush WCs, Woodland Hall at the Green Wood Centre is one of the most energy-efficient buildings in the country. Here you'll find Cherry's Real Food Café run by Polly Cherry, who places strong emphasis on organic, seasonal, free-range and local produce. The café is bedecked with fairy lights and more than a smattering of yoga leaflets, but Polly's chunky chips, Herefordshire cider and steak burgers squaring up alongside a veggie and vegan-friendly menu (think chilli bean enchiladas or hearty homemade nut roast) make everything far less worthy and a bit more wow. Dogs are welcome. You'll find secondhand books for sale for charity and a few craft items too.

THE LIFE & DEATH OF JOHN 'IRON MAD' WILKINSON

Of the many pioneers whose lives make up the industrial history of Ironbridge Gorge, it is the bullish John Wilkinson (b1728) to whom my imagination keeps returning. His was a great engineering mind. One of his patented inventions could accurately bore cylinders for steam engines, an innovation in machine tools that would have many wider applications. John Wilkinson became fabulously wealthy. While his fellow industrialist Richard Reynolds, a Quaker, refused on moral grounds to make armaments for the French war, Wilkinson's Bersham Ironworks did a roaring trade in cannons and guns.

Wilkinson was instrumental in the construction of the gorge's world-famous bridge, heavily influencing the decision to use iron rather than wood. He contributed a significant amount of money to the project, although sold his shares before the bridge came to fruition. It may have been around this time he acquired the nickname 'Iron Mad'; certainly his love for the material was becoming increasingly ardent.

In 1787 in Broseley Wilkinson cast the first iron barge to carry freight and launched it on the River Severn at Willey, much to the disbelief of onlookers. From 1787 to 1795, during a shortage of copper coins and therefore small change, he issued his own controversial copper tokens bearing an image of his bust and the inscription: 'JOHN WILKINSON IRON MASTER'. In the 1790s his obsession with iron grew – and well it might

3 IRONBRIDGE

🏠 **Iron Bridge House** (page 249), **The Library House** (page 248)

Here I've taken Ironbridge to mean the area around the gorge continuing on from Coalbrookdale, starting more or less at the Museum of the Gorge, and running along Wharfage Road to near the old police station, currently a restaurant called Pondicherry. Look for the unusual iron kerbsides. This stretch, for me, is the greatest place to admire the River Severn on its powerful downward course, sheltered by the steep wooded slopes of the gorge into which attractive cottages and smart Georgian houses nestle. Visible from various points here – although not from the iron bridge itself – are the 1960s cooling towers of Buildwas (page 116). It's also at Buildwas where 'above level datum' is taken to predict risk of the Severn flooding so that warnings may be issued in the area. The Museum of the Gorge has been flooded many times and is now poised for action: plug sockets are positioned halfway up the walls and all displays can be dismantled and moved swiftly whenever heavy rainwater falling on to the Cambrian mountains threatens to run the length of the river.

for by 1796 his empire was producing an eighth of the country's cast iron output.

Now advanced in years, John Wilkinson dreamed up a way to express his affection for iron even in death. He had two cast iron coffins forged, one for him and one for anyone similarly enthused by iron. He kept them at his home in Broseley – surely a talking point for any dinner guest. He also designed his own iron obelisk, standing 40 feet high.

Iron Mad's death in 1808 does not end this story. By the time he died, not in Broseley but at his Castle Head mansion house near Lindale in Cumbria, the coffin had become too small for his hefty figure. Forged from cast iron, it couldn't be altered, so a new one was made

at Wilkinson's Shropshire ironworks. He was buried in the garden of Castle Head; twice, because the ground over the first site would not support his 20-ton monument.

In 1828 the house's new owners decided they did not want a corpse in their grounds, so Wilkinson's remains were moved to the burial grounds of Lindale Parish Church (where their exact location is now a mystery). The obelisk was not allowed to accompany him and lay hidden in undergrowth for some years until erected by the roadside near Lindale. It's still there.

Iron Mad's Shropshire mansion is on Church Street in Broseley. In his day it was called the New House; now it's The Lawns (a private home).

Museum of the Gorge

TF8 7DQ ⊙ 10.00–17.00 daily; the adjacent car park is managed by the local authority, more expensive than the Gorge-owned car parks & limited to three hours' parking

Be grateful you weren't standing at the site of the Museum of the Gorge on 12 February 1795. A flood mark on the wall shows the height of the River Severn on that fateful day and I'm not sure even Captain Matthew Webb (who is well represented in the museum) could have battled the rushing water. The museum stands proud on the banks of the river, with a castellated roof like a miniature sandstone castle. In fact it was once a warehouse, built in the gothic revival style for the Coalbrookdale Company, storing products made in Coalbrookdale ready to be shipped along the Severn.

ROWING A CORACLE

The coracle bobbed on the mere beside a homemade jetty of wooden pallets. 'On' being the operative word: coracles are keel-less, lightweight circular boats resembling giant half-walnut shells atop the water, at the mercy of currents and the slightest breeze. *I'm definitely going to fall out,* I thought, footsure not even of the jetty as I swung one, then two legs into my wobbly bowl and bumped rear-first on to the wooden slat that would be my seat. The knowledge that coracles have existed for hundreds of years offered little reassurance: hardly anyone outside of Wales and Shropshire has heard of them ... *so obviously they are a terrible and long-abandoned idea*, I decided. Why not row something more streamlined: a canoe or a dinghy? The answer is that coracles are easy to build, light to transport and (in theory) highly manoeuvrable, allowing fishermen to catch eels and migratory fish in the shallows of rivers – places inaccessible to wading or long lines.

'One coracle family, the Rogers, were well known for locating the bodies of people who'd drowned in the Severn,' said Terry Kenny, a retired coracle maker who'd built the vessels my friends and I were rowing today. They were constructed in the 'Ironbridge style', lathes of ash wood covered in calico and bitumen. 'They knew the Severn so well, they understood the currents, and could predict the places where corpses could be secreted. But they never accepted any rewards.'

The Barn at the Green Wood Centre (page 121) has a display of coracles, and the Rogers' coracle shed has just been saved for posterity by the Ironbridge Coracle Trust. My first glimpse of coracles was at the **Ironbridge Coracle Regatta**, which takes place from Dale End Park every August bank holiday. It has to be said that, in the pouring rain, even the rowers who'd considered themselves skilled enough to enter a coracle race made the whole thing look rather hard. I decided,

The museum would be another useful starting point for your Ironbridge Gorge adventure, as a film running every 15 minutes details the history of this special place. It's also home to the **visitor information centre**.

In summer on the first Sunday of the month a **local produce market** takes place on the car park outside.

The iron bridge, Toll House Museum & nearby

In this age of skyscrapers and space travel (and even that makes me sound stuck in the past, like the narrator for a 1980s science video), it's hard to imagine what a magnificent feat of engineering the iron bridge was when constructed in 1779.

against my own better judgement, that I wanted to have a go.

And so here I was, just about upright, in a mere north of Whitchurch on a chilly Sunday morning, my friends chuckling from the grassy banks as they awaited their own drenching. A traditional village fair was being set up nearby and crackling dulcimer music drifted from a rented loudspeaker like a surreal soundtrack. 'Henry Mancini's *Baby Elephant Walk* – that should be your coracle theme tune,' my brother had said, ducking before I could whack him with my oar.

I began paddling in the way I'd been told – with a figure-of-eight motion in front of the coracle – and made a little progress. I spun around a few times, but I had achieved propulsion. And a little more. I was upright!

And not wet. I would paddle to the middle of the mere and wave at my friends who waited their turns.

I didn't notice that a light wind was carrying me and my coracle east towards the church until I found myself in the shallows of the great kettle hole, my paddle striking the mere bed. I pushed away with the paddle and tried again, only to find myself spinning into an argument with a tree, the low-hanging soft branches of a dying alder tangled up in my hair. A worrying quantity of water had gathered in the bowl of the coracle, a result of my inefficient strokes. I couldn't stop laughing. Eventually I was towed back to the jetty with a canoe, hardly triumphant but delighted not to have swallowed a mouthful of mere.

My coracle experience at Marbury (just over the Shropshire border) was organised by **Sue Tuerena Outdoor Adventure** (☏ 07803 560455 ☌ www.suetuerena.co.uk), a Shropshire-based family business I'd highly recommend for activity days including bushcraft, canoeing, hill walking and of course coracle rowing.

The bridge was built by Abraham Darby III to link Coalbrookdale, the manufacturing town of Broseley and the mining town of Madeley, replacing an old ferry service. (The ferry masters were, quite rightly, exempt from paying the new toll.) But it was much more than a bridge. At the behest of John 'Iron Mad' Wilkinson (pages 124–5) it was to be constructed not from wood but cast in iron, to showcase the genius of the Coalbrookdale ironmasters. No-one had before done anything so ambitious and the Shrewsbury architect Thomas Farnolls Pritchard was consulted for the design.

"The small exhibition tells the stories of the bridge, including how in 1934 even Queen Mary, wife of George V, was not exempt from paying her halfpenny to cross it."

The iron bridge was built in the manner of a wooden bridge, with joists rather than the rivets we would expect from modern bridges. There are no eyewitness accounts but its construction must have been a spectacle, baffling and marvellous. Certainly the opening attracted great attention and before long the bridge's image would appear on crockery, letterheads, handkerchiefs, brooches and even fire grates. Sadly, Pritchard did not live to see the realisation of his construction: he died in 1777 aged just 54. Darby saw the grand design fulfilled, though, and was awarded a gold medal from the Royal Society of the Arts.

Today the bridge remains, toll-free and available to cross on foot, a 378-ton monument to industry and endeavour.

While the bridge is a public access monument and therefore always open, the **Toll House Museum** at the southern end keeps limited hours (☉ w/ends during local school holidays; admission free). If it happens to be open when you visit the gorge it's worth looking inside. The small exhibition tells the human stories of the bridge, including how in 1934 even Queen Mary, wife of George V, was not exempt from paying her halfpenny to cross it.

While you stand on the iron bridge, look back to the Wharfage side of the gorge and the gothic church of **St Luke's** in its imposing position on the hillside. Most churches are built with the tower at the east end and sanctuary at the west, but St Luke's is the reverse since the earth at the east end would not sustain the weight of a tower. The sides of the gorge are prone to subsidence: major stabilisation work is underway at Jackfield to avoid a repeat of the 1952 landslide which saw several houses disappear into the river.

FAMILY DAYS OUT

Shropshire offers limitless scope for exploring, hill scrambling, wildlife spotting and gleeful welly muddying. History is easily absorbed too: conservation efforts, excellent museums and a largely unblemished landscape make the past a tangible concept, and never dull.

1 Blists Hill Victorian Town. **2** Workshop at Coalport China Museum. **3** Hawkstone Park Follies. **4** Hoo Farm Animal Kingdom.

ARENA PHOTO UK/S

HISTORY & HERITAGE

Scratch away at Shropshire's tranquil surface and you'll find a county with a history that has changed the world, from Clive of India to the modern-day Olympic movement. Perhaps most significant was the impact of Ironbridge Gorge on the Industrial Revolution.

SCT

DEATONPHOTOS/S

1 Severn Valley Railway engine, Hampton Loade. 2 The canalside bottle kiln houses part of the Coalport China Museum. 3 Heavy horse, Acton Scott Historic Working Farm. 4 The world's first iron bridge was built in 1779. 5 Canal warehouse, Ellesmere. 6 Wood bodger, Acton Scott Historic Working Farm. 7 Jackfield and Coalport Memorial Bridge. 8 Tar Tunnel, Coalport. 9 Trevithick locomotive replica, Blists Hill Victorian Town.

THE GREAT WAR
1914 ... ✦ ... 1918
THIS BRIDGE IS FREE
O TREAD IT REVERENTLY
IN MEMORY OF THOSE
WHO DIED FOR THEE
ERECTED BY PUBLIC SUBSCRIPTION
1922

SCT

LOCAL EVENTS

Shropshire's calendar is illuminated year round with festivals and fairs, celebrating everything from apples, flowers, steam machinery and ale to sweet peas, coracles and storytelling.

1 Morris dancers at Bridgnorth Folk Festival. 2 Green Man Festival, Clun. 3 Wellington Town Charter Day. 4 Shrewsbury Flower Show.

WELLINGTON H2A

SHROPSHIRE HORTICULTURAL SOCIETY

DEATONPHOTOS/S

Cross the bridge with the Toll House on your right and a number of **walking possibilities** open up to you. Turn left to follow signs to Jackfield, Coalport and Madeley, including Blists Hill Victorian Town (which is 1¾ miles away). Turn right into the woodland of **Benthall Edge**, where an interpretation panel and waymarkers await. You can pick up the **Severn Valley Way** (♿ flat & surfaced track) to the cooling towers at Buildwas (a 1½-mile return walk); make a short (half-mile) circular woodland walk to former **lime kilns**; or take steep wooden steps up through the forest-dense sides of the gorge to a rewarding view of Ironbridge 300 feet above Patten's Rock Quarry. The latter is a challenging 1¾-mile round walk, with optional footpath diversions to **Broseley** and **Benthall Hall**. The paths are uneven in places and get muddy in wet weather and there are some narrow walkways along Benthall Edge with steep drops.

Market Square & around

Market Square consists of a short stay car park and Market Hall, a row of shops that would once have been open-fronted. Most of its buildings date to the 1780s when the expanding town became known as Ironbridge. Church Steps, to the right of the Tontine Hotel, lead to St Luke's Church.

�𝗬𝗢 FOOD & DRINK

Eighty Six'd 1a Waterloo St ✆ 01952 432620 ☺ 10.00–18.00, closed Mon & Tue ♿ situated upstairs, so not easily accessible. A coffee shop and art café in a quirky flat-iron-shaped building, exhibiting work by local artists. Serves light, freshly made lunches (sandwiches, big salads, tarts) and an excellent selection of homemade cakes: think delicate frangipane, vegan banana bread and yummy chocolate blondies.

Eley's 13 Tontine Hill ✆ 01952 432504 ⬦ www.eleysporkpies.co.uk. If you like pork pies, call in at Eley's to pick up a 'world-famous' hand-raised specimen. The success of this business, established in the 1960s, has mirrored the growing tourist trade in Ironbridge Gorge. Give the team three days' notice to make, bake and dispatch a personalised pork pie; you can also order online for home delivery.

Restaurant Severn 33 High St ✆ 01952 432233 ☺ open from 18.30 & for occasional Sun lunch (see website), closed Mon & Tue. An intimate venue overlooking the river, for two AA-rosette fine dining. The chef patron specialises in classical French and British cooking with fusion techniques. Everything's made in house and the produce is seasonal and local, much of it grown on the restaurant's smallholding.

4 BROSELEY & BENTHALL HALL

The former manufacturing town of Broseley and leafy village of Benthall aren't in the Telford & Wrekin district but I've swiped them from southeast Shropshire because of their geographical and metaphorical closeness to Ironbridge Gorge, just south of the River Severn. Indeed, both are fun to access by foot from the gorge, up through the steep thick woodland of Benthall Edge (see page 129).

Broseley

It was from his Broseley forge in 1787 that John 'Iron Mad' Wilkinson (pages 124–5) made the first iron ship. One of James Watt's first steam engines was constructed here too. Sir John Betjeman in his 1951 *Shell Guide to Shropshire* described Broseley as a 'decayed manufacturing town of great beauty, textural and forlorn'. I think he must have found beauty and texture in Broseley's juxtaposition of architectural styles: workers' cheerful cottages crouched alongside grand former homes of wealthy industrialists. It feels, to me, both thrown together and entirely harmonious. There is little sign of decay now, nor forlornness, just a town glad to celebrate its heritage.

Broseley Pipeworks (⌀ 01952 433424 ⊙ mid-May–late Sep 13.00–17.00) is one of the ten Ironbridge Gorge Museum Trust properties, a 'time capsule' museum in the form of a factory that was abandoned in the 1950s and little altered since. Broseley clay tobacco pipes were once world famous; 'Would you take a Broseley?' the social refrain of smokers. Abraham Darby I is interred in the Quaker burial ground next to the former factory. From the museum you can follow a trail to the **jitties**, a jumble of narrow lanes and passageways that emerged in the 1590s as a way of joining squatters' cottages inhabited by very poor immigrant miners. The jitties include the irresistibly named Ding Dong Steps.

The Arriva **bus** services 88 and 88A linking Telford Town Centre and Much Wenlock (via Ironbridge) stop in Broseley.

Benthall Hall

Broseley TF12 5RX ⌀ 01952 882159 ⊙ varies; please check website; free parking
♿ grounds partly accessible; mobility toilet; National Trust

One mile northwest of Broseley town, this distinguished stone house, wispy with wisteria, resides like an elderly gentleman on a plateau above the River Severn. Built between the 1530s and 1580s, Benthall Hall is said to have offered refuge for travelling Catholic priests. Note the five circular symbols above the main entrance: they're thought to represent Jesus's stigmata, a secret symbol that Roman Catholics would be safe here. The Benthall family has lived in this house for 500 years, seeing Civil War skirmishes, the clanging and banging of the Industrial Revolution, and the infinitely gentler moving in of the National Trust. George Maw lived here from around 1852. A great botanist, as well as famously establishing the tile-manufacturing company Maw & Co with his brother, he left a legacy in the gardens which yield colourful crocus displays in the spring and autumn.

"The circular symbols above the main entrance are thought to represent Jesus's stigmata, a secret symbol that Roman Catholics would be safe here."

Benthall Hall's current residents Edward and Sally Benthall are tenants of the National Trust (the house was given to the nation in 1958) and the occasional glimpse of their occupancy – a toothbrush mug in the bathroom or an upturned book in the master bedroom – enhances the visitor experience, I think, by allowing you to view Benthall Hall as a warm and treasured family home. Look for the late 17th-century carved oak panel depicting the future King Charles II being escorted secretly from Boscobel House (page 104); the bushy oak that concealed him the day before is also present in the scene.

The **tea room**, serving hot drinks and cakes, offers a welcoming fire on chilly afternoons. Outside, besides George Maw's green-fingered influence, you'll find a dovecote housing gently cooing fantail doves and an Elizabethan skittle alley for play.

The **church of St Bartholomew**, in a walled churchyard within the grounds, is unusual for having an apiary, which would have provided income for the church. Bees would fly from the mouth of a stone lion and an inscription reads 'Out of the strong forth came sweetness'.

The Arriva **bus** service number 88 which runs from Telford bus station to Much Wenlock via Ironbridge and Broseley every two hours (Mon to Sat only) stops at Benthall Hall Junction. The **Shropshire Way** passes through the woodland and you can also make the short walk back to Ironbridge by following the footpath signs.

In case you need to ask for directions, most (but not all) local people agree that Benthall for the Hall rhymes with 'gentle', while the name of Benthall village is pronounced with a soft 'th', rhyming with 'menthol'.

⫡ FOOD & DRINK

Clays 67 High St, Broseley ✐ 01952 884667 ⊙ closed Mon & Tue. How fortunate that owners David and Trudy should have a surname to match the very substance that helped Broseley prosper. They are working magic at Clays, supporting local suppliers and delighting residents. Reasonably priced, the menu is predominantly British and Mediterranean. Lunch is as light or substantial as you want: imagine baked eggs with local black pudding, chicken paella, rarebit made with local cheeses, or beef meatballs and gnocchi in a rich tomato sauce.

The King & Thai The Forester Arms, Avenue Rd, Broseley ✐ 01952 882004. A stylish Thai restaurant to which diners travel from far and wide. The puddings are very special. Multi award-winning chef Suree Coates is a familiar face in the demo kitchens of the Ludlow Food Festival; at the King & Thai you can benefit from her culinary expertise in a more personal setting by signing up for a masterclass in Thai cookery.

5 COALPORT

⌂ **Coalport Station Holidays** (page 248), **YHA Coalport** (page 248)

Built on hayfields, Coalport was the 'new town' of the 1790s, sprouting houses, warehouses, wharves and quays within a few years, thanks to its excellent connections to the river, road and canal. The ingenious **Hay Inclined Plane** (♀ SJ694027), in operation from 1792 to 1894, represented a huge feat of engineering. Worked by just four men, it would raise a pair of 5-ton, 20-feet tub boats up 207 feet to Blists Hill Victorian Town in four minutes, a task that would otherwise require 27 locks and up to three hours.

Coalport is an easy walk from Jackfield and Ironbridge but if you're driving, use the long-stay pay and display car park attached to Coalport China Museum.

Coalport China Museum

TF8 7HT ⊙ 10.00–17.00 daily

We tend to give Staffordshire much of the credit for British ceramics, but in the late 18th and early 19th centuries Shropshire was at the heart of china making. In 1796 John Rose, who had learned his trade with Caughley china, founded a porcelain factory in Coalport, the 'new town' that was already heaving with industry. Rose had the impeccable timing of every great entrepreneur. Thanks to a cut in tax in the previous decade, tea had ceased being an exotic luxury and was now the refreshment of choice for all. In 1795 imports of tea had increased fourfold and, simply, people needed cups and saucers to drink from.

In a riverside location in part of the later factory (including a bottle kiln), Coalport China Museum tells the manufacturing and social stories of Coalport and Caughley china. In the Long Workshop you can see craftspeople in action and, on certain days, try your hand at clay modelling, painting and glazing.

If you're in need of refreshment, YHA Coalport over the courtyard has a clean and welcoming **licensed café**. It's in the John Rose Building, the earliest surviving part of the China Works.

Tar Tunnel

TF8 7HT ✐ 01952 433424 ◷ 10.30–16.00 daily

It's a five-minute walk along the canal behind the China Museum and over the bridge to the Tar Tunnel. This was dug in 1786 under William Reynolds's watch, with the aim of building a canal to transport coal from the mines at Blists Hill Victorian Town. After driving through for about 300 yards, the miners struck a spring of natural bitumen. This oozy, treacle-like substance isn't actually tar (a by-product of coal production) but the microscopic remains of plants and animals, millions of years old, useful for lining the bottoms of ships, creating lamp oil, even for medicinal preparations. It's thought that in the early days around 1,000 gallons of bitumen were extracted here every week. In 1787 (published in 1824) Italian diplomat Carlo Castone della Torre di Rezzonico Comasco said:

> The workmen who gather the pitch, are, of a truth, like the imps described by Dante in his Inferno as gathering with a hook the souls of the damned into a lake of pitch – so horribly disfigured and begrimed are they.

Largely forgotten after World War II when it was used as an air raid shelter, the tar tunnel was rediscovered in 1965 when the Shropshire Village Mining Club persuaded the owner of Coalport's village shop to explore the darkness extending out from a door in his cellar …

You won't find Dante's imps in the tunnel today but you can walk the first 100 yards before coming to a stop at a locked iron gate. The tunnel has never been explored in full, but may have stretched as far as pits in the Madeley area. The walls still ooze, so be sure to stick to the central pathway. If you have an Ironbridge Gorge Museum Trust Annual Passport it's worth visiting the Tar Tunnel, but the whole experience lasts only a few minutes so don't make it the main focus of your day.

If, instead of returning to Coalport China Museum, you cross the **Jackfield & Coalport Memorial Bridge** and turn right, it's only a short walk to Jackfield and the Maws Craft Centre.

⅋ FOOD & DRINK

The Woodbridge Inn TF8 7JF ✆ 01952 882054. This sumptuous pub on the banks of the Severn was built in around 1785, long surviving the wooden bridge it was named after, which connected the inn to Coalport. It has many airy, bright spaces as well as cosier nooks for more intimate drinking and dining. The food is pricier than an average pub but excellent (summer examples: smoked haddock and salmon fishcakes, Moroccan-seared lamb; pea, broad bean and asparagus risotto) with a good wine list and local ales.

6 JACKFIELD

> Heaven preserve me from having to live at such a forsaken place as that.
> Henry Dunnill (1865)

Despite Henry Dunnill's reaction to his first glimpse of Jackfield – which at that time was mired in squalor and brothels – he would soon go on to establish the Messrs Craven Dunnill tile factory here, alongside the equally famous tile producers Maw & Co. Jackfield's industrial history was already well established, a port town growing up at the confluence of the River Severn. In 1605, the coalmaster James Clifford had constructed a wooden railway (the first in Shropshire and only the second in Britain) from his mines at Broseley down 'tylting railes' to Jackfield.

All the places listed below are a short, well-signposted walk from Coalport and Ironbridge.

Jackfield Tile Museum

Salthouse Rd, TF8 7LJ ⊙ 10.00–17.00 daily

I never expected to feel enthused by a tile museum, but enjoyed my first visit to Jackfield Tile Museum thoroughly – recounting as it does the history of Jackfield industry and British tile making, celebrating the joint aesthetic and hygienic function of tiles (which should appeal to anyone with even a passing interest in interior design). The extensive museum includes reconstructions of a tiled Victorian pub and Edwardian tube station, and adorably unfashionable pictorial tile panels rescued from 1960s children's hospital wards. Housed in the still-operational Craven

Dunnill factory, it's a living museum where on certain days you'll find tile makers busy in their workshops. I was lucky enough to see Minton encaustic floor tiles being made for the Palace of Westminster; such is the calibre of the workmanship here in Jackfield.

Artisans at Fusion

Church Rd ◌ www.artisans-at-fusion.org ◌ studio opening times vary: check individual listings at the website; free parking

Adjacent to Jackfield Tile Museum is Fusion, so called because the original building on its site was a foundry of non-ferrous metals. Fusion houses the workshops of talented craftspeople and artists; you can buy their artwork, glass and prints and occasionally attend courses.

Maws Craft Centre

192 Salthouse Rd, TF8 7LS ◌ 01952 883030 ◌ www.mawscraftcentre.co.uk ◌ daily but hours vary from unit to unit: the best time to visit is generally 12.00–15.00; free parking

Housed in the Victorian factory buildings of Maw & Co, once the world's largest encaustic tile manufacturer, are around 20 units and studios selling craft and hobby supplies, handmade gifts, photography, picture framing, jewellery, wall art, and vintage items. Some of the units hold crafting workshops – and alternative therapy sessions are available at the Gorge Therapy & Training Centre. **Scarlett's** is the on-site licensed tea room. It's useful to take cash because a number of the craftspeople don't have debit or credit card facilities.

7 MADELEY

Madeley, just east of Ironbridge Gorge (and officially a part of Telford New Town), was purchased by Milburga of Wenlock Priory (page 93) in AD727. The name means Mad(d)a's clearing, with Madda a first name of Anglo-Saxon origin. John Betjeman called it 'an unspoiled specimen of early industrialism'. The reputedly haunted **Madeley Court** (currently a Mercure hotel), with its handsome gabled attic dormers, was built by Robert Broke in 1553 (see Claverley listing on page 87) and leased for a time in the early 18th century by Abraham Darby I. The mysterious Elizabethan cuboid sundial device outside is grade II listed.

Madeley's history is rich, with Parliamentary forces occupying the church during the English Civil War; a barn on Church Street (now smart mews houses) sheltering Charles II after his defeat at the

Battle of Worcester. In the mid 18th century Madeley was an important centre of Methodism, with John Fletcher (a contemporary of John Wesley) the vicar of **St Michael's Church**.

In 1864 at nearby Brick Kiln Leasow Pit, the chain loops on an apparatus known as 'the doubles' (used to raise miners in and out of the deep shaft) came unhooked – probably due to human error – and nine workers plunged to their deaths. The youngest were only 12 and 13 years old. **The Nine Men of Madeley Project** is a community undertaking to honour the miners and tell their story, also revealing the social and working conditions of people in Victorian Madeley. A two-hour trail starts at the miners' iron-topped communal grave in the churchyard (⬧ www.ninemen.org), itself a green and intriguing place to explore.

Blists Hill Victorian Town

Legges Way, Madeley TF7 5DU ✆ 01952 433424 ◷ 10.00–17.00; pay & display car park

Of the ten museums run by the Ironbridge Gorge Museum Trust, the open-air attraction at Blists Hill is undoubtedly the biggest crowd-pleaser. Blists Hill once comprised blast furnaces, a brick and tile works, and mines. Now the industrial landscape has been reimagined as a 'living museum' across more than 50 acres, allowing you to experience with all five senses a small English Victorian town. It is populated by real Victorian characters (or, rather, volunteers happy to play the part) pottering about their daily lives in shops, workplaces, cottages and gardens. Their commitment to detail is impressive: I once overheard a bonneted lady, briefly and forgivably out of character, apologising for squinting because she'd had to leave her plastic-rimmed glasses at home.

If you feel similarly inspired to enter into the Victorian spirit, exchange your money at the bank (modelled on the still-existing Lloyds in Broseley) for pre-decimal sterling to spend in the shops, where skilled trades are preserved wherever possible – including in tallow candle making and typesetting and printing. (Either way, do take some cash as no ATM exists on the site.) Other establishments in which you can lighten your pocket include a sweetshop, bakery and a traditional fish and chip shop. The chemist's shop was the filming location for BBC Two's *Victorian Pharmacy*. Your farthings and pennies can't be used in the entrance gift shop, coffee shop or refreshment pavilion, although any money remaining can be exchanged back to modern sterling when you leave.

Other jolly experiences include dressing up and sitting for a portrait photograph (extra charge), taking part in a music hall singalong in the New Inn Pub and, in summer, enjoying the swingboats and carousel at the old time funfair. For a couple of pounds extra you can take a short trip on a mine railway. Exhibits and demonstrations vary from day to day so if there's something special you're keen to see, it's best to check the line-up in advance.

As with all the Trust's museums, Blists Hill offers sound learning experiences amidst the merriment, and it's a popular destination for school parties (who can compare their lives with those of Victorian children in the schoolroom). Some of the buildings were moved here, brick by brick, from other sites: the pub, for example, used to stand in Walsall and the squatters' cottage is from Dawley. On a short stretch of narrow gauge track near the ruins of the brick and tile works, you can see a working replica of the Trevithick locomotive.

Look out for special events, especially those in the evenings: my first visit to Blists Hill was one Bonfire Night and the atmosphere crackled with warmth and fun. The ghostly gaslit Halloween is another popular occasion, as are Blists Hill's Victorian Christmas weekends and the 1940s extravaganza, Blitz Hill (it had to be).

ᛦ FOOD & DRINK

All Nations Inn 20 Coalport Rd, Madeley TF7 5DP ℘ 01952 585747. A no-frills drinking pub up a steep slope opposite Blists Hill Victorian Town (and yet far enough off the beaten track to feel like a secret). All Nations has just launched its own brewhouse and serves just the grub you need to mop up a pint: filled rolls and ploughman's lunches.

Fried Fish Dealers Canal St, Blists Hill Victorian Town ☉ 11.30–15.00 when the museum is open. If you're at Blists Hill and have no objection to beef fat, then lunch simply has to be traditionally battered fish and chips with lashings of vinegar. On the one occasion I made do with a sandwich, I had to wrestle my own hands back into my coat pockets to avoid pinching chips from the paper cones of passing strangers.

8 TELFORD

When I think of Shropshire's 'new' town I recall a meme on the Facebook wall of a friend who lives near Shrewsbury. It comprised a series of stills from Disney's *The Lion King,* where Simba and his father are gazing over a shimmering valley. 'Look Simba, everything the light touches is Shropshire,' says the doctored caption. The cub asks, puzzled: 'What about that shadowy place?' The last image shows the father lion looking sternly down at his son. 'That's Telford, you must never go there, Simba.'

The meme made me smile because of the truth it contained, if only in terms of some people's attitudes. Telford, developed in the 1960s and 1970s on industrial and agricultural land (and merging together smaller settlements including Oakengates, Dawley, Madeley and Wellington), does indeed have a reputation for blighting Shropshire's beauty. Michael Raven, author of the 1989 *A Shropshire Gazetteer,* referred to its 'garish plastic-covered factories and spartan, treeless housing estates'.

"Telford has one of the most wonderful town parks you'll find anywhere."

Let's not judge the new town too harshly. It's not possible to compare roundabouts and retail outlets to medieval market towns and heather-topped hills. I'd rather celebrate Telford for what it represents to us: a useful gateway to central Shropshire and an ideal rainy-day destination. It also has one of the most wonderful **town parks** you'll find anywhere and, on the outskirts, big-dreaming steam enthusiasts at **Telford Steam Railway.**

Telford is named after **Thomas Telford** (1757–1834), the Scottish civil engineer who left his mark on roads, bridges and canals around Shropshire and beyond. He's buried in Westminster Abbey, an honour bestowed on very few of history's engineers.

TOWN CENTRE

Technically Telford does have a town centre but it's probably unlike any other you've encountered. Shropshire's new town is more of a retail park, with copious roundabouts; some of which were built to allow for future expansion and currently appear to go nowhere. Telford's a useful landing point in Shropshire. You can catch a train to Telford Central and travel by bus to Ironbridge Gorge, Bridgnorth, Much Wenlock, Shrewsbury, and so on. When you alight at Telford Central, follow signs to the town centre and onward to the bus station.

The mechanical **frog clock** (also known as the Telford Time Machine) in the 25-acre Telford Shopping Centre gives an automated, bubble-blowing performance on the hour. For **Oakengates Theatre** (www.theplacetelford.com), alight at Telford Oakengates station – the modern playhouse is a five-minute walk away.

TELFORD TOWN PARK

Hinkshay Rd (for Visitor Centre), TF3 4EP ✆ 01952 382340 ⌖ www.telfordtownpark.co.uk
♿ accessible, with an inclusive playground (see below)

However you feel about the planners who created Telford New Town, we've got to hand it to them for allowing space for Telford Town Park. You can reach it by exiting Telford Shopping Centre at the Southwater end and heading for the glorious green stretching almost two miles into south Telford. Having grown up on a site of brickworks, coal mines and quarries, much of the park is now a designated Local Nature Reserve, nurturing diverse flora and fauna on its acid heathland, as well as rare spotted orchids from more alkaline soils. The gentle ghost of the industrial past has yielded to nature: Stirchley Chimney towering 203 feet into the sky looks down on pit mound remains that have given way to heathland and woodland, to former quarry pools that are now flitting haunts for dragonflies and damselflies, to hedgerows running in almost mocking abandon alongside remnants of canals and railway tracks.

To explore the past, or discover the nature that has reclaimed it, follow the waymarked **Heritage Trail** (2½ miles) or **Nature Trail** (four miles – including two sets of steps). To enhance your journey, pick up a trail leaflet from the centrally located visitor centre (☉ 09.00–18.00 daily in summer, earlier closing times from autumn onwards). Next to the centre, as well as a **café**, is **Telford Cycle Centre** (✆ 0845 4348451 ⌖ www.cycleexperience.com/telfordcyclecentre ☉ summer 10.00–16.30 Tue–Sun; winter 10.00–16.00 Thu–Sun) for bike hire, sales, repairs or training. You can rent cycles to enjoy on the hard surfaces of the park, or take them further afield. For walkers or cyclists, it's worth noting that the **Silkin Way** connects with Ironbridge Gorge from here, following disused railway lines and dry canal beds.

Telford Town Park offers a great deal to keep young families amused: adventure playgrounds and a trim trail with age guidance, a huge rocket slide, water play and sandpit. ♿ The **inclusive playground** (built around the incongruous remains of a Norman chapel, moved to the park from nearby Malinslee in the 1970s) has thoughtfully designed apparatus for young children and children with disabilities, including a roundabout that is flush with the ground to allow wheelchair and buggy access.

Chelsea Gardens (with sensory garden) and Japanese-style **Maxell Garden** (look for radiant cherry blossom in spring) provide a peaceful retreat from the delighted screeching of pre-schoolers. And if you're looking for an even more substantial day out, there are a couple of paid-for options to enjoy: the 12-hole **Telford Adventure Golf** (⊘ daily; pay and collect clubs and balls from the visitor centre) and **Closer to the Edge** high ropes course (✆ 0845 8802477 ⊘ Feb half-term until end Oct ⊘ www.closertotheedge.co.uk).

Wonderland

✆ 01952 591633 ⊘ www.wonderlandmidlands.com ⊘ late Mar–early Sep & selected dates in winter

At the southern end of Telford Town Park is Wonderland, a low-key theme park set in nine acres of woodland. Its fairytale characters and fibreglass cottages are a little tired and may not impress anyone over the age of four. But having carried my two-year-old out kicking at the end of a long day ('Play MOOOORE!') I can confirm that, for tots, this place is enthralling. For now, that makes Wonderland wonderful for me too. One admission fee grants unlimited rides and there is soft play for when the weather sends you indoors. If you're often dismayed by theme park catering, consider bringing a picnic.

It's best to access Wonderland through Telford Town Park: it doesn't have dedicated parking and can be hard to locate if you're driving. Simply follow signs (the paths are suitable for buggies) or, in the summer season, catch the little red Wonderland train from near the high ropes course: it's £1 per passenger and there is space for foldable pushchairs. If you are approaching Wonderland by car, the closest free car park is on Randlay Avenue (TF3 2LS).

9 PRIORSLEE

On the face of it, there's not a huge amount to do at Priorslee, one of the more affluent suburbs of Telford and characterised by new executive housing. Birders may find interest at Priorslee Lake, accessed by foot mid-way down Priorslee Avenue, via Teece Drive (⊘ www. friendsofpriorsleelake.blogspot.co.uk). But thanks to **Lakeside Plant & Garden Centre** with small resident animal park (TF2 9UR; just off Salisbury Avenue ⊘ www.lakesideplantcentre.co.uk ⊘ daily); **Quackers Play Barn** (⊘ daily) just behind it; and one branch of **Green Fields Farm Shop** (⊘ www.greenfieldsonline.co.uk – they make home deliveries), my son and I managed to spend an entire Friday there *and* source everything we needed for dinner that evening.

If you head north out of Priorslee, look for the **Limekiln Bank Roundabout** at the eastern end of the St George's bypass. The sculpture in the middle, two triangles linked by a bar and saltire cross, depicts the mason's mark of Thomas Telford.

10 TELFORD STEAM RAILWAY

The Old Loco Shed, Bridge Rd, Horsehay TF4 2NF ✆ 01952 503880 (phones operated Tue eve & Sun) ⌂ www.telfordsteamrailway.co.uk ⊙ Sun & bank holiday Mon

The village of Horsehay (whose Anglo-Saxon name means 'an enclosure of horses') around two miles southwest of Telford may still be just a farm today had Abraham Darby II not built a blast furnace next to the expanse of water now known as Horsehay Pool. The Old Loco Shed is on the outskirts of the village, delightfully visible and audible on days when Telford Steam Railway is having a steam-up. My toddler and I were greeted by a puffing Morris's of Shrewsbury sentinel steam wagon which he insisted was Elizabeth, the Fat Controller's long-lost lorry.

Please don't think Telford Steam Railway is on the same scale as the **Severn Valley Railway** (page 80): it isn't and if you approach with similar expectations, you may be disappointed. As commercial director Mark Paynter told me with more than a ring of self-deprecation: 'You could walk the current length of the line faster than you could travel by train'. It takes 20 minutes for a restored diesel or steam locomotive to travel the ¾ mile of track between Spring Village station at Horsehay and Horsehay & Dawley station, including a quick stop at Lawley Village station (newly opened in 2015).

Instead, think of Telford Steam Railway as an ongoing project in the care of enthusiastic volunteers. Since forming Telford Horsehay Steam Trust in the 1970s, they have succeeded in restoring not only

"My toddler insisted the sentinel steam wagon was Elizabeth, the Fat Controller's long-lost lorry."

the short stretch of line but also handsome rolling stock to chug along it, including a 1926 Rocket steam locomotive. THST is currently extending the track south to Doseley and has plans to reconnect the line with Ironbridge. As the Trust continues with its fundraising, the Bridge Road site in Horsehay remains a little rough around the edges. My son, one of the latest generation of Thomas the Tank Engine fans forced to attribute human qualities to both rail and road vehicles, was relieved to hear the rusty carriages and broken-down engines are soon to be repaired.

As well as being a registered charity, Telford Steam Railway represents a fun Sunday outing and good value for money. (A family ticket currently costs £12, which includes unlimited train travel and rides on the cheery **steam tram** around Horsehay Pool.) At Horsehay & Dawley station you'll find **Furnaces Tearoom** (☉ summer, Sun & bank holiday Mon 11.00–16.30) and the **Railway House** exhibition shed containing two extensive layouts of 00 model railway with scenery that includes a fairground, colliery and village green with morris dancers.

Visit on the last Sunday of the month or a bank holiday Monday for a sweet little bonus: the **Phoenix Miniature Railway** (small extra charge) runs alongside the platform at Spring Village, complete with tunnel, bridge and cuttings.

11 WELLINGTON

Technically Wellington falls under Telford New Town, but I think it has a character all its own – and I know many who would agree with me. There are several theories as to how Wellington got its name, but the

DID PHILIP LARKIN REALLY HATE WELLINGTON?

Marc Petty

The Library is a very small one, I am entirely unassisted in my labours, and spend most of my time handing out tripey novels to morons. I feel it is not at all a suitable occupation for a man of acute sensibility and genius.

When Philip Larkin arrived in Wellington in late 1943 at the age of 21 to take up a post as the town's nascent librarian, it's clear he was not particularly enamoured of a place he infamously likened to a 'hole of toads' turds'. The inevitable local uproar that followed the publication of his criticism of Shropshire's second town (which came to light in a volume of private letters published posthumously in the 1990s) has never truly diminished and, to paraphrase the man himself, continues to deepen like a coastal shelf. The real picture, however, is less straightforward and closer scrutiny reveals a more nuanced view of a setting that many scholars of Larkin's work now see as crucial to establishing an individual style separate from the writers he sought to emulate, while moulding his views towards life, love and relationships – the subject of much of his greatest work.

So what is Wellington's claim on the Larkin legacy? Well, it was in the town's answer is not thought to come from any duke. More likely it derives from *wealla*, a Saxon word meaning spring, making Wellington the 'town of springs'. It's an unassuming, friendly place, blessed with a heated **indoor market** with 60 further stalls outside (☉ Tue, Thu, Fri & Sat: check out Lesley's Larder for local cheese, Wroxeter wine and Coopers Gourmet Sausage Rolls) and cheerful drinking pubs – although the high street has seen a sad decline in recent years. The **centre** is pedestrianised and recent investment has brought the community a new library and leisure centre, just footsteps away from the main shopping area.

In 1244 Wellington was one of the first towns in Shropshire to be awarded a market charter, an achievement celebrated on **Wellington Town Charter Day**, the first Saturday in March. A volunteer rides on horseback into town dressed as Henry III's messenger to read the charter to amused onlookers. Street theatre and morris dancing ensue – and in a tradition dating from 1345 one lucky soul is given the title of Ceremonial Ale Taster. Another great time to visit Wellington is in October during the council-run **Wellington Literary Festival**, which combines free walks, talks and readings and attracts well-known writers to the town.

library, between shifts in the reading room, that he wrote his only two novels, while his first poetry collection *The North Ship* was also published when he was resident. His friendship with local schoolgirl Ruth Bowman (later his fiancée) blossomed into his first serious relationship – and set many local tongues wagging. Larkin's achievements in the job he later claimed 'determined the course of my life' shouldn't be overlooked either: in just under three years, he helped drag the archaic institution into the 20th century, doubling library loans and readership numbers in the process.

Larkin left Wellington in 1946 for another library job at University College Leicester. Following his departure, his opinion of the town softened and in 1962 he returned to open an extension to the (now redundant) Walker Street facility. In later years, he would go on to praise the town's 'treasured community spirit' but in true curmudgeonly style was scathing of its administrative subordination to Telford, which he imagined 'a rather horrific place' and 'very unlike the Wellington I knew'. Thankfully, many of Larkin's old haunts (including his former lodgings and favourite hostelries) remain. Anyone interested in exploring the finer points of the poet's tenure in this ancient Shropshire town can visit ⊘ www.wellingtonla21.org.uk/discover.

The architect of Wellington's 18th-century **All Saints Church**, which presides over a green above the station, was George Stueart, who also designed Attingham Park and Shrewsbury's St Chad's. The smoky-dirty exterior is a remnant of Wellington's industrial history and the Wellington and Drayton section of the Great Western Railway, which once linked the Midlands to the north and northwest of England. One of several notable former curates is **Patrick Brontë**, whose modest forays into poetry during his year in Wellington could not have predicted the literary dynasty he would eventually father, in the form of Charlotte, Emily and Anne.

Wellington is a breeze for Slow travel, with train links from Shrewsbury and mid Wales in the west and Wolverhampton and Birmingham in the east. You can travel directly from London Euston too, although when the service was launched in late 2014 Wellington was missed from the printed pocket timetable, prompting disbelief from Wellingtonians and a formal apology – plus a batch of 'We love Wellington' cupcakes – from Virgin Trains. The bus station has good links to Telford. Just off the M54, Wellington is easily accessible by car and offers plenty of free parking (including at the train station). If you arrive by car or bus, look for Watling Street: it's the old Roman road that ran from London to Uriconium (Wroxeter – page 179). 👆 Read about the campaign to save **The Clifton** – a redundant Art Deco-style cinema building – at ⌂ www.bradtguides.com/savetheclifton.

🍴 FOOD & DRINK

The Old Orleton Inn Holyhead Rd, TF1 2HA ✆ 01952 255011. What a welcome sight the Old Orleton Inn must have been to 17th-century travellers in transit between London and Holyhead. The former coaching inn on the southwestern corner of Wellington has retained its inviting Georgian exterior, while the inside has been restyled to super-modern specifications. Too modern, according to some locals. But you'll never please everyone, and those in favour are delighted by the extensive menu of contemporary British food, often with cheerfully local twists (Wenlock Edge salt-cured bacon chops or Shropshire fidget faggots for meat eaters; perhaps a Wrekin Cheddar homity tart for veggies). The pub is a member of Slow Food UK's Supporters' Scheme and has ten boutique-style bedrooms.

The Pheasant Pub & Brewhouse 54 Market St ✆ 01952 260683. After nearly 50 years' absence, Wrekin Brewing Company returned to its original home on Market St in 2014 where it makes popular concoctions (including Ironbridge Gold and Wrekin Pale Ale) just behind the newly renovated Pheasant.

Sunnycroft

200 Holyhead Rd, TF1 2DR ✆ 01952 242884 ⊙ w/ends throughout year & other times on website with tours daily in main season & free flow at other times; cash only ♿ adapted toilet close to house, separate mobility parking, & the grounds are partly accessible; National Trust

A mile's walk outside the town centre (you could follow the first part of the walk outlined on page 146) is Sunnycroft. Bequeathed to the nation in 1997 complete with original interior décor, fixtures and fittings, this is as near perfect an example of a pre-World War I suburban villa and miniature estate you can hope to find. Knowledgeable and friendly guides are stationed in every room to bring Sunnycroft's stories and artefacts to life. Often referred to as a gentlemen's residence, two of its notable owners were female: Mary Slaney, a businesswoman in the wine and spirits trade, was credited with Sunnycroft's sizeable expansion, while Joan Lander was a Red Cross nurse, radiographer and, later, a much-admired needlewoman. Some of her celebrated embroidery is on display. I love the Wellingtonia redwood and lime tree avenue driveway. The former smoking room is now a **tea room** serving Shropshire-made cakes and sandwiches; you can also make your way outside to a small **secondhand book shop** and a children's trail. In the warm weather you can play badminton or croquet on the lawn – and you may be able to buy produce grown in the kitchen garden when in season. Christmas is an extra special time at Sunnycroft, with the rooms dressed for an Edwardian celebration.

"Bequeathed to the nation complete with original décor, Sunnycroft is as near perfect an example of a pre-World War I villa you can hope to find."

12 APLEY WOODS

Peregrine Way, TF1 6TH ⚲ www.apleywoods.co.uk; limited parking in roadside on Peregrine Way ♿ accessible path for wheelchairs & buggies

Apley Woods are a 25-minute walk northeast of Wellington if you cut through on Whitchurch Road. The remains of a moated castle built here in around 1270 have been converted into modern dwellings, while its Georgian successor is a ghost beneath silver birch trees and remnants of landscaped gardens. The loss to the Charlton family, who owned the site from the early 14th to late 18th century, is an entire community's gain: the 56 acres of woodland, meadows and pools are now managed by the Friends of Apley Woods who won a Queen's Award for Voluntary

Wellington to the Ercall & the foot of The Wrekin

Kindly devised for this book by Wellington Walkers are Welcome

❀ OS Explorer map 242; start at Wellington station ticket office ♥ SJ651116; 5–6 miles depending on route chosen; generally moderate with steep ascents in places; allow 2–3 hours. For details of walk extensions, see the double-sided leaflet *Maps of Wellington Historic Town & The Wrekin Forest Walks* published by Wellington Town Council at ⬧ www. wellingtonwalkersarewelcome.org.uk.

O n this walk you'll pass through ancient oak woodland and see evidence of 500 million years of history in the Ercall (pronounced 'Arkle') quarries. You'll visit the foot of Shropshire's beloved 'little mountain' The Wrekin, with optional access around or over it. You can also make a circular route extension to Limekiln Wood with its industrial heritage.

1 Take the road up towards the town, turn left and go through Market Square, keeping to the left of the black-and-white building (currently a branch of Subway). Walk along Crown Street, then carry straight on up Tan Bank. Cross Victoria Road and continue through the pedestrian access way into the next section of Tan Bank. After just over 30 yards take the brick footpath on the right. Cross the next road (Roseway) and take the rising footpath immediately opposite. Carry on past the allotments on your right and **Sunnycroft** (page 145) on your left.

2 Cross **Holyhead Road** by the pelican crossing and head straight on to **Golf Links Lane**. Continue up the lane and pass under the motorway bridge.

3 Immediately after the bridge, turn right to follow the signposted footpath through **Ercall Wood**. (Directly opposite this entrance you'll find steps leading to a possible three-mile walk extension using a circular path through Limekiln Wood.)

Once in Ercall Wood, cross the footbridge and bear left into the main part of the wood. After a short distance the route forks right (following the mustard-coloured Wrekin Forest Trails waymark) and rises steeply. (For a gentler alternative bear left at the fork and keep to the wider main path which rises more slowly along the side of the hill. You will re-join the main walk at point 4.)

Follow the main path where it opens out uphill, bearing left to join the ridge. Turn left along the ridge and take in the fine view over **Wrekin Golf Club** as you approach the top. (If you wish you could continue along the ridge for more views over quarries and The Wrekin, then return to the junction of the path just up from point 4.)

4 The two routes recombine at the foot of the short sharp descent on the left. Continue straight on to follow the main route (or, from the gentler alternative, turn left). After a few yards the path will begin to swing right and descend. Follow the path downhill as it bends to the right and approaches our first quarry.

5 About mid-way down the hill you will come to a junction with a waymark on the left.

The main route carries on down the hill but the short 'mountain goat' path on the right leads to a ledge inside the quarry and, above that, the base of the **Ercall Geological Unconformity**, where Ercall granophyre meets Wrekin quartzite and clearly marks a shift from volcanic to sedimentary rock. Be sure to turn around here for a special view of The Wrekin not many people get to see.)

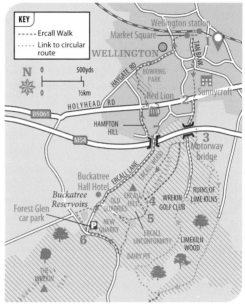

KEY
- - - - - Ercall Walk
· · · · · Link to circular route

N
0   500yds
0   ½km

WELLINGTON

Wellington station
Market Square
Bowring Park
Red Lion
Sunnycroft
Holyhead Rd
B5061
Hampton Hill
M54
Motorway bridge
Buckatree Hall Hotel
Buckatree Reservoirs
Forest Glen car park
Old Quarries
Ercall Hill
New Quarry
Wrekin Golf Club
Ruins of Lime Kilns
Ercall Unconformity
Limekiln Wood
Dairy Pit
The Wrekin
Haygate Rd
Tan Bank
Ercall Lane
Ercall Wood

Upon reaching the base of the first main quarry you'll find an interpretation board and a large stone inscribed with a **poem**. Looking up on a sunny day you'll see the colourful rocks shining out near the top of the quarry face.

Continue downhill until you reach a pool on the left. Take the hairpin left at the end of the pool and follow the path uphill to the **Dairy Pit**, after which the path steeply descends to the **Little Wenlock Road**. Turn right at the road and follow it to the **Forest Glen car park**. Cross the road and continue on a few yards to the entrance to The Wrekin.

6 This is the main access point to **The Wrekin**, from which routes over and around the hill can be made. A straight up and down will add 3 miles and 800 feet to your walk, while a circuit midway up the hill will add 4 miles. Refreshments may be available at The Halfway House, which was being renovated at the time of writing.

Continue along the road until you reach a footpath on your right (at a road junction, with a sign marked Uppington on your left). Turn right along the footpath, follow the path around the reservoir with its views of the Ercall, and then turn right to reach **Ercall Lane**. ▶

Wellington to Ercall & the foot of The Wrekin (continued)

◄   Follow the road until you pass the **Buckatree Hall Hotel** on your left. Cross into the fringe of the woodland where you see a wooden footpath sign, turning left to head towards Wellington. Follow the paths that run alongside the road as closely as you can until you reach the **motorway bridge**.

7 Immediately after crossing the motorway bridge, turn left along the footpath which emerges at a small roundabout at the top of Hampton Hill (offering great views over north Shropshire). Take the road which descends steeply down **Hampton Hill** to reach Holyhead Road. Turn right, cross the road and turn left into **Bowring Park** (opposite the Red Lion pub). Follow the path to the main entrance (where there is a pavilion café) on Haygate Road. Turn right, heading towards the town centre and cross the road by the **John Bayley Club**. At the junction, turn left along **Bridge Road** and walk until you reach the traffic lights. Turn right here, walking down Market Street (past the Pheasant Inn) and back to **Market Square**.

Service for their work in preserving the woods for present and future generations. The variety of habitats – glades and grassland, reedbeds and scrub – gives rise to a diversity of wildlife and bird species, including field and bank voles, five types of bat, rabbits, woodpeckers, moles and the occasional fox.

The information panel at the Peregrine Way entrance outlines several walking routes. Fun things to look out for include stone armchairs and tree carvings.

To reach Apley Woods by **bus** take the Arriva Midlands North 44 to Leegomery from Wellington and alight at the Princess Royal Hospital; the woods are just behind it.

13 THE WREKIN

At 1,335 feet high, The Wrekin is not Shropshire's tallest hill (that plaudit goes to Brown Clee) but it is arguably Shropshire's most famous landmark, rising surprisingly from a flat plain, and being the very embodiment of home to the people who live here. I have been warned by people living nearby that The Wrekin's definite article must always take a capital T, reflecting the hill's importance to the area. Etched into the hearts of Salopians, this 600 million-year-old 'little mountain' has given rise to a local toast: 'To friends all around The Wrekin'.

Further into the Midlands, people talk about going 'all around The Wrekin' to describe wasting time in doing something in an overly complicated way (when other Brits might say they've been 'all around the houses'). This tells you about The Wrekin's domination of the landscape of mid Shropshire, where it can look crouching or mountainous depending on where you're standing. Some people cite it as JRR Tolkien's inspiration for Middle Earth.

Naturally for this land of folklore, The Wrekin was built by a Welsh giant: one with a grudge against Shrewsbury. He planned to dump a spadeful of soil in the River Severn, flooding the town and drowning its inhabitants. A quick-witted cobbler told the giant he was a long way from Shrewsbury. He dropped a sack of old shoes at the giant's feet, saying he'd worn them all out himself on the journey from the town. Giving up his idea, the giant left his spadeful of soil by the road: this became The Wrekin. The smaller hill beside it, the **Ercall** (see walk on pages 146–8), was formed by the brushed-off soil from the giant's boots. (This legend is conveyed with charm in the children's book *The Wellington Cobbler and The Wrekin Giant* by local author Dave Weston and illustrator Toni Siân Williams.)

The Wrekin's real heritage is almost as intriguing: it was an Iron Age hillfort, possibly the capital of the Cornovii tribe, and probably invaded by Romans in the mid 1st century AD (Roman javelin heads have been discovered at the Ercall and northeast gate sides).

Today, walking up the steep paths through oak woods to reach The Wrekin's heathland summit is a popular activity all year round, but especially on Boxing Day and New Year's Day. Perhaps that reflects our human need to mark holidays by doing something special – or maybe we're all clearing hangovers and burning off Christmas pud. Either way, standing on The Wrekin's gentle whale-backed top, looking out over 15 counties on a clear day (some say 17), leaves you feeling you're at the edge of the world.

"Standing on The Wrekin's gentle whale-backed top, looking out over 15 counties on a clear day (some say 17), leaves you feeling you're at the edge of the world."

To get there by **car**, take the Wellington turn-off along the A5 and follow the direction of Little Wenlock. You can park in the Forest Glen car park (TF6 5AL) above which, when I last visited, peregrines were nesting.

THE WEALD MOORS TO NEWPORT

The Weald Moors – which look wild and marshy as their name suggests – stretch from north and west of Newport towards Wellington, providing an unspoilt and interesting area for peaceful walking and cycling. A leaflet created by Wellington LA21 contains trails to follow: visit ⌂ www. wellingtonla21.org.uk and select 'Along the Moors'.

Preston upon the Weald Moors, on the outskirts of which you'll find Hoo Farm Animal Kingdom, is thought to be the longest name of any village in England.

The privately owned Chetwynd Park estate outside Newport may have a literary claim to fame. Some people think Charles Dickens, who travelled in this area, based *Great Expectations*' mournful Miss Havisham on Elizabeth Parker of the great house, who became reclusive after being jilted on her wedding day.

🖐 North of the Weald Moors is the village of **Great Bolas**, remarkable for the story of the Cottage Countess; go to ⌂ www.bradtguides.com/cottagecountess to find out more.

14 HOO FARM ANIMAL KINGDOM

Preston upon the Weald Moors TF6 6DJ ✆ 01952 677917 ⌂ www.hoofarm.com ⊙ late Mar–Christmas 10.00–17.30 (17.00 from Sep), closed Mon in Sep, Oct & Nov

The Dorrells, a family of dairy farmers, moved to the site of Hoo Farm in 1988. At first they used the land as the council had done before them, for growing and selling Christmas trees, but soon realised the visiting public was more interested in seeing their resident cows, goats, horses, pigs and sheep. In 1991 the family reopened their business as Hoo Farm Animal Kingdom, adding more exotic animals in the early 2000s as a protective response to the foot and mouth epidemic that had devastated farms across Britain. Now they have around 120 species, including pythons, cockatoos (some of them talk), wallabies, otters, meerkats, lemurs and ostriches. Spread over 32 acres of paddocks and woodlands, Hoo Farm specialises in up-close animal encounters and is famous for its sheep steeplechase. If you're staying in the area the farm's 'return for free within 14 days' offer makes Hoo Farm's admission fee decent value: there is plenty to amuse younger guests (particularly those of pre-school age), including a playbarn and ride-on tractors. Weekdays during term time are often blissfully peaceful.

The on-site catering doesn't deviate far from jacket potatoes and chilled sandwiches, but you're welcome to take your own food and there are plenty of benches for picnicking.

15 NEWPORT

Newport, sin no more, lest a worse punishment befall thee!
A comment in the Newport parish register beneath a description of the damage caused by the Great Fire of Newport in 1665.

Newport, ten miles northeast of Telford, reminds me of a smaller Northallerton in North Yorkshire, with a thriving town centre, good number of independent shops and wide high street to accommodate the market, flanked with handsome Georgian and Victorian buildings. Newport's market is now held on Fridays and Saturdays in the Victorian indoor market hall, its entrance on Stafford Street. The red sandstone **church of St Nicholas** is imposing in its location on an island in the middle of High Street: parts of the building date to the 14th century.

Mr Moyden's Handmade Cheese, based in Market Drayton, makes an artisan cheese called Newport 1665, named after the Great Fire of Newport which tore through the town in the 17th century. It has the same sweet mellow taste of the original Newport cheese but is smoked (⊘ www.mrmoyden.com).

🖐 Be on your guard when you visit Newport for here, they say, is the haunt of one of Shropshire's most feared ghosts. Go to ⊘ www. bradtguides.com/madampigott to read more.

16 Shropshire Lavender

Wellbank Farm, Pickstock TF10 8AH ⊘ 01952 550303 ⊘ www.shropshirelavender.co.uk
☉ late Jun–mid-Aug 12.00–17.00 Fri–Sun; free

Although Shropshire Lavender sells dried lavender and other lavender products on its website all year round (teas, soaps, essential oils), the best time to visit this dreamy smallholding – about four miles north of Newport – is in July when you can inhale the purple flowers during their short, brilliant season, and fresh lavender bunches are available to take away. Joanna and Robin Spencer cultivate several varieties of intermedia and angustifolia lavender without chemicals or pesticides so bees, butterflies and moths can thrive in the gently sloping fields. Essential oils are distilled on site in a copper still which the Spencers call Big Bertha.

A must-do for visitors is **afternoon tea** on the scented garden terrace: Joanna's lemon and lavender cake is heavenly.

Joanna and Robin are medieval fans and their farm hosts the **Chetwynd Medieval Fair** in early July each year (⌖ www.chetwyndmedievalfair. co.uk), lively with musicians, puppet shows, falconry displays, archery, artisan crafts, battle re-enactments and beer.

FOOD & DRINK

The Fox Pave Lane, Chetwynd Aston TF10 9LQ ✆ 01952 815940. This roomy pub-restaurant about two miles southeast of Newport is styled in an Edwardian fashion with fireplaces, talking-point pictures and just the right number of knick-knacks. Many dishes cost a few pounds more than you might expect for this region, although they're delicious: think beer-battered haddock, red onion marmalade sausages, tandoori-roasted cod. The ale selection is great too, featuring several Shropshire breweries. On warm days you can dine on the expansive south-facing terrace.

Smallwood Lodge Upper Bar, Newport TF10 7AP ✆ 01952 813606. Some people think Anne Boleyn may have stayed overnight at Smallwood Lodge, although the tea room owner told me every time she looks into the history of the half-timbered house in Newport centre, conflicting evidence emerges. Inside, low ceilings and wood panelling lend an elegant yet cosy atmosphere to your breakfast, light lunch or afternoon tea, or you can sit in the secluded front garden. The homemade scones are perfect.

17 LILLESHALL

You can spot Lilleshall from miles away thanks to **Lilleshall Monument**, a 70-foot high obelisk completed by tenants of the village in 1833 in memory of their landlord George Leveson-Gower, the First Duke of Sutherland. The other claim to fame here is the **Lilleshall National Sports & Conferencing Centre**, a centre of excellence for elite sportspeople. The current England men's football team may do well to decamp to Lilleshall for a spell: it's where the 1966 squad trained before their World Cup win.

Lilleshall Abbey

Unclassified road off A518, four miles north of Oakengates ♀ SJ737140 ☉ daylight hours; free entry; dogs on leads welcome; English Heritage

I stumbled across Lilleshall Abbey, or rather its atmospheric ruins, one Tuesday afternoon in late winter while driving aimlessly and joyfully alone. Overshooting the entrance, I turned around and navigated the wobbly dirt track to the unheralded remains of this once-great Augustinian abbey, where I parked my car. I wandered among the crumbled cloisters in a ghostly silence occasionally broken by distant gunshot rendered to a muffled pop by the fields that separated me from a lone hunter. Founded in around 1148, the abbey would once have been held in high prestige: you can still feel this, oddly, in its large scope and ornately sculpted door. During the English Civil War in 1645, now converted to a house and garrison, it fell under siege to Parliamentarians. This was fascinating to me but I didn't stay long because I couldn't dismiss the conflicting feelings of being isolated from the road yet not entirely alone. Monastic spectres hadn't spooked me (although I've since read some chilling tales about a small shuffling man in a black robe); rather the idea that any common or garden psychopath could be crouched behind the archways awaiting their next victim, and no-one knew where I was. I jumped back in my car and drove off in a cloud of topsoil, resolving to return with companions. Lots of companions.

UPDATES WEBSITE

You can post your comments and recommendations, and read the latest feedback and updates from other readers online at ◊ www.bradtupdates.com/shropshire.

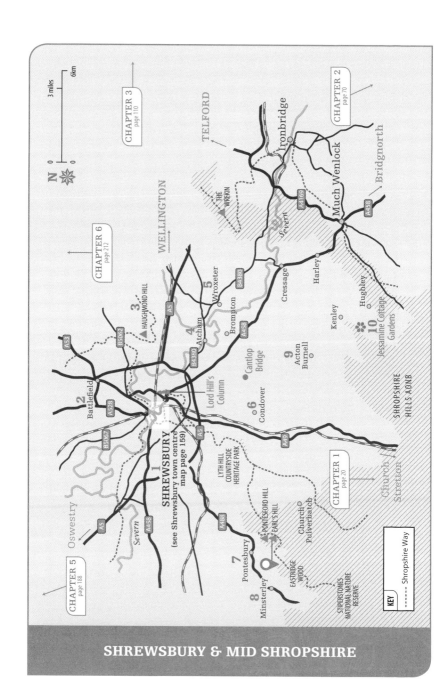

SHREWSBURY & MID SHROPSHIRE

4

SHREWSBURY &
MID SHROPSHIRE

As Shropshire is a land of contrasts, its centre – dominated by the genteel town of Shrewsbury – has a touch of everything great about the county: medieval architecture, ancient woodland, castle ruins and, to the south, Mary Webb country and some highly respectable hills.

Shrewsbury, declared by that famous scholar of art and architecture Nikolaus Pevsner to be a 'fine example of a Tudor town' is at the physical heart of the county and, for many, is where Shropshire's emotional heart beats too. Salop, the old word for Shropshire, is sometimes used to mean Shrewsbury; it's also the nickname of Shrewsbury Town Football Club, who play at New Meadow on the southern outskirts of the town. An old story goes that the oft-used term 'Proud Salopians' recalls the town burgesses' refusal of Charles I's (some say Henry VIII's) offer to endow Shrewsbury with the status of a cathedral city, pleased with their town the way it was. And indeed there is much to be proud of now. As well as the castle, Quarry Park and excellent museum, Shrewsbury has a lively arts scene, many independent shops, and some outstanding places to dine and drink.

In 1809 Shrewsbury was the birthplace of **Charles Darwin**, the naturalist whose 1859 *On the Origin of Species* furthered our understanding of the creation of the world and every living being in it. Several walks and landmarks, outlined in this chapter, will guide you around his boyhood haunts.

Just outside the town is the site of the **1403 Battle of Shrewsbury**, now a farm shop, visitor centre and award-winning café. Elsewhere in mid Shropshire we have the estate and Palladian-style manor house of **Attingham Park**, the Kiwi-style **Jessamine Cottage Gardens**, the remains of the fourth largest **Roman city** in Britain at Wroxeter – with a nearby **vineyard** – and the ruins of a fortified mansion, near to where Edward I assembled England's first ever parliament.

GETTING THERE & AROUND

Shrewsbury benefits from a direct **rail** link to London Euston. It's on four other main networks too, giving us easy access to mid Wales, Cardiff, Chester, Birmingham and Manchester. Locally it connects with all other Shropshire stations, making it an excellent base for a car-free adventure. National Express tends to run three coaches a day from London to Shrewsbury.

Once you're here, the mid Shropshire region is reasonably well served by **buses**, notably the 70 to Oswestry, 511 to Whitchurch, 64 to Market Drayton, 436 to Bridgnorth and 81 to Telford. GHA Coaches' service number 96 between Shrewsbury and Telford is particularly useful because it stops at Atcham, Wroxeter, Buildwas and Ironbridge too.

On Saturdays, Sundays and bank holiday Mondays from May to October, an open-top 'hop on hop off' bus makes several stops in the region: see page 72 for more information.

WALKING

Away from Shrewsbury (which is in itself a rewarding town to stroll around, thanks to the Severn loop and refined Quarry Park) walkers will find much to enjoy in mid Shropshire – even though it doesn't possess the big-name hills of the south. This is Mary Webb country (see pages 98–9): you can follow in her footsteps over **Lyth Hill** and at **Pontesbury**. Shropshire Tourism has shared **three Mary Webb trails** at ⟨ www. shropshiretourism.co.uk/mary-webb.

For child-friendly woodland walks, head to **Haughmond Hill** which is managed by the Forestry Commission.

❋ OS Explorer map 241 covers this area, stretching up to Wem in north Shropshire.

CYCLING

Although Shrewsbury, with its narrow lanes and steep Wyle Cop, isn't the most cycle-friendly town, it is pretty much at the centre of Sustrans' National Cycle Network. The Shropshire section of route 44 (which will eventually connect Shrewsbury with Cinderford in Gloucestershire) is called the **Six Castles Cycleway**, thanks to the strongholds and ruins it takes in along the way. Route 81 runs from Aberystwyth to Wolverhampton; the leisurely stretch from Shrewsbury will take you *i* **TOURIST INFORMATION**

Shrewsbury The Music Hall, The Square, SY1 1LH ℰ 01743 258888 ☉ Easter–Oct 10.00–17.00 daily, Nov–Thu before Easter: 10.00–16.30 Tue–Sun. See ⌂ www. shrewsburymuseum.org.uk for Christmas & New Year opening hours.

13 miles to Wellington alongside the river and old canals, and then to Albrighton in southeast Shropshire. Mountain bikers will find challenging trails in the hilltop woodland of **Eastridge** near Habberley (⌂ www.forestry.gov.uk) – and **Haughmond Hill** might provide some off-road downhill fun too.

Phil Roe of Urban Bikes UK in Shrewsbury recommended a route. 'From Shrewsbury you can cycle to **Attingham Park** without encountering too much traffic and, if you turn up on a cycle, they'll let you into the grounds for free.' You're welcome to swing by his stall at the Market Hall for route maps and more ideas. Another of Shrewsbury's bike retailers, Stan's Cycles on Wyle Cop, organises bike rides on Thursdays (18.15; just for women) and Saturdays (09.15; catering for differing levels of ability).

BIKE HIRE

Urban Bikes UK Stall 13/14 Market Hall, Shrewsbury SY1 1QP ℰ 07828 638132 ☉ 09.00–15.30 Tue, Wed, Fri, Sat; 09.00–13.00 Thu. This friendly stall rents out bikes and helmets and will also supply you with route maps. 'We talk to you too!' says owner Phil Roe.

BIKE SALES & REPAIRS

Stan's Cycles 53–54 Wyle Cop, Shrewsbury SY1 1XJ ℰ 01743 343775 ⌂ www.stanscycles. co.uk. A long-established bike and accessories shop and service centre. The in-house coffee shop serves locally sourced coffee and 'cycling fuel' (OK, cakes).
Urban Bikes UK Stall 13/14 Market Hall, Shrewsbury SY1 1QP ℰ 07828 638132. For new and secondhand cycles and specialist parts, as well as repairs and servicing. Bike maintenance classes are sometimes available.

HORSERIDING

The Humphrey Kynaston Way, named after an infamous highwayman (page 210), passes through this region at Church Pulverbatch and near Pontesbury: see ⌂ www.shropshireriding.co.uk. You'll also find a great route at Battlefield on the Albrighton estate, allowing you to take in the church and farmland. See page 18 for more on the permissive route information shared by Natural England.

Set in a bow of the River Severn, The Isle Estate at Bicton (page 249) has a luxurious **B&B with horse accommodation** and a thousand-acre cross-country course with plenty of natural fences. Hard-standing parking and a route card are available.

HORSE HIRE & RIDING LESSONS

Wenlock Edge Riding Centre Hughley SY5 6NT ℘ 01746 785645. In the south of this region, brushing up against Wenlock Edge, you can take riding lessons, own a pony for a day or take your own horse on a guided hack or a ride out with a pub lunch for you. Wenlock Edge Riding Centre B&B allows you to holiday with your horse.

WET-WEATHER ACTIVITIES

Shrewsbury Museum & Art Gallery (page 163)
Shopping in Shrewsbury's independent shops
House at Attingham Park (which includes a children's room; pages 177–8)

1 SHREWSBURY

 Drapers Hall (page 249), **Ferndell Bed & Breakfast** (page 249), **The Golden Cross** (page 249), **The Isle Estate**, Bicton (page 249), **Lion & Pheasant Hotel** (page 249), **The Old Police Cells** (page 249), **Porterhouse SY1** (page 249)

> High the vanes of Shrewsbury gleam
> Islanded in Severn stream;
> The bridges from the steepled crest
> Cross the water east and west.
>
> A E Housman, from 'The Welsh Marches', *A Shropshire Lad* (1896)

With a few deft pen strokes, Housman painted Shrewsbury in a poem. Shropshire's handsome county town is indeed almost islanded by the River Severn – a sweeping loop of water whose one-time virtue as a defence is often overshadowed now by its potential to invite floods. The 'steepled crest' comprises the spires of the churches of St Mary, St Alkmund and St Chad, while road, foot and rail bridges give us easier access to the water-encircled town.

To go beyond Housman's poetic sketch, there is much more to love about Shrewsbury: black-and-white Tudor mansions; a noble riverside park; medieval 'shuts' (or shortcuts) and passageways which enable us to disappear temporarily into a bygone time and reappear on a different street. As with all old towns and cities, a closer inspection of Shrewsbury will reward the curious-minded. You'll find street names describing what was once sold there (Butcher Row, Milk Street … and don't think too hard about the dark and narrow Grope Lane). In the half-timbered shopfronts on High Street you'll see carvings recalling the Tudor tradition of depicting faces of controversial characters in wood. Mick Jagger, Michael Heseltine and Margaret Thatcher are all here. And while a fast food restaurant may not seem a classic contender for a history tour, visit the basement of McDonald's on Pride Hill to view remains of **medieval walls**.

It's easy to reach Shrewsbury by **train**, with five main lines meeting here. Built in 1848 in imitation Tudor style, to serve the county's first railway (the Shrewsbury to Chester line), **Shrewsbury station** looks to me like a squat castle. A plaque on Platform 3 is testament to the power of Slow travel: it commemorates Arwel Hughes OBE who, in 1938, composed the Welsh hymn 'Tyddi a roddaist'(Thou Gavest') while waiting for a connecting service.

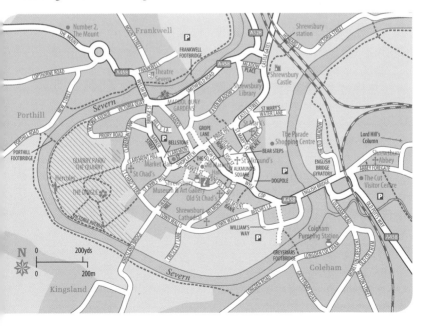

SHROOSBURY OR SHROWSBURY?

I feel certain that, in the Midlands at least, debates concerning the correct pronunciation of Shrewsbury have filled more hours of radio phone-in shows than the emotive jam-first/cream-first scone quandary. (Come to think of it, should scone rhyme with *one* or *own*?) Purveyors of the Shroosbury argument say we should pronounce it by sight. Shrowsbury aficionados point out that in Middle English, *shrew* was pronounced *shrow*. They also refer back to the 'o' in the Saxon name for the town, Scrobbesbyrig.

The question always stirs up strong feelings, perhaps due to a spurious association with Shrowsbury as the pronunciation adopted by 'posh' people, born within the boundaries of the River Severn; Shroosbury for commoners and outsiders. In 1937 E Moore Darling, Canon of Oswestry stated in *Seeing Shropshire* that Shrewsbury should not be pronounced Shrewsbury 'as in the *Taming of the Shrew*, but so that "Shrews" rhymes with throws. This is not a matter of choice. One is wrong and the other right'. But having read the whole book, I'm inclined to think the vehemence of Canon Darling's stance is not matched in strength with evidence.

In 2015 the *Shropshire Star* attempted to settle the argument with an online poll. Over 1,000 people responded and over 81% of people plumped for Shroosbury.

Personally I like people who drop the 'r' and a syllable and just say 'Shoosbree'. An older tradition is to call it Salop.

Parking spaces are neither plentiful nor cheap in Shrewsbury (although you may get a Sunday bargain). If you have to drive, the long-stay car park at Frankwell is a good bet (SY3 8HQ). You'll need to cross Frankwell footbridge to reach the town centre. An even better bet might be one of the three park and ride sites, at Harlescott (SY1 4AB), Meole Brace (SY3 9NB) or Oxon (SY3 5AD), operating Monday to Saturday with cheap fares and the last bus at 18.30. Cycle parking is available at the latter two.

A serene way to see Shrewsbury is from the river. **Drummond Outdoor** hires out boats from the canoe ramp at Frankwell: see ⬧ www.docanoe.com/index.htm for information. More relaxing still, **Sabrina Tours** (⬧ 01743 369741 ⬧ www.sabrinaboat.co.uk ☉ Mar–Oct daily, six cruises on the hour) gives you a 45-minute cruise of the Severn loop in a Sabrina passenger boat (Sabrina was the Roman goddess of the River Severn), which leaves from Victoria Quay near the Welsh Bridge. A live commentary will keep you entertained and the boat is licensed, with table service, so you won't go thirsty. A roof over the top deck makes this outing suitable for both wet and dry weather. Look out for special ghost cruises and other themed evenings, plus live music on Tuesdays. Buy your tickets from the visitor information centre at Shrewsbury Museum & Art Gallery for 10% off.

Also head to the museum for **daily walking tours** (☉ 14.00 Mon–Sat, 11.00 Sun; Sat only in winter) which offer an inspiring introduction to the town in the knowledgeable company of green and blue badge guides. As well as standard tours, look out for ghost walks and, in December, *A Christmas Carol* tour. The 1984 production (the one starring George C Scott) was filmed in Shrewsbury and, although that's over 30 years ago, it's still relevant today if you're interested in architecture, Dickens or the logistics of producing a feature-length film in narrow medieval streets.

THE SQUARE & AROUND

Fronted by a statue of **Clive of India** and dominated by Old Market Hall, The Square (also known as Shrewsbury Square, linking High Street and Market Street) is the centre of Shrewsbury. This has been a market area since the 13th century: today you'll find two open-air markets a month: the **Made in Shropshire market** on the second Saturday (⟁ www.madeinshropshire.co.uk – perfect for handmade gifts and artisan food) and a **Shrewsbury Farmers' Market** on the first Friday.

Samuel Taylor Coleridge once preached at the Unitarian church on nearby High Street.

OLD MARKET HALL

The Square ⟁ 01743 281281 ⟁ www.oldmarkethall.co.uk ♿ book in advance if you need a wheelchair space in the cinema, giving you & a companion tickets at half price

Dominating The Square is this stilted beauty in Grinshill stone built between 1595 and 1596 by the Corporation of Shrewsbury. Originally the upper room would have been used by drapers and the lower floor, exposed by archways, used by farmers selling corn. By the stone steps underneath, look for the small holes that puncture the wall. Their purpose is a mystery, although many believe they were used as a kind of abacus for medieval traders. This site has seen public hangings, a travelling crocodile exhibition and, in The Square in Victorian times, a live unwrapping of an Egyptian mummy with little pieces given away to spectators.

"This site has seen public hangings, a travelling crocodile exhibition and a Victorian unwrapping of an Egyptian mummy."

Earlier still, there was a pool or bog here where it's said irksome wives and deceitful traders were subjected to the ducking stool.

Nowadays Old Market Hall's entertainment is rather more civilised. Sensitive to the loss of many great Shrewsbury buildings in the 1950s and 60s, and wary of the building's status as a scheduled ancient monument, developers in the late 1990s worked with English Heritage and the people of Shrewsbury to decide on the best way to utilise the building. Redevelopment carried out in 1999 created a smart new **café** and **81-seat independent cinema** which uses the original beamed Tudor ceiling built by wool merchants. The cakes available here, I'm pleased to confirm, are excellent.

SHREWSBURY FLOWER SHOW

Held in Quarry Park in the middle of August, the Shrewsbury Flower Show is a descendant of the Shrewsbury Show – itself a more formalised version of the old fairs and pageants introduced by burgesses in the 1800s to bring trade to the town. The Shropshire Horticultural Society held the first Shrewsbury Flower Show in 1857, near Coton Hill. Alongside botanical displays and lectures from expert gardeners, the show has always featured family entertainment, with military bands providing much of the happy noise. In the early days before powered flight, high-wire acts and balloon ascents wowed the crowds; today you're likely to see falconry displays, show jumping and pretend jousting. Eating and drinking are a big part of the experience now too, with catering vans, pop-up restaurant stalls and brewery bars scattered around the site, and demonstrations from celebrity chefs in the food marquee.

Shropshire Horticultural Society gives a great deal back to Shrewsbury in community donations and education, but it's nevertheless understandable when some locals complain that the high ticket prices keep them away from their own park for a weekend. To achieve the best value for money, I'd recommend booking in advance to save a few pounds (⬀ www.shrewsburyflowershow. org.uk) and making a full day and evening of the show, staying for the headline music act and spectacular fireworks.

Other Shrewsbury calendar highlights

Shrewsbury Bookfest (children's book festival) May, various venues

Shrewsbury International Cartoon Festival April, various venues

Shrewbury River Festival June, The Quarry

Shrewsbury Food Festival June, The Quarry (with fringe events around town)

Shrewsbury Folk Festival August bank holiday weekend, West Midlands Showground

Shrewsbury Steam Rally August bank holiday weekend, Onslow Park

Shrewsbury Museum & Art Gallery

The Square ☏ 01743 258885 ⌂ www.shrewsburymuseum.org.uk ⊙ daily, but closed Mon Oct–Easter ♿ fully accessible

Shrewsbury Museum & Art Gallery opened in 2014 in a brave conversion of the town's 1840 Music Hall (whose bill over the years featured Charles Dickens and also the Beatles), joined artfully with other buildings that include Vaughan's Mansion, a medieval merchant's hall house. The new museum branding plays on the 'roll up, roll up' excitement of a Victorian music hall: variable circus-style typefaces and bold invitations to discover the wonders within. This approach helps to draw coherently together centuries of artefacts that might, aside from their connection to Shropshire, appear disjointed. Instead you advance logically through the building, starting with Hadrian and the Romans until you reach the Special Exhibition Gallery. Along the way you'll learn about Caughley porcelain, the woolly mammoth skeletons unearthed at Condover, and Charles Darwin. One of my favourite exhibits is an oil painting of **Old Parr**, a man from Wollaston who allegedly lived from 1483 to 1635, fathering an illegitimate child at 100 and marrying for the second time at 122.

The ground floor hosts Shrewsbury's **visitor information centre**: a friendly first port of call for ideas, leaflets, maps and books on exploring Shrewsbury and the rest of Shropshire. It's also home to the welcoming **Stop Café Bar**, serving fresh coffee, a big range of teas and locally made savouries and cakes.

CHARLES DARWIN'S SHREWSBURY

Although Shrewsbury is rightly proud of being Charles Darwin's birthplace, the town doesn't currently offer a surplus of Darwin-related visitor experiences. One cannot help but feel that the Darwin Shopping Centre is not a fitting tribute to the naturalist, even with a major new Primark store. The Georgian house into which Darwin was born, on The Mount in Frankwell, is currently Shrewsbury's Valuation Office and not open to the public.

Perhaps some may consider this understated celebration a good thing. One Sunday in Stratford-upon-Avon I overheard a bewildered man saying, 'They just seem a bit … Shakespeare *mad* around here.' But if you wish to seek out the man whose theory of evolution changed the way we understand the world, here are a few places to find him:

BENJAMIN DISRAELI & THE SURPRISING YELLOW PARROT

The flamboyant Conservative politician Benjamin Disraeli, a contemporary of Charles Darwin and twice Prime Minister, was MP for Shrewsbury from 1841 to 1847. He was friendly with the third Earl of Bradford and his wife. In later life, Disraeli gave Lady Selina Bradford a gift: a yellow parrot which everyone assumed was male. The poor bird's true gender became apparent when it laid 24 eggs in 23 days, then promptly keeled over and died. You can pay your respects to its stuffed remains at **Weston Park** (page 103): some people have remarked that it retains a surprised expression.

Statue outside Shrewsbury Library

1A Castle Gates

The Grade I-listed library building housed Shrewsbury School from 1580 to 1882 and Darwin is still its most famous alumnus (with apologies to Michael Palin and the late John Peel). His bronze likeness stands in the courtyard; or rather sits, looking up from a newspaper with a kindly expression as though considering the answer to a question. Some people think it significant that the statue has its back to the building, since Darwin wrote of school: 'Nothing could have been worse for the development of my mind … the school as a means of education to me was simply a blank'. In the Old School Room on the library's first floor, take a look at the etchings in the wood panelling, scratched out by his schoolboy contemporaries.

Darwin Festival

🖉 www.discoverdarwin.co.uk

Darwin's birthday was 12 February and at 12.00 on that date every year, people gather by the **bellstone** outside Morris Hall (on the road also named Bellstone) to toast his memory. This unassuming granite boulder is an erratic, pushed here from (probably) Cumbria by glacial ice during the Ice Age, and perhaps one of the touchpapers that ignited young Darwin's brilliant mind. The bellstone toast marks the beginning of the **Darwin Festival**, comprising two days of walks, lectures and children's events around the town. It tends to focus not on the serious, bearded adult Darwin but the mischievous boy who grew up in Shrewsbury; the one nicknamed 'Gas' for conducting laboratory experiments in his garden shed.

Geo Garden
Mardol Quay Gardens

On the bank of the River Severn (the town centre side) is a garden celebrating both Charles Darwin and the geological diversity of Shropshire. Towering above a 'rock timeline' (which uses stone samples from each geological time period) is the focal point: a 40-foot stone sculpture called **Quantum Leap**, erected in 2009 to commemorate the 200th anniversary of Darwin's birth. The design, with ribs or blades, came from patterns and forms found in nature: flowers, shells and DNA double helix. It's meant to represent the arches of Shrewsbury's bridges and other nearby sights. Many locals, still smarting from the £1million council bill, refer to it as Slinky, due to a perceived likeness to the coiled toy.

Darwin River Walk
Starts from behind Theatre Severn, Frankwell Quay

A circular Darwin River Walk of just under 1½ miles with five interpretative boards begins behind Theatre Severn, taking in The Mount (the road on to which Darwin was born), and his family's 'Thinking Path', which was acquired by Shropshire Wildlife Trust in 2012. (The path is steep and fenced off, so look out for open days.) A separate **town trail** (you can download the leaflet from ✑ www.discoverdarwin. co.uk) has commemorative waymarks set into the pavements. It starts on Mardol Head at Darwin Gate, a parallax modern sculpture inspired by St Mary's Church (which Darwin attended as a boy).

THE LOWER CURVE OF THE RIVER

The south of Shrewsbury town centre, gently cupped in the meander of the Severn, is dominated by a 29-acre ornamental park with iron entrance gates cast at Coalbrookdale. Known as **The Quarry** or **Quarry Park**, its history as a working mine is revealed only in name, the past hidden now by the lime tree-lined riverside promenade, children's playground, Victorian bandstand and rose garden opened to celebrate the Queen Mother's 100th birthday. Over the swan-gilded river, whose banks in the summer blossom with fragrant pink flowers of Himalayan balsam, you can see Shrewsbury School and the toll-charging Kingsland Bridge under which one daring Captain Collett flew his plane in 1918. Prebendary Auden compared this view over the river to the Backs of Cambridge.

The parkland's intimate centrepiece is **The Dingle**, once a stone quarry and now a sunken flower garden with lake and winding paths. In it you'll find a bronze bust of **Percy Thrower** who was for 28 years Parks Superintendent for Shrewsbury. Percy was also one of Britain's first celebrity gardeners, presenting *Gardener's World* for the BBC and establishing the *Blue Peter* garden.

As you wander down Victoria Avenue, don't forget to wink at the **statue of the Farnese Hercules**. He's from the early 18th century, probably by sculptor John Nost, and an inexact copy of the original marble Farnese Hercules in Naples. The Quarry isn't Shrewsbury Hercules's first home: he stood at Condover Hall originally and has also been stationed opposite St Chad's. Locals may tell you his fig leaf was installed to spare the blushes of Victorian churchgoers, but we now know otherwise. Extensive restoration in 2003–04 revealed that poor old H never had bits to boast of in the first place and so the fig leaf, an original feature, was reinstated.

St Chad's Church

St Chad's Terrace, SY1 1JX ✆ 01743 365478 🖱 www.stchadschurchshrewsbury.com
🕘 08.00–17.30 Mon–Sat, Sun all day (services at 08.00, 10.00 & 18.00); limited pay & display parking outside ♿ accessible, apart from organ loft & balcony

Overlooking The Quarry and affectionately referred to as the 'salt and mustard pot' (although less affectionately thought upon during its building in the 1790s: the radical design led to riots), St Chad's is the only grade I-listed circular Georgian church in England. The architect was George Stueart, who also designed the manor house at Attingham Park. He was assigned to the project when the original St Chad's collapsed in 1788. Having produced at least three designs Stueart forged ahead with the wrong one (the Parochial Church Council had approved

THE GRANDFATHER OF SKYSCRAPERS

A notable occupant of St Chad's churchyard is Charles Bage, the late 18th-century designer of the world's oldest iron-framed building just north of Shrewsbury town centre. Despite being only the height of a modern five-storey building, Ditherington Flax Mill and its construction principles have paved the way for skyscrapers. The site recently received Heritage Lottery Fund money and a grant from the European Regional Development Fund to be restored for community use: 🖱 www.flaxmill-maltings.co.uk.

a rectangular design) 'due to a misunderstanding'. Charles Darwin was baptised at St Chad's – although the christening bowl used to wet his clever head is no longer here.

As well as an elegant staircase showing fine Shropshire ironwork, an early product of the Industrial Revolution, the church has first-rate acoustics which you can experience during **Free Friday Concerts in the Round** (🖰 www.stchadschurchshrewsbury.com).

In the churchyard, see whether you can find the **grave of Ebenezer Scrooge**. Don't worry – your literary knowledge hasn't let you down: it's a remnant of the 1984 production of *A Christmas Carol*, which was filmed in Shrewsbury.

SHREWSBURY CATHEDRAL
11 Belmont ⊖ Easter–end Oct 13.00–16.00 Mon–Fri, 10.00–16.00 Sat; rest of year Sat only 10.30–14.30

Along Belmont at the Town Walls is Shrewsbury's Roman Catholic cathedral. Commissioned by John Talbot, the 16th Earl of Shrewsbury, its architect was Augustus Welby Pugin – a convert to Catholicism who had a pioneering role in the gothic revival style. Pugin, who regarded the classical style as 'pagan', was also responsible for the sumptuous gilt work, panelling, carvings and other fine details in the Palace of Westminster. He died in 1852 before the first Shrewsbury Cathedral plans had taken flight, having spent a sorry spell in London's Bethlem Royal Hospital, the institution from which derives the word 'bedlam'.

Also along Town Walls is Shrewsbury's last remaining 14th-century watchtower. It's managed by the National Trust and open a handful of days each year.

LONGDEN COLEHAM
From Town Walls you can cross the river from St Julian's Friars and over Greyfriars Footbridge, the name of which recalls the grey robes of the monks who settled in Shrewsbury in the 13th century. Here you'll find Longden Coleham, part of Coleham district to which Shrewsbury owes not a little of its gentility. The steam-driven beam engines of **Coleham Pumping Station** (🖰 www.colehampumpingstation.co.uk) were installed in 1897–98 as part of the town's new sewage disposal system. The neat brick building (rather resembling a Victorian chapel, which is no coincidence given the Victorian connection between

cleanliness and godliness) is now owned by Shropshire Council and run by Shrewsbury Steam Trust volunteers who open it to the public for a few days each year.

WYLE COP TO ABBEY FOREGATE

Back in Shrewsbury proper runs **Wyle Cop**, a road lined with interesting independent shops and inviting cafés which takes its unusual name from the Welsh 'hwylfa' meaning 'road up a hill' and 'coppa' meaning 'summit'. From this you can surmise that the road is steep.

Follow Wyle Cop down and cross the Severn over the **English Bridge**, where a stone plaque claims the rebuilt bridge 'was opened by Her Majesty the Queen on the 19th August 1927'. She didn't. As noted by Dorothy Nicolle in her fascinating book *Shropshire's Oddities*, George V had been due to do the honours, but the death of a minor member of the royal family meant all his public engagements were cancelled. The practical people of Shrewsbury remembered that his Queen Consort Mary of Teck had recently crossed the otherwise closed bridge by special arrangement while repairs were underway and decided that this constituted her reopening of it.

Shrewsbury Abbey

Abbey Foregate, SY2 6BA ✆ 01743 232723 ⌘ www.shrewsburyabbey.com ☺ Apr–Oct 10.00–16.00, Nov–Mar 10.30–15.00. Limited free parking ♿ for level access use the door on the right-hand side; ramps indoors will assist your access to the chancel & high altar

Cross under the railway bridge to reach Abbey Foregate and Shrewsbury Abbey. The size of the building today represents neither its humble beginnings as a wooden Saxon chapel nor its monastic span of Norman times. You can gauge the latter by looking for the 14th-century refectory pulpit, which stands in ruined isolation across the road.

In 1137 the monastery acquired what every 12th-century monastery needed: holy relics. The remains of St Winefride were brought from Gwytherin in north Wales and interred in a shrine, attracting pilgrims, wealth and power. For insight into medieval abbey life we can turn to the novels of Edith Pargeter (writing as Ellis Peters), who made Shrewsbury Abbey the home of her fictional crime-solving monk, Brother Cadfael.

While Shrewsbury Abbey has lost much of its glory, there is plenty to reward the modern visitor, including a **13th-century effigy** thought to be of Roger de Montgomery (former Earl of Shrewsbury who founded

BROTHER CADFAEL

While pilgrims in the Middle Ages were drawn to Shrewsbury Abbey for its holy relics, today's visitors are just as likely to be seeking out links to the fictional medieval monk and sleuth, Brother Cadfael. The creation of Shropshire author Ellis Peters (*nom de plume* of Horsehay-born scholar and translator Edith Pargeter), Brother Cadfael is a worldly Welsh Benedictine monk with an extensive knowledge of herbs and a less than celibate past.

You can pick up Cadfael books and trail leaflets in the abbey bookshop. The abbey also houses a contemporary stained-glass Brother Cadfael window by Shropshire artist Jane Gray.

The adaptions of the novels to TV starring Derek Jacobi weren't filmed in Shropshire, sadly, but in Budapest. To discover the Shropshire and Welsh borders landscape envisaged by Ellis Peters as she wrote the Cadfael stories, check out a book called *Cadfael Country* with colour photography by Rob Talbot and text by Robin Whiteman, with a foreword from Cadfael's creator herself. It's out of print, but I've seen copies in secondhand bookshops throughout the county and plenty are available online.

the abbey in 1083) and **chest tombs** acquired in the 18th century when Old St Chad's fell down and Old St Alkmund's was pulled down.

The **World War I memorial** inside, below the tower, lists a certain Lieut. W.E.S. Owen M.C. who is, of course, the war poet Wilfred Owen (page 194). He worshipped here after his family moved to Shrewsbury in 1907. The modern granite memorial in the churchyard is an interpretation of a pontoon bridge, a symbol of both Owen's bravery and death, with inscriptions that include the line 'I am the enemy you killed, my friend' from 'Strange Meeting'.

Look out for **Wednesday-at-One music recitals** (⊙ 13.00 Wed, lasting about 45 minutes; free admission but donations welcome).

🖐 For more on the history of the abbey, take a look online at ⊘ www.bradtguides.com/shrewsburyabbey.

The Cut Visitor Centre (Shropshire Wildlife Trust)

193 Abbey Foregate, SY2 6AH ⊘ 01743 284280 ⊘ www.shropshirewildlifetrust.org.uk ⊙ 10.00–16.30 Mon–Sat; parking & bike racks

Opposite Shrewsbury Abbey the 18th-century house with large sash windows, and a bee-buzzing walled garden, is the main base of Shropshire Wildlife Trust. You're welcome to call in for light refreshments, to chat to staff and to pick up thoughtful, wildlife-friendly gifts and bird food.

Lord Hill's Column

See ⟨⟩ friendsoflordhillscolumn.co.uk for details of 'climb it' days

If you continue along Abbey Foregate it's impossible to miss the sight of **Lord Hill's Column** near Shirehall, Shropshire Council's headquarters. Built between 1814 and 1816 to commemorate Lord Rowland Hill (one of the Hills of Hawkstone: see page 230), who fought alongside the Duke of Wellington at the Battle of Waterloo, this lofty monument hides a 172-step spiral staircase. A campaign is underway to rebuild the column in hard-wearing coade artificial stone.

ST ALKMUND'S & ST MARY'S TO SHREWSBURY CASTLE

This is where you'll find the infamous Grope Lane (see page 159) and some of Shrewsbury's most intriguing little shuts and passages, the narrowest of which is behind St Mary's Church.

Nearby in St Mary's Place, housed in the former Royal Salop Infirmary with its four distinctive columns, is **The Parade** shopping centre. Here are nearly 30 independent shops (many specialist, such as the Period Houses in Miniature studio) and The Snug café, with a balcony terrace and views over the Severn.

Church of St Mary the Virgin

St Mary's Place ⊙ 10.00–16.00 Mon–Sat ♿ accessible, apart from steps to sanctuary & Jesse window & the coffee shop has a ramp

Now redundant as a place of worship, the weathered sandstone St Mary's is the only complete medieval church in Shrewsbury. As you gaze up at its 500-year-old spire, one of the tallest in England, spare a thought for daring young steeplejack Robert Cadman who, in 1738, slid down it headfirst in an attempt to cross the Severn. You can read his stone-engraved obituary – in witty poetic form – outside the west door.

The church has a humbling interior: above your head find graceful stone arches and an oak nave ceiling ornately carved with animals, birds and angels, while below your feet are Minton tiles, testament to Victorian manufacturing prowess in this region. Illuminating it all are exquisite stained-glass windows, the most famous of which is the vast and colourful 14th-century **Jesse window** in the east of the chancel, moved here from Old St Chad's after its collapse in 1788. Jesse windows aim to depict through art Jesus Christ's line of descent. Sharing the

THE CHURCH THAT FELL DOWN

When the central tower of St Chad's collapsed in July 1788, no-one was less surprised than Shrewsbury's county surveyor, Thomas Telford. He wrote in a cheerful letter to a friend:

… these fractures were said to have been there since time immorial [sic] – and it was said even by sensible people that professional men always wish'd to carve out employment for themselves: and that the whole might be done at a small expense which they proceeded to do – and I gave myself no disturbance when lo and behold on the morning of the ninth inst the very parts I had pointed out gave way – and down tumbled the mighty mass – forming a very remarkable, magnificent Ruin!

This 'magnificent Ruin' (still evident as a chapel between Princess Street and Belmont, referred to as Old St Chad's) resulted in panic: the medieval section of St Alkmund's was swiftly demolished, leaving just the tower and spire, with local architect John Carline commissioned to build a new church in the gothic revival style.

St Mary's was saved – but only by a whisker.

chancel are the St Bernard windows, featuring scenes from the life of the Cistercian abbot, with Latin captions serving a similar purpose to speech bubbles in contemporary cartoons.

On the wall of St Catherine's chapel you'll find a stone memorial to Shrewsbury-born hero **Admiral John Benbow** (d1702): the 'Nelson of his times'. The story goes that when he ran away to sea, young Benbow left his front door key nailed to a poplar tree in an orchard at Coton Hill. That very key (or at least an old-looking key befitting of the legend) is encased behind glass on the front steps of Shrewsbury's modern Benbow Quay apartments, site of his birthplace.

If you find yourself in St Mary's and in need of refreshment you're in capable hands: the **café** serving sandwiches, cakes and hot drinks is run by the people from Battlefield 1403 (page 175) and keeps the same opening hours as the church.

Shrewsbury Castle & Regimental Museum

Castle St ✆ 01743 358516 ⊙ Jun–mid-Sep 10.30–17.00, closed Thu; rest of year 10.30–16.00, closed Thu & Sun); grounds & gardens open year round 09.00–17.00

Shrewsbury Castle may not be the finest-looking fortress in the land, but it sure was placed in a sensible position, overlooking the Severn's meander on the site of an Anglo-Saxon fortification. The Victorian artist H Thornhill Timmins quoted an 'old writer' who said the castle was 'built in such as brave Plott that it could have espyed a Byrd flying in every Streete'. Like Shrewsbury Abbey, this red sandstone building is a Roger de Montgomery legacy, although little of the Norman structure remains.

Since 1985 the castle's dignified interior has held the collection of the **Shropshire Regimental Museum Trust**: medals, pictures, weapons and uniforms dating from the 1700s. One of the most significant exhibits is the decorative baton given to Grand-Admiral Karl Dönitz by Adolf Hitler in 1943. Dönitz succeeded Hitler following his suicide and, when Dönitz and his remnant Nazi government were arrested by the 159th Infantry Brigade, the baton was handed over as a token of surrender. For its military connections the museum was the target of an IRA firebomb attack in 1992 which caused extensive damage (although, mercifully, no human injury) and closed the building for three years. Today it takes the regimental motto *Aucto Splendore Resurgo:* 'I rise again in greater splendour'.

"One of the most significant exhibits is the decorative baton given to Grand-Admiral Karl Dönitz by Adolf Hitler in 1943."

You'll need to pay a small admission fee for the castle, but you can visit the grounds and **Laura's Tower** on the Norman motte summit for free. This octagonal folly was built by Thomas Telford in 1790 and presented to Laura Pulteney, daughter of Shrewsbury MP Sir William Pulteney, as a coming-of-age gift. The inside of the one-room sandstone tower is currently inaccessible to visitors but the plateau on which it stands has long views over Shrewsbury Abbey to Lord Hill's Column and beyond to The Wrekin.

The private **Castle Gates House** is located at the entrance to Shropshire Castle, but it wasn't always. This late 16th-century black-and-yellowish half-timbered building was originally built on Dogpole (just off High Street) and moved to its present position by the Earl of Bradford in around 1702.

A shopfront on the opposite side of Castle Street bears a plaque commemorating one Mr Palin who 'first made the unique Shrewsbury cakes to his original recipe in the year 1760'. Shrewsbury cakes, perhaps better known as **Shrewsbury biscuits** because of their hard texture, were once commonly bought by visitors to the town just as holidaymakers to Scotland might buy shortbread.

ARTS

Bear Steps Art Gallery St Alkmunds Pl 01743 344994 www.shrewsburycivicsociety.co.uk. This tiny art gallery in an exquisite 16th-century timber-framed building also serves as the headquarters of Shrewsbury Civic Society, which had restored the building by the early 1970s. The bear in the name probably refers to a now-extinct pub.

The Buttermarket Howard St 01743 281712 www.thebuttermarket.co.uk. Shrewsbury's biggest entertainment venue has a Wurlitzer organ.

Theatre Severn Frankwell Quay 01743 281281 www.theatresevern.co.uk. In 2009, Shrewsbury's new performing arts complex was nominated for the Carbuncle Cup, a celebration of the year's worst architecture. However you feel about its steel and curved glass, this theatre hosts a varied and exciting programme of plays, comedy, music and talks.

SHOPPING

Market Hall Shrewsbury Claremont St ⊙ Tue, Wed, Fri & Sat (some stalls open on Thu morning: see www.markethallshrewsbury.co.uk. Market Hall has retained its 1960s green-and-white-striped tarpaulin vibe but stallholders have moved with the times. It contains over 60 stalls selling the good stuff in life: secondhand and rare books and records, vintage clothes, specialist board games, deli treats, wholefoods (there's a gluten-free shop), cake craft and handmade gifts.

Pomona Grocery 1–2 Castle St 01743 366660. I wish there were more grocery stores like Pomona (whose name of course refers to the Roman goddess of fruits). The crates outside are treasure chests of fresh, colourful and often local produce that invariably makes me want to cancel any dining-out plans and cook instead. Indoors, alongside more produce and specialty ingredients, you'll find nifty gift ideas: bamboo socks, Shropshire mugs, notebooks and garden accessories.

Tanners Wine Merchants 26 Wyle Cop 01743 234500. It's often the mark of a good Shropshire restaurant when you see a wine list procured from Tanners. James Tanner is the fourth generation of his family to lead this distinguished Shropshire business. If you think the warren-like Shrewsbury shop has Dickensian charm, you're in agreement with the makers of 1984 film *A Christmas Carol*, as the cellar doubled up as Mr Fezziwig's warehouse for a party scene.

FOOD & DRINK

The Boathouse New St SY3 8JQ 01743 231658. On the banks of the Severn by Porthill Bridge, overlooking Quarry Park, is one of Shrewsbury's best-loved pubs. The setting's so relaxing it's hard to imagine that the building served as a pest house during the plague of 1650. But don't be put off your food, which is good: well-presented grills and pub classics with a twist.

Chez Sophie 10 Mardol Head ✆ 01743 588560. Serving sweet and savoury crêpes, Belgian and craft beers (several on draught) and freshly made milkshakes, Chez Sophie's an authentic-feeling French crêperie which grew out of its unit at the Market Hall thanks to the hard work of Sophie Carron and Matt Hocking. The atmosphere's laid back and pretty cool; upstairs you can sink into old cinema seats.

CSONS 8 Milk St ✆ 01743 272709. This informal café/restaurant is owned and run by brothers Reuben, Josh, Ben and Adam Crouch (the C 'sons'), all with impressive backgrounds in catering or hospitality. The décor's pared back but elegant, the service is warm and friendly, and the menu by Josh (who trained alongside Clive Green at the Green Café in Ludlow) is updated daily and flawlessly executed, using local suppliers (a scroll on the wall lists them all) and global influences.

The Golden Cross 14 Princess St ✆ 01743 362507. Even if the food weren't great at this upscale inn, it would still provide an atmospheric hideaway for a drink – and indeed it's been keeping the people of Shrewsbury watered for almost 700 years. Luckily, the posh pub food matches the stylish ambience. **The Golden Cross** is also a boutique hotel.

Lion & Pheasant 49–50 Wyle Cop ✆ 01743 770345. Widely regarded to provide the best fine-dining restaurant experience in Shrewsbury, the menu at this chic hotel is always exciting and makes clever use of the season's freshest produce.

Market Hall Shrewsbury Claremont St ✆ www.markethallshrewsbury.co.uk ⊙ Tue, Wed, Fri & Sat: check website for individual traders' opening hours. For a bargain-price lunch you can't go far wrong with Market Hall. I'm especially impressed with the **Bird's Nest Café** – a fairy-lit space serving wholesome, tasty and often local, fairtrade and organic food (such as open sandwiches and huge slabs of cake).

Optimum Joy 81 Wyle Cop ✆ 01743 240037. This small, sweet place is also a wellbeing retreat. Even if laughter yoga and amethyst bio mats aren't your bag, give this organic wholefood café a try. The food is unusual and nicely cooked: imagine spiced Caribbean stew or deliciously seasoned dhal with beetroot bhajis.

Palmer's of Shrewsbury Claremont St ✆ 07850 741555. A not-for-profit coffee house on the ground floor of Shrewsbury Baptist Church which sells reasonably priced drinks and cakes while supporting charities. On a hot day the cucumber and mint green iced tea is a cooling treat.

Panacea Lower Claremont Bank ✆ 01743 233332. Considered by many to be the best Indian restaurant in town. All the classic dishes, cooked authentically, with delicious specials for when you feel like trying something new.

The Peach Tree Abbey Foregate ✆ 01743 355055. Executive chef Chris Burt is passionate about supporting local suppliers, a policy that sings out through his classy dishes. See also the interconnecting, simply great **Momo.No.Ki** ramen noodle bar (that's *peach tree* in Japanese) and Cuban-style **Havana Republic** bar.

NORTH & EAST OF SHREWSBURY

You need not travel far from Shrewsbury to find gloriously open spaces. National Trust-managed **Attingham Park** holds a special place in my family's heart for its captivating mansion house, deer park and enormous playfield. Heading east towards The Wrekin, you'll find a vineyard and the remains of an important **Roman city**.

2 BATTLEFIELD

🏠 **The Old Station**, Leaton (page 249)

Three miles north of Shrewsbury in the parish of Albrighton is the village of Battlefield, named because it was here – or near here – that the 1403 **Battle of Shrewsbury took place**. The bloody skirmish between Henry IV's men and the rebel army led by Henry 'Hotspur' Percy was immortalised in Shakespeare's *Henry IV Part I*. A farm shop may seem an odd way to mark this site, but it does work, I promise …

The **Adventure Rope Course** in the grounds of nearby Albrighton Hall Hotel & Spa gets rave reviews from visitors seeking a treetop challenge (www.adventureropecourse.co.uk). And Battlefield is now home to the new and ambitious **Battlefield Brewery**, with a shop due to open soon (www.battlefieldbrewery.co.uk).

Battlefield 1403

Upper Battlefield SY4 3DB 01939 210905 www.battlefield1403.com 09.30–17.30 Mon–Sat, 10.00–16.00 Sun

Part of the Albrighton Estate, Battlefield 1403 is a visitor centre featuring a free exhibition on the Battle of Shrewsbury. The pleasingly stocked **farm shop** on the site has its own deli and butchery: the beef and lamb are raised on the estate, while most of the other produce is sourced from Shropshire and bordering counties. **Sparrow's Café** has won Great Taste and Countryside Alliance Awards; it wins my heart for its super-local menu and knight-size slices of homemade cake.

Behind Battlefield 1403, some startling-looking owls and an African Grey parrot called Henry will greet you in the small and welcoming **Battlefield Falconry Centre** (01939 210204 www.battlefieldfalconrycentre.co.uk 10.00–15.30 daily). Bird-handling sessions and day-long falconry experiences can be booked in advance, including the popular Hawk Walk.

Collect the key from the shop at Battlefield 1403 and make the quarter-mile walk across the alleged battlefield (no bones have ever been unearthed) to the **church of St Mary Magdalene**. It was the eve of the feast day of St Mary Magdalene in 1403 that King Henry IV triumphed over rebellious marcher lords. Built soon afterwards, between 1406 and 1408, to commemorate the thousands killed in the battle, the church was restored by Shrewsbury architect Samuel Pountney Smith in 1860–1862 and funded for the main part by the Corbet family. The hammerbeam roof, from the restoration, features the heraldry of knights who fought in the battle. The bright light in the vestry belies its former function as the Corbet mortuary chapel, but don't miss the floor tiles shaped like a coffin. The chancel houses a rare and mournful 15th-century sculpted oak pietà – the Virgin Mary cradling her dead son – thought to have been salvaged from a chapel at nearby Albright Hussey. The church of St Mary Magdalene no longer sees regular worship but is still consecrated, and is managed by the Churches Conservation Trust.

"It was the eve of the feast day of St Mary Magdalene in 1403 that King Henry IV triumphed over rebellious marcher lords."

3 HAUGHMOND HILL

SY4 4PW ♀ SJ545147 ✆ 0300 0676977 (recreation manager) ⬧ www.forestry.gov.uk/haughmondhill ⊙ car park open 06.00–20.30 daily (06.00–18.00 in winter) & costs £1

Five miles east of Shrewsbury, near Uffington, with views over the River Severn and Shrewsbury to south Shropshire and beyond, is the working woodland of Haughmond Hill. Like the Callow Hill entrance to the Wyre Forest (page 92) it's managed by the Forestry Commission and brilliantly geared up to visitors, with toilets, picnic benches and children's play equipment (in this case a giant wooden coil for running around).

The **café**, in a wooden cabin (⊙ 09.30–16.30), sells bacon sarnies, tuck shop-style treats, tea, coffee and cold drinks. ♿ Two of the **four well-marked trails** (Geo and Corbett) are accessible for buggies, wheelchairs and mobility scooters.

Afterwards, you might fancy procuring a wooden sword from the entry kiosk at **Haughmond Abbey** (SY4 4RW ✆ 0370 3331181 ⊙ end Mar–end Sep 10.00–17.00, closed Mon & Tue; English Heritage) and venturing around the extensive ruins of this Augustinian monastery, which was probably founded in the early 12th century.

CHRISTOPHER ELWELL/S

RURAL LIFE

Shropshire is predominantly agricultural, with over 85% of its land area given over to farming. This cannot help but influence the feel of the county, preserving quietude, long green vistas and a pace of life that moves gently with the seasons.

1 Farmland in the Shropshire hills. 2 Fordhall Organic Farm has been on an exciting journey over the last ten years. 3 Beekeeper, Acton Scott Historic Working Farm. 4 Pedigree British White cattle.

TOWNS OF SHROPSHIRE

From Whitchurch near the Cheshire border to Ludlow in the Welsh Marches, Shropshire's towns give us black-and-white half-timbered buildings, thriving markets, characterful pubs and independent shops.

1 Ludlow is known as the UK's Slow Food capital. 2 Bridgnorth's High Town and Low Town overlook the River Severn. 3 Castle Gates House, Shrewsbury. 4 St Chad's Church from The Quarry, Shrewsbury. 5 Ellesmere welcomes shoppers with flags and hanging baskets.

LUDLOW FOOD FESTIVAL

SAVOURING THE TASTE

Across Shropshire you'll find beautifully presented farm shops, food festivals, breweries, and innovative chefs pushing at the boundaries of what can be achieved with produce from the county and its neighbours.

1 Fresh pasta at Ludlow Food Festival. 2 Celebrating Great British cheese. 3 Paddle of Joule's ales, Market Drayton. 4 Kerry Vale Vineyard.

SCT

MARIE KREFT

KERRY VALE VINEYARD

4 ATCHAM

🏠 **Brompton Farmhouse B&B** (page 249)

Atcham (three miles southeast of Shrewsbury on the B4380) took its name as an abbreviation of Attingham which means 'the home of the children of Eata'. The English chronicler and Benedictine monk Orderic Vitalis was born here in 1075. The **church** has a Saxon foundation but none of the original building survives. It's the only church in Britain dedicated to St Eata, who's commemorated in a late Victorian stained-glass window over the west door. Buried in the churchyard is Anna Bonus Kingsford (d1888) whose husband – and cousin – Algernon Godfrey Kingsford was priest at the church. Dr Kingsford was one of the first English women to obtain a degree in medicine and, as an anti-vivisectionist, the only medical student of her time to graduate without experimenting on a single animal.

The rushing **River Severn** is spectacular at Atcham and crossed by two bridges. Designed by John Gwynn, a founder member of the Royal Academy, the older seven-arched stone bridge stands as a scheduled ancient monument.

In its glorious setting by the river, the Georgian red-brick **Mytton & Mermaid Hotel** was once a dower house to Attingham Park. John 'Mad Jack' Mytton's (page 218) funeral cortege stopped here in 1834; his ghost is said to haunt the building on 30 September, the Squire's birthday.

Arriva's' 81 **bus** service between Shrewsbury and Telford Town Centre stops outside the Mytton & Mermaid, giving you easy access to Attingham Park and other nearby attractions.

Attingham Park

Atcham SY4 4TP ✆ 01743 708123 ⊙ park 09.00–17.00 year round; check website for house opening times & other facilities; National Trust

There's so much to see at Attingham Park, it's worth setting aside at least a day to enjoy it. The Palladian-style mansion house was designed by George Stueart (he of unpopular St Chad's fame: see page 166) and built from Grinshill stone in 1785 for the first Lord Berwick. Inside the mansion are three floors to view, telling the fascinating story of the Berwick family whose motto 'Let wealth be his who knows its use' is poignant once you know how dramatically their fortunes ebbed and flowed over the years. In 1805 the extravagant second Lord Berwick (who in his 40s married an 18-year-old courtesan, Sophia Dubochet) appointed architect John Nash to create the glazed roof picture gallery. Nash would later work on Brighton Pavilion and Buckingham Palace to great acclaim, but his design for Attingham Park was flawed and the roof always leaked. A recent £1.4 million conservation programme has seen a new steel and glass roof placed over the original.

"John Nash would later work on Brighton Pavilion and Buckingham Palace, but his roof design for Attingham Park was flawed and it always leaked."

Attingham's parkland covers around 4,000 acres and, although that's only half the area it claimed in the early 1800s, you can still spend entire afternoons getting joyfully lost, exploring the woodland, deer park, walled garden and – for children and their parents – the expansive **Shoulder of Mutton Playfield** (so called because of its uneven shape), with tunnels, dens and logs. Look for the Parkland Walks leaflet as you enter the estate, detailing the gentle **Mile Walk** (♿ on even ground, suitable for wheelchairs and pushchairs), as well as the **Woodland**, **Deer Park** (with more than 250 fallow deer – look out for feeding times) and **World War II Walks**.

Attingham Park is the regional headquarters of the National Trust and, like most of the charity's properties, is child-friendly. Baby slings can be borrowed in the mansion; there are pushchair parks and lockers; baby changing facilities are found in most toilet blocks. The mansion has an **activity room** with dressing-up and toys, plus a dedicated children's trail. Four-legged family members are welcome too (in keeping with the Berwick family tradition: look for the memorial bench to pet dogs on the east side of the mansion), although do check the guidelines on where they should be kept on short leads.

Catering-wise, you have a choice of the **Carriage House Café** near the stables (savoury snacks, cakes, tea and coffee), the **Mansion Tearoom** (soups, homemade pies, veggie tartlets, cold desserts – many of the ingredients are grown in the walled kitchen garden) and the most refined offering: **Lady Berwick's** by the Outer Library, serving seasonal set luncheons and afternoon tea. Or for a bacon sandwich outside, **The Greedy Pig** van is open most weekends and in the school holidays, stationed in the playfield. Two shops raise funds for the National Trust: the **Butler's Pantry** gift shop in the Mansion plus **Grooms' Rooms**, a two-floor secondhand bookshop accessible from the Stables Courtyard.

Elsewhere in Atcham

The celebrated architect John Nash may not have done justice to Attingham Park's picture gallery (see page 178) but the nearby Italianate villa of Cronkhill, which he designed during the same period, is sublime. It's also owned by the National Trust but privately tenanted: look out for the few open days each year.

Located by the driveway for Attingham Park, the small organic arable and dairy farm at **Home Farm Attingham** (⌀ 01743 709243 ⌀ www. homefarmattingham.co.uk) was once part of the Attingham estate. It remains today as a working example of a traditional Shropshire farm (with the addition of Merlin the robotic milking machine). There's not a huge amount on offer for visitors at the moment, although the owners' intentions are clearly good and the entrance fee isn't unreasonable so it could be worth an hour's visit, especially if you have little ones. The **tea room** serves homemade cakes.

A mile away, still on the Attingham estate, is Brompton, home of **Brompton Cookery School** (⌀ www.bromptoncookeryschool.co.uk) run by celebrity chef Marcus Bean.

5 WROXETER

A valley village in sight of The Wrekin, Wroxeter has the substantial remains of Viroconium/Uriconium, the fourth largest **Roman city** in Britain (and almost as big as Pompeii). Established in the 90s AD, it was inhabited until the 7th century when the region was conquered by the Anglo-Saxon kingdom of Mercia.

The Anglo-Saxon **church of St Andrew** is noteworthy for its recycled Roman stone, as well as the striking alabaster effigies of Sir Richard Newport and his wife Margaret. Sir Richard was one of the Queen's Counsel during Elizabeth I's reign.

Arriva bus number 96 from Telford to Shrewsbury stops at Wroxeter – and it's a great idea not to drive as the village is also home to a **vineyard**.

Wroxeter Roman City

SY5 6PH ⌀ 01743 761330 ⊙ 10.00–18.00 daily; free parking ⌀ mostly accessible; English Heritage

The remains of the Roman City at Wroxeter may not be extensive, but with aid of the audio guide and well-written interpretive panels, it's easy to envisage the glory days of Uriconium, when the vast open basilica was used for exercising, socialising and relaxing before the city's Roman residents retreated to their bath house, kept humid with furnaces. At 23 feet high, the **Old Work** – the ruined wall at the centre of the site – is the biggest piece of freestanding Roman wall in Britain. The relatively undeveloped landscape around Wroxeter gives archaeologists valuable insight into how Roman towns related to their surroundings.

Over the years the site has yielded one of the most extensive collections of **artefacts** from Roman Britain. A solid silver mirror found in the 1920s now resides at Shrewsbury Museum and Art Gallery, alongside other treasures, and you'll find excavated pottery, coins and jewellery in the museum at Wroxeter.

In a memoir, the Shropshire poet-novelist Mary Webb wrote of the Roman camp: 'Nothing dies if one has the love to keep it alive'. I think that's true of Wroxeter more today than ever, with English Heritage working hard to bring new audiences and understanding to the site. In 2010 as part of a Channel 4 programme called *Rome Wasn't Built In A Day,* six builders with help from volunteers reconstructed a **Roman town house** (*villa urbana*) using only tools known to the Romans, and local materials. The finished product is partly furnished and laid out so you can imagine it occupied, complete with dressing-up box in case you feel moved to don a toga.

While it makes for an absorbing visit, the site probably won't comprise a full day out. Better, perhaps, combined with a tour of Wroxeter Roman Vineyard.

The shop adjacent to the museum sells drinks and ice cream but no food of great substance.

Wroxeter Roman Vineyard

SY5 6PQ ✆ 01743 761888 🖱 www.wroxetervineyard.co.uk 🕓 09.00–17.00 daily ♿ level, with good accessibility

English wine is having more than a moment – and long may it last. A few hundred yards from St Andrew's Church is Wroxeter Roman Vineyard, planted in 1991, where the Millington family uses their sheltered smallholding with free-draining soil to produce well-regarded red, white, rosé and sparkling wine and cider. You can roam freely around the vineyard before sampling Wroxeter wares in the large **shop and café**. Guided tours and tasting sessions are available.

TOWARDS SOUTH SHROPSHIRE

🏠 **Caro's Cottage** (page 249), **Pitchford Estate** (page 249)

It makes sense that, where the A49 heads south from Shrewsbury towards the Shropshire Hills Area of Outstanding Natural Beauty with its farms, open countryside and artisan food producers, there should be a high density of excellent places to eat. Combine these with intriguing local stories and you have several satisfying stops on your way to or from Church Stretton and the Shropshire Hills.

An exhilarating place to walk is **Lyth Hill Country Park** (📍 SJ475070), five miles south of Shrewsbury and just west of the A49. It was here in 1917 that **Mary Webb** (pages 98–9) built Spring Cottage, a simple retreat where she could write, drawing inspiration from the countryside around her. The cottage is much changed since Mary's day; in 2014 Shropshire Council rejected the current owners' plans to demolish it and build a six-bedroom house in its place, although the future of Spring Cottage is still uncertain. Lyth Hill comprises woodland, scrub and grassland and offers many pleasing walks, with panoramic views of the Stiperstones, Wenlock Edge and The Wrekin.

6 CONDOVER

Almost encircled by Cound Brook, Condover is six miles south of Shrewsbury just off the A49. While the large parish isn't exactly a tourist destination, it's notable for several reasons – not least for being the site of an exciting discovery. In 1986 a woman named Eve Roberts who was walking her dog in the quarry discovered the remains of what was later confirmed as the bones of an adult **woolly mammoth** and three young, newly uncovered by quarry workers. When the bones were carbon dated, scientists realised that mammoths had still been present in Shropshire around 13,000 years ago – 5,000 years later than previously thought. This gave nationally important insight into many areas of study, including climate change, habitats and human hunting activity. You can learn more about the Shropshire woolly mammoths at Shrewsbury Museum, and Shropshire Hills Discovery Centre in Craven Arms.

"In 1986 a woman named Eve Roberts walking her dog in the quarry discovered the remains of what was later confirmed as the bones of an adult woolly mammoth and three young."

The three-storey Elizabethan manor house of **Condover Hall** is now a JCA residential centre for schools and groups. Presumably children who stay over are not informed of its alleged curse, from a butler who was condemned to death after being falsely accused of murdering his master. 'As I perish an innocent man, may those who follow my murdered lord be cursed,' he is reported to have said at the gallows. On his way down the stairs at Condover Hall he left a bloodied handprint on the wall,

The sleeping dragon:
Pontesbury to the summit of Earl's Hill

Adapted from *20 Walks in and around Shrewsbury* with kind permission from Shrewsbury Ramblers

❀ OS Explorer map 241 & 216; start at Pontesbury Hill Rd adjacent to School Rd ♀ SO398061; 3½ miles (around 2 hours); strenuous: initially minor roads & open countryside then a sustained ascent followed by a steep but short descent, & on rough paths.

This walk is well worth the uphill scramble for the 360-degree panorama at the top of Earl's Hill. Until the late 1800s this hill, sometimes likened from afar to a sleeping dragon, was the venue for popular Easter festivities – including a race down the hillside to the brook at its base. If the winner dipped the fourth finger of the right hand in the water it was said they would marry the first person of the opposite sex they next encountered.

1 Walk along Pontesbury Hill Road away from the church, following the road past the phone box and turn left at Birch Row, until you reach the ford adjacent to the Plough Inn. Don't cross the ford but turn right up **Whitwell Lane**. Follow the stream past houses on the left and take the lane to the right until you reach a metal kissing-gate on the left. Go through it. Walk along the hedgerow to the next metal gate and turn right following the waymark. Cross the field to the metal kissing-gate. Turn left, following the hedgerow on the left. Cross a stream and continue to pass through the metal kissing-gate in the corner of the field.

2 Turn right along the road until you reach a farm driveway on the left. Turn left and then go through a metal gate on the right. Follow the fence line on the left, staying in the field and following the hedgerow on the left to the metal gate in the corner of the field. Continue in the same direction through the field, crossing two stiles until you reach a stile in the left-hand corner, taking you to face the route to Earl's Hill.

3 Cross the stile and walk towards Earl's Hill. Cross another stile and footbridge until you reach the stile in the top right-hand corner of the field.

which defied all attempts to be cleaned. Eventually the brick around the bloodstain had to be chipped away. Before the activity centre was opened in 2010, it was blessed by a priest.

Cantlop Bridge, an English Heritage-protected cast iron bridge (possibly designed by Thomas Telford and certainly approved by him) crosses Cound Brook. It's listed among VisitEngland's top ten bridges for playing Poohsticks.

4 Cross the lane to enter **Earl's Hill Reserve**. Follow the path up the hill, ignoring another path on the left. Continue to the top of the hill until there you see a stile and pine woods on your left.

5 Turn right up Earl's Hill until you reach the summit, marked by a trig point. Take a while to soak up the extensive views from here. Looking north you will see Shrewsbury and notably the white Shelton Water Tower. To the east, The Wrekin and Buildwas Power Station. To the west, extensive views into Wales. Here you will see the outline of a hillfort which occupied the hilltop in the first millennium BC.

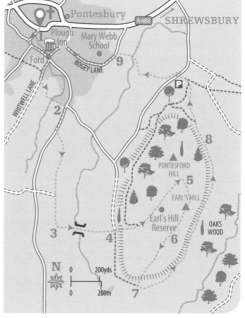

6 From the trig point continue in the same direction to descend Earl's Hill. Follow the path until you reach a steep descent to a stile at the bottom of the hill. Go over the stile and walk 10 yards to join a path. Turn left.

7 Follow this path on the eastern side of Earl's Hill, through ▶

The sleeping dragon:
Pontesbury to the summit of Earl's Hill (continued)

◀ woodland. Continue walking in the same direction, ignoring footpaths to both left and right, to reach a metal gate. Pass through a further metal gate where you arrive at an open field with gorse. Go through another metal gate and continue in the same direction, heading for woodland.

8 Go through the metal gate on to a woodland track and continue until you reach **Earl's Hill car park**. Go through the car park on to the road and turn right heading downhill for about 55 yards to a sharp left turn signposted, over the cattle grid. Head down the track to the hedge line, then turn right at a cattle grid through a metal gate, walking diagonally across the field to the kissing-gate. Turn right down the tarmac driveway to the road.

9 Turn left on the road, passing **Mary Webb School** on your right. Walk past the school entrance and continue to the T-junction at the bottom of the road. Turn left, arriving at the **Plough Inn** and the ford on your right, which you passed at the beginning of the walk. Cross the ford to the road leading back to the start.

¶❙ FOOD & DRINK

The Old Hall Persian Main Rd, Dorrington SY5 7JD (about 2 miles southwest of Condover) 🖉 01743 719100. Dr Lal Haider is a Shropshire surgeon who swapped his scrubs for chef's whites to pursue his dreams. A charismatic and warmly welcoming host, Lal has created an ambience in a half-timbered house at Dorrington that feels equally special occasion and come-as-you-are. The Persian food combines modern and traditional cooking techniques: hearty dishes delicately flavoured with fresh herbs, spices and dried and fresh fruits. The menu's great on value, especially the tasting banquet.

7 PONTESBURY

🏠 **The White Horse**, Pulverbatch (page 249)

Eight miles southwest of Shrewsbury on the A488, Pontesbury is Mary Webb country. She had a triangular garden at her house at Rose Cottage, where she grew produce and flowers to sell at Shrewsbury market. The village shop **Hignetts** (🖉 01743 790228) is a fruitful place to source a picnic: as well as having a butchery they sell homemade Scotch eggs, local cheeses and other deli goods.

Nearby **Pontesford Hill** (a twin to Earl's Hill to which the walk on pages 182–4 will take you) was recently purchased by Shropshire

Wildlife Trust with help from the Mary Webb Society and donations from more than a thousand people. Mary's novel *The Golden Arrow* featured an old Palm Sunday tradition which took place on the hill, wherein young people sought an arrow lost in a 661 battle in the hope of also finding good fortune.

¶¶ FOOD & DRINK

Red Lion Longden Common SY5 8AE ✐ 01743 718889. Almost equidistant between Pontesbury and Condover, this inviting 19th-century coaching inn has its own microbrewery. One of the two handcrafted beers is called The Golden Arrow (see above). Outside are free-range chickens and ducks; inside you'll find traditional pub food.

The White Horse Pulverbatch SY5 8DS ✐ 01743 718247. Another country pub flying the flag for Shropshire produce and real ale. It's popular with both locals and walkers so you're advised to book ahead for a table. The Arriva bus 546 from Shrewsbury stops conveniently outside this warm 15th-century inn. Three B&B en-suite rooms are available.

Zenna Main Rd, Pontesbury SY5 0RR ✐ 01743 792955. Clean, welcoming and serving consistently great food, long-established Zenna is considered by many to be Shropshire's best and most authentic Chinese restaurant.

8 MINSTERLEY

⌂ **Haymakers Cottage** (page 249)

Two miles west of Pontesbury – and only a little way north of the Stiperstones in south Shropshire – is the village and civil parish of Minsterley, described by John Betjeman in 1951 as a 'slightly industrialised dairy village'. (It still is: the long-established creamery came into Müller's ownership in 2013.) See whether you can spot the Victorian pissoir and inscription on its green iron panels: 'PLEASE ADJUST YOUR DRESS BEFORE LEAVING'. The **church of the Holy Trinity** is special, built in 1689 to the design of William Taylor who also oversaw the Palladian-style mansion at Weston Park. Don't miss the *memento mori* stone carvings above the west door. Inside is another reminder of the frailty of human existence: a collection of **maidens' garlands** (page 186).

9 ACTON BURNELL

Acton Burnell is an idyllic village and parish about seven miles southeast of Shrewsbury. In 1977 it became a dedicated conservation area thanks to its architectural importance (look for the gabled timber porches

MAIDENS' GARLANDS

Rosie Morris & www.maidensgarlands.com

A child of the 1950s, I attended Sunday school at Holy Trinity Church in Minsterley. I remember gazing up in wonder at seven dusty bags, which resembled upside-down hanging baskets and looked to be full of moss.

Maidens' garlands, also known as virgins' crowns (and, in Derbyshire, 'cransties'), were funeral mementos of paper, flowers or ribbons for young, usually female, virgins – although bachelor garlands also exist. Funeral garlanding was commonplace in the 17th, 18th and 19th centuries. At a funeral procession, they were carried before the coffin and then placed upon it during the reading of the funeral service. In some locations they were buried with the coffin; in others they were hung in a conspicuous place within the church and remained on display either for a period of 12 months' mourning, or permanently.

The maidens' garlands at Minsterley are particularly fine and represent a collection of national importance. Conserved in 2000, they are all authenticated as being made of 18th-century paper. Their colour, which I would describe as a Madonna blue, is unique. The basic shape is that of a beehive. As described by Syer Cumming in the 1875 *Journal of the British Archaeological Association*, 'Each measures a full foot in height; they have a wooden framework covered with linen and decorated with paper flowers and cockades. Within these crowns are hung several pairs of white paper gloves.'

Maidens' garland associations are very sad. For example, the one found at Astley Abbotts, Bridgnorth (page 85) was made for Hannah Phillips who drowned on the eve of her wedding in 1707. At Minsterley, bereaved fiancées who remained unmarried were also eligible for one.

There are examples of funeral garlanding to be found in Europe – for example in Berlin – but the form the custom took in rural Britain is particularly touching and deserves to be better known.

on the black-and-white houses, remodelled in the 19th century) and spectacular scenery, pressed as it is into hills overlooking the Severn flood plain. The suffix Burnell was present by 1198 and commemorates the family of Robert Burnell (c1239–92) who served both as Bishop of Bath and Wells, and Lord Chancellor to Edward I.

In this village Burnell built a red sandstone castle – or rather a semi-fortified mansion house like the one at Stokesay (page 39). According to English Heritage, which manages the site, the large upstairs windows suggest **Acton Burnell Castle** (☉ daylight hours; free entry) was designed less as a defensive measure and more to impress. It certainly makes for impressive red ruins now, set in quiet woodland.

Next door is the cruciform **church of St Mary**, one of the best-preserved 13th-century churches in Britain. Highlights include the enormous table tomb of Sir Richard Lee (d1591) in the north transept, a knight portrayed with his wife beside him, three sons at his head and nine daughters behind him. The detail on the carvings is exquisite, with every one of the children markedly different. The small square window low down in the chancel is thought to be a leper's window, allowing people with leprosy to see services they were not allowed to attend.

The stuccoed mansion nearby is **Concord College**, an independent boarding school which serves mainly international students. In its grounds are the end walls of a large hall where it is said Edward I called England's first parliament, to deal with the 'Welsh problem'. Local people still refer to the two gable ends as those of Parliament Barn.

FOOD & DRINK

The Pound at Leebotwood SY6 6ND ✐ 01694 751477. This country pub and restaurant in a 15th-century drovers' hostelry is polished, warm and inviting. It's 11 miles south of Shrewsbury; around 5½ miles southeast of Acton Burnell (well on the way to Church Stretton). The innovative menu, which champions suppliers and artisan producers from within a 30-mile radius, also includes pub favourites, yet always with a special twist.

10 JESSAMINE COTTAGE GARDENS

🏠 **Wenlock Edge Riding Centre B&B** (page 249)
Kenley SY5 6NS ✐ 01694 771279 ⊙ May–Aug 14.00–18.00 Thu, Sun & bank holidays; park on the verge outside

In quiet countryside about three miles southeast of Acton Burnell is Kenley, a small village and civil parish. Here in 1999 Pam and Lee Wheeler returned home inspired from their years in New Zealand to create a garden in Shropshire. The time and thought they've invested in transforming bare paddocks into Jessamine Cottage Gardens are evident throughout their three acres: in the neat parterre, the peaceful spinney, the bountiful kitchen garden which in the summer months supplies fruit for jams and chutneys. (The latter are available, alongside homemade cake, in the wood-built **tea room**, which is constructed in the Kiwi style). A much-admired *Cornus controversa variegata* ('wedding-cake tree') blooms in May and there are plenty of seats for quiet contemplation in sight of Wenlock Edge. Visit in June to see the outlandish pink Gertrude Jekyll roses from David Austin in full flower.

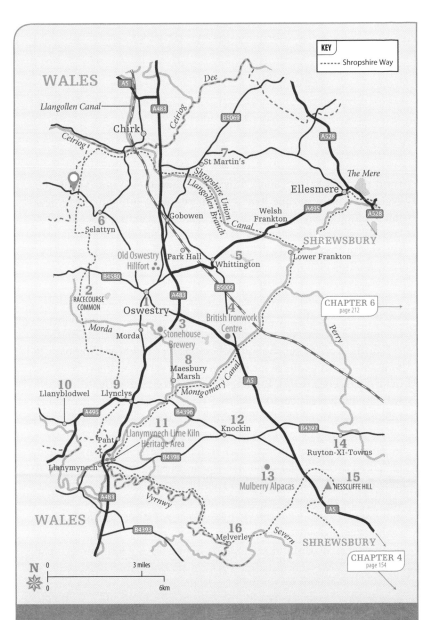

WALES

Llangollen Canal

Dee

A5

A483

Ceiriog

B5069

A528

Chirk

Ceiriog

7

St Martin's

The Mere

Shropshire Union

Llangollen Branch

Ellesmere

6

Selattyn

Gobowen

Welsh
Frankton

A495

A528

SHREWSBURY

Canal

Old Oswestry
Hillfort

Park Hall

5

Lower Frankton

B4580

Whittington

2

RACECOURSE
COMMON

A483

B5009

4

CHAPTER 6
page 212

Oswestry

1

3

British Ironwork
Centre

Perry

Morda

Morda

Stonehouse
Brewery

8

Maesbury
Marsh

Montgomery Canal

A5

10

Llanyblodwel

9

Llynclys

A495

B4396

12

Knockin

B4397

11

Llanymynech Lime Kiln
Heritage Area

Pant

14

Ruyton-XI-Towns

B4398

Llanymynech

13

Mulberry Alpacas

15

NESSCLIFFE HILL

A483

Vyrnwy

A5

WALES

B4393

16

Melverley

Severn

SHREWSBURY

CHAPTER 4
page 154

N

0   3 miles

0   6km

5

OSWESTRY &
NORTHWEST SHROPSHIRE

Until the 1536 Act of Union, Oswestry belonged to Wales. Nearly 500 years later many people here still identify as Welsh: you'll overhear lovely lilting accents all over the region and see road signs rendered in Welsh as well as English. Life in this fiercely fought-over border country is peaceful now, of course, although I've seen some ITV regional news footage from 1972 in which several shoppers insisted Oswestry was in Wales and were surprised, if not affronted, to be told otherwise.

Spectacular views over Cymru can be found at the churchyard in Welsh Frankton and on Racecourse Common. On the fourth hole at Llanymynech Golf Club you can tee off in England and putt out in Wales.

Nevertheless, the temptation to describe Oswestry (or Croesoswallt, to use its Welsh name) as a gateway to Wales serves an injustice to the many attractions within the English border, especially the town itself with its lively café culture, Wilfred Owen heritage and exceptional hillfort. At Whittington you'll find Britain's first community-run castle, while the partially restored Montgomery Canal allows us to enjoy a horse-drawn cruise. This compact region has several special churches, including the black-and-white oak-framed St Peter's at Melverley and St John the Baptist, the 'tin tabernacle' in Maesbury. We also have heritage railways. The Cambrian Heritage Railway has a museum in Oswestry and operates rides from the town as well as at Llynclys. At the time of writing the group working to revive Tanat Valley Light Railway was building a new platform in time for the railway's 150th anniversary; operating dates will be listed at ⊘ www.nantmawrvisitorcentre.co.uk.

So don't go racing up to Chirk or overlook Oswestry on your way to Lake Vyrnwy. Stay awhile, enjoy the scenery, meet the alpacas. This is England, but with a uniquely Welsh twist.

This chapter covers the area that constituted the pre-2009 Borough of Oswestry, plus Nesscliffe Hill due to its proximity to the area.

GETTING THERE & AROUND

The small town of Gobowen, three miles north of Oswestry, has the only station served by a mainstream **railway** in this region: it's on the Shrewsbury to Chester line which runs south to Shrewsbury, Cardiff Central and Birmingham New Street, and north to Wrexham General, Chester and Holyhead. Oswestry is well connected by **bus**: the Arriva service number 70 from Shrewsbury is particularly useful as it stops at Nesscliffe and Whittington *en route* to the town's bus station on Oswald Road. Arriva service number 53 heads into Ellesmere in north Shropshire, stopping at Park Hall, Gobowen and St Martin's.

National Express operates one service a day to and from London (stopping also at Telford and Shrewsbury).

See *Getting there & around* in *Chapter 6* for details of canals.

WALKING

One of Britain's most famous walking routes passes through this region: Offa's Dyke Path enters Shropshire at Bronygarth and heads west of Oswestry towards Llanymynech (see page 199).

Oswald's Trail (⚲ www.oswestryramblers.org.uk) is a 12½-mile walking route around Oswestry, conceived by the Ramblers' Association Oswestry Group. Divided into five shorter sections, it takes in several sights included in this chapter, including Racecourse Common and Old Oswestry Hillfort – both excellent places for revitalising walks and wonderful views.

Ron Bond, who kindly supplied the route to Selattyn Tower on pages 202–3, has written three informative walking guides to the area, available from Booka (page 197) and the Visitor & Exhibition Centre in Oswestry. Other great places for walks, as gentle or exhilarating as you choose, are Llanymynech Lime Kiln Heritage Area, accessed via Pant, and Nesscliffe Hill, where afterwards you can reward yourself with a perfect pub lunch at the Old Three Pigeons.

This region is covered by ❋ OS Explorer map 240.

CYCLING

Oswestry is on National Cycle Network route 455, a peaceful 28-mile journey connecting Oswestry, Gobowen, Ellesmere and Whitchurch. The 'North West' stretch of Shropshire Council's Shropshire Cycleway routes will take you through Oswestry past the meres of north Shropshire and over to Whitchurch. For leaflets on both see the cycling section of ⌖ www.shropshiresgreatoutdoors.co.uk.

Around Oswestry many of the roads are quiet: from the town you could devise scenic routes to Selattyn or Llanymynech Lime Kiln Heritage Area. To encourage more women into cycling, Claire Barkley of Stuart Barkley Cycles in Oswestry organises ladies-only bike events called Bike with Claire (see ⌖ www.oswestrycycles.co.uk for more details).

BIKE SALES & REPAIRS

BikeWorks 93 Beatrice St, Oswestry SY11 1HL ✆ 01691 654407 ⌖ www. bikeworksoswestry.co.uk. Specialists in mountain bikes, plus accessories, clothing and spares. The workshop can offer a same-day turnaround on many repair jobs.
Stuart Barkley Cycles Salop Rd, Oswestry SY11 2NR ✆ 01691 658705 ⌖ www. oswestrycycles.co.uk. A family business trading for over 30 years, now run by husband and wife team Peter and Claire Barkley. They offer a click and collect service on new bikes through their website, and a wealth of cycling information (plus a repair service) in store.

HORSERIDING

If you're a novice rider or don't have a horse of your own, Penycoed Horse Riding Centre in Llynclys is the place to start. They have around 20 horses and ponies to suit all abilities (♿ and are especially keen to help nervous riders and people with disabilities) become confident in the saddle. With miles of bridleways near to a nature reserve at Llynclys and easy access to Llanymynech, they can take you out on an hour-long ride without encountering any roads. The site also has four heated log cabins and offers 'bring your own horse' holidays for experienced riders.

Route 7 of the Humphrey Kynaston Way starts at Nesscliffe: see ⌖ www.shropshireriding.co.uk.

TOURIST INFORMATION

Oswestry Mile End Visitor Information Centre Mile End Services, Oswestry SY11 4JA ✆ 01691 662488 ◷ summer 09.00–16.00, Sat 10.00–16.00; winter 09.30–15.30, Sat 10.00–14.00. Always closed Wed & Sun.
Oswestry Visitor & Exhibition Centre 2 Church Terrace, Oswestry SY11 2TE ✆ 01691 662753 ◷ summer 10.00–16.30 Mon–Sat; winter 10.00–16.00 Mon–Sat

JUST OVER THE BORDER

- **Chirk Castle** National Trust
- **Lake Vyrnwy Nature Reserve & Estate**
- **Pontcysyllte Aqueduct & Canal World Heritage Site** www.pontcysyllte-aqueduct.co.uk
- **Rodney's Pillar**, Breidden Hills

HORSE HIRE & RIDING LESSONS

Penycoed Horse Riding Centre 01691 830608 www.penycoedridingstables.co.uk.
Springhill Farm Riding Stables Springhill Farm, Selattyn SY10 7NZ 01691 718406
www.springhillfarm.co.uk. Located near the Welsh border, Springhill Farm offers pony sessions, riding lessons, longer trail rides and riding holidays especially aimed at teenagers. The bunkhouse sleeping up to 21 people would make an excellent base for families and friends on an activity break.

WET-WEATHER ACTIVITIES

Showroom at the British Ironwork Centre (page 200)
Cambrian Antiques Emporium (page 197)
Beer tasting at Stonehouse Brewery (page 199)
Willow Gallery in Oswestry (page 197)

OSWESTRY & AROUND

Pen-y-Dyffryn Country Hotel, Rhydycroesau (page 250)

Oswestry's narrow streets of terraced houses, which grew up with the dawn of railway in the town, swiftly yield to big Victorian and Edwardian residences and then rural lanes and verdant, open countryside. The low stone walls, gently hilly landscape and fields of grazing sheep will inevitably remind one of being in mid Wales – and of course you may well be soon.

Oswestry's name is thought to be a corruption of Oswald's Tree. The grisly legend goes that Oswald the King of Northumbria fought a great battle near here in AD641 against Penda, the pagan King of Mercia. Penda defeated and killed Oswald and, as warning to those who might challenge his rule, dismembered his body and hung his limbs from the branches of a tree. Another version is that a raven carried one of Oswald's severed arms to a nearby ash tree. St Oswald's Well, just off

Maserfield Road in Oswestry (although several wells are dedicated to St Oswald, including those in Cheshire, North Yorkshire and Cumbria), is said to have sprung up where the bird dropped the arm.

1 OSWESTRY

🏠 **Sebastians** (page 250)

Many Oswestry place names conjure images of the turbulent past: English Walls, Welsh Walls, Bailey Head. Behind the latter, near the marketplace, are the scant remains of Oswestry Castle, first built around 1085 and razed, re-raised and razed again in the following centuries.

In 1559 a plague killed almost a third of the town's population. A hollowed-out cuboid stone, known as the Croeswylan Stone (set into the boundary wall of The Marches School on Morda Road), marks the place near which markets were held at the time. Some people think the stone was the base of a wayside weeping cross, while others say money was washed in the hollow to prevent contamination.

Today the town markets are plague-free and thriving: the indoor and outdoor market at Bailey Head takes place on Wednesday, Friday and Saturday, with the farmers' market on the last Friday of

> *"Many Oswestry place names conjure images of the turbulent past: English Walls, Welsh Walls, Bailey Head. Behind the latter, near the marketplace, are the scant remains of Oswestry Castle."*

the month. When it comes to shops, several chainstores have suffered a decline in recent years and, as with many British high streets, many empty units stare blankly at passers-by. But independent gems may be found amid the closed businesses, including Booka, one of the best indie bookshops in the country.

The Booka team is instrumental in organising Oswestry's **LitFest** which takes place in March, around the time of Wilfred Owen's birthday. The festival brings a raft of well-known writers and speakers to the town.

To learn more about the history of Oswestry, you could join a town tour, taking place at 11.00 every Saturday from Easter to September. Just turn up at the Visitor Centre.

Oswestry Town Museum (☺ Apr–Oct 10.30–13.00 Tue, Wed, Fri & Sat) in Oswestry Town Hall is mainly of local interest, telling Oswestry's stories through civic documents and artefacts. The guides are friendly and a small activity room may keep young children amused.

Church of St Oswald & around

St Oswald's (or the church of St Oswald, King and Martyr to use its full title) is a centrepiece for Oswestry. Its oldest part is the tower, thought to be Norman, which was used as an observation point by Parliamentarians during the Civil War, in which the church was severely damaged. Mounted on the north wall is a stone monument to the Yale family, relatives of the Welsh merchant Elihu Yale who was benefactor to a college in Connecticut; known today as the prestigious Yale University.

Oswestry Visitor & Exhibition Centre (⊙ Mon–Sat) is set within the churchyard. This handsome timber-framed building used to be called Holbache House and was the site of Oswestry's first school (founded in 1407). The Oxford don William Archibald Spooner was educated

WILFRED OWEN (1893–1918)

Oswestry's most famous son is the poet and soldier Wilfred Owen, whose writing on the 'pity of war' now shapes our collective cultural memory about what it meant to serve in World War I. Born to Tom and Susan Owen in a house called Plas Wilmot, Owen experimented with poetry from a young age but was virtually unknown in literary circles during his lifetime, publishing only four poems. Enlisted to the Army in 1915, it was while convalescing from injury and shellshock in Edinburgh's Craiglockhart War Hospital that Owen met Siegfried Sassoon. A few years older than Owen, and already established as a poet, Sassoon would have a profound influence on the work for which Owen is remembered: angry, bitter, and deploring of life on the frontline.

Owen returned to active service in France in the late summer of 1918 and was awarded the Military Cross for bravery in October 1918. He was killed by German machine gunfire, aged 25, while building a pontoon bridge over the Sambre-Ors canal. His death came exactly one week before the war ended. The Owens, who now lived in Shrewsbury, received the dreaded telegram as the bells rang out for Armistice Day.

You'll find memorials to Wilfred Owen at Shrewsbury Abbey and here in Oswestry. Above a stone bench on Broad Walk near St Oswald's Church (the avenue linking Church Street with Welsh Walls), a commemorative plaque is inscribed with Owen's poignant 'Anthem for Doomed Youth' and 'Futility'. A leaflet outlining a self-guided tour, the Wilfred Owen Town Trail, is available from the Visitor & Exhibition Centre, taking you to Oswestry sites that include Wilfred Owen Green (accessed by the side of Sainsbury's) with its wildflower meadows, wooden play equipment and children's labyrinth.

To find out about readings, talks and other events relating to this extraordinary man, visit the Wilfred Owen Association website at ⊘ www.wilfredowen.org.

there, he who became famous for muddling up consonants, vowels or morphemes and giving rise to the term spoonerism. The house has also been used in turns as a workhouse, laundry and residential dwellings. Today it's a valuable place for planning your visit to Oswestry, the rest of Shropshire and Wales; it also houses a tea room and, upstairs, a small museum and gallery of mainly civic items.

Cae Glas Park

Pass through the imposing memorial gates dedicated to Oswestry's war fallen and you'll find yourself in the seven-acre Cae Glas Park. Alongside neat bedding and lawns are facilities that include a play area, bowling green, tennis courts, bandstand, pavilion, toilets and cheaply priced mini golf. You'll also find African giraffes and British red deer – highly tame as they're forged from iron, sponsored by the British Ironwork Centre (page 200) and part of the Oswestry Urban Safari Adventure Trail (⌀ www.oswestrysafaritrail.co.uk).

Cambrian Heritage Railways Museum

Oswald Rd, SY11 1RE ⌀ 01691 688763 ⌀ www.cambrianrailways.com ☉ Easter–Sep 11.00–15.00 Tue–Fri plus during special events; free; parking £2 all day; cycle stands in forecourt

Oswestry is – or was – a town of great importance where six major roads converge and, in the 19th century, where Cambrian Railways built its headquarters. Housed now in an 1860s goods depot is the Cambrian Heritage Railways (CHR) Museum, crammed with signs, lamps, photographs and other memorabilia from Oswestry's great age of rail.

Next door the fine Italianate Cambrian station building stands testimony to the importance of the town in the Victorian era. Recently restored, the ♿ wheelchair-accessible building now contains a friendly café with carriage booth-style seating: perfect for a strong cuppa and chip butty on a chilly afternoon. Short train rides commence from this site on heritage days, as well as from the CHR's Llynclys site (page 206). Exciting future plans may see an eight-mile section of the line opened up, connecting Oswestry and Llynclys and joining with the main Network Rail line at Gobowen. Would-be engine drivers: look for details of affordable Drive a Train courses on the CHR website.

"The CHR Museum is crammed with signs, lamps and photographs from Oswestry's great age of rail."

BARBARA PYM (1913–80)

A blue plaque at the former site of 72 Willow Street in Oswestry tells us this was the birthplace of novelist Barbara Pym. I wouldn't call Pym a forgotten author, for many articulate voices still extol her virtues (see ⊘ www.barbara-pym.org), but she's not as well remembered as her talent should demand. Even while living she endured a spell of obscurity, until Philip Larkin and Lord David Cecil in the January 1977 *Times Literary Supplement* described her as 'the most underrated novelist of the century'. The same year her *Quartet in Autumn* was shortlisted for the Booker Prize. Sometimes compared to Jane Austen's, Pym's writing feels arrestingly modern even now, conjuring parochial worlds, populating them with ordinary people and poking gentle fun at the absurdities of their behaviour. To quote Larkin again, she was 'a chronicler of quiet lives'.

Pym studied in Liverpool and at Oxford, served in the Women's Royal Naval Service in World War II and worked in London for many years before moving to Oxfordshire. But Shropshire's influence is present in her novels. Her mother Irena was assistant organist at St Oswald's in Oswestry, for example, and the clergymen who visited their family home found their way into many of her stories.

Pym's father Frederic had a solicitors' practice which is still in operation today on Willow Street: look for the brass sign bearing the names Crampton Pym & Lewis.

Old Oswestry Hillfort

Follow Llwyn Rd from Oswestry by foot or, if driving, park for free at the Gatacre Pavilion: SY11 1DR; free access ♿ not easily accessible due to steps & steepness of location

Ten minutes' walk from the town centre, unexpected in its location behind a crowded housing estate, stands a testament to the Iron Age in northwest Shropshire. Old Oswestry Hillfort is a 3,000-year-old settlement and one of Britain's best-preserved hillforts, with clear multiple ramparts and mysterious ditches. In late summer blackberries grow in the thickets. A circuit of the hillfort takes 30–40 minutes, which is energising in the wind and rewards you on clear days with views of Nesscliffe to the southeast and Wrexham to the north as well as glimpses of Wat's Dyke. (This rampart and ditch, similar to Offa's Dyke, runs from Dee Estuary to Morda Brook, south of the town. Wat's Dyke Way is a 61-mile waymarked trail from Llanymynech in Powys to Holywell in Flintshire: see ⊘ www.watsdykeway.org.)

At the time of writing plans for a large housing development in the hillfort's vicinity were being sternly opposed by local campaigners, working under the banner of HOOOH (Hands off Old Oswestry Hillfort).

🎭 ARTS

Kinokulture 9 Arthur St ✆ 01691 238167 ⬧ www.kinokulture.org.uk. Oswestry's independent community cinema, seating 79 people.

Willow Gallery 56 Willow St ✆ 01691 657575 ⬧ willowgalleryoswestry.wordpress.com. The former premises of a used car showroom are perfect for not-for-profit Willow Gallery, offering a light and contemporary space for exhibitions, workshops and art classes. The independently run, licensed café serves light, locally sourced lunches (quiches, salads, cakes), while the small craft shop stocks handmade cards and small gifts. Regular events alongside the art exhibitions include live music.

🛍 SHOPPING

Booka 26–28 Church St ✆ 01691 662244 ⬧ www.bookabookshop.co.uk. If browsing a well-curated bookshop makes you feel cheerier, warmer and full of resolutions (in my case: read more, scribble more, buy thoughtful gifts and wrap them neatly in hand-printed paper), then indie bookshop Booka is for you. Its many prizes include Independent Bookshop of the Year from the Bookseller Industry Awards. If you need further excuses to visit, Booka houses a small café and hosts regular literary events and author signings.

Cambrian Antiques Emporium Cambrian Works, Gobowen Rd ✆ 01691 652257. Located in one of Oswestry's former railway buildings, Cambrian Antiques Emporium is 8,000 square feet full of antiques, collectables and vintage items, with the bonus of delicious homemade cakes in the Cambrian Coffee Lounge (where everything on display is for sale). ♿ Cambrian Coffee Lounge is up a steep staircase, but downstairs seating is available: just ask.

Upstairs Downstairs 35–37 Leg St ✆ 01691 658591 ⬧ www.globalcookshop.co.uk. A specialist cook shop hosting reasonably priced workshops in everything from basic kitchen and knife skills to Moroccan, Greek, Italian or French cuisine, and lots more.

🍴 FOOD & DRINK

The Curious Tea Room 11 English Walls ✆ 07508 148297 ⊙ 10.00–17.00 Mon–Sat. Packed with nostalgia and knick-knacks (much of which is available to buy), this tea room serves ethically sourced teas and coffee in bone china teacups to a soundtrack of vinyls drifting out from an old record player. Snacks and light lunches (soup, toasties, sarnies and slabs of cake) are available too – and I'm a fan of their ice cream milkshakes.

Gillhams 27 Church St ✆ 01691 653187. This welcoming delicatessen and coffee shop is the birthplace of the heavy and delicious Coopers Gourmet Sausage Roll. In 2009 Gillhams owner Ivan Watkiss saw a way to diversify through the recession and disappeared into his kitchen to create the perfect sausage roll. Judging by their delicious taste, and the huge number of Coopers stockists from Whitchurch to Weston Park (and outside Shropshire, in the upmarket foodhall of Harrods), I think he succeeded at both.

Sebastians Restaurant with Rooms 45 Willow St ✐ 01691 655444 ◔ 18.30–21.30 for dinner Tue–Sat. Often cited by local people as their special place to go for a celebratory dinner, Sebastians is one of Shropshire's longest established fine-dining restaurants, serving French cuisine. For best value, look for the mid-week market menu.

Townhouse 35 Willow St ✐ 01691 659499. The newest offering at the upmarket end of Oswestry's dining scene, with a French-inspired menu designed by the two Michelin-starred Michael Caines (executive chef at Gidleigh Park, Devon). A special place for afternoon tea.

Wot's Cookin' 24 Willow St ✐ 01691 652904. A chippy with chairs and waitress service, Wot's Cookin' is also a five-star member of the National Federation of Fish Friers. It uses gluten-free batter and sustainably caught fish.

2 RACECOURSE COMMON

♥ SJ258310; free car park at South Common off the B4580 ♿ mostly flat and easy going in places; Owens of Oswestry bus service 78 between Oswestry and Llansilin passes on Wed & Fri

Straddling the B4580 just northwest of Oswestry, on the plateau of a hillside called Cyrn y Bwch – the Horns of the Buck – Racecourse Common is a bracing place to walk off your Sunday lunch. On a clear day you can see across Shropshire and the Cheshire Plains to the east and Wales to the west: a double-headed stone horse shows you which way you're facing. Installed in the 1990s, this statue commemorates the common's history from the early 1700s to 1848 as the venue for an

"Visit in spring for bluebells or in early autumn when rowan trees are at their bright berry best."

annual race meeting. Chains were draped across the road separating North Common and South Common to stop carriages getting in the way of the races, while turf laid on the road provided grip for horses' flying hooves as they thundered the two-mile, figure-of-eight circuit. Most of the famous families from the area were involved in some way at some time; John 'Mad Jack' Mytton (page 218) is known to have revelled with the best and worst of them. (The squire even named his son Euphrates after one of his winning horses.) Spectators who could afford it cheered from the stone grandstand, the ruins of which you can see today. They're ruins because in the 1840s the races became rowdy with drinking and rife with pickpockets. There was a dramatic reduction in revenue generated by entrance fees and rents from stallholders, and the emergence of railway meant punters could reach larger meetings further afield, such as in Chester. The last race took place in 1848 and the racecourse was

OFFA'S DYKE

King Offa's kingdom of Mercia stretched from the Trent and Mersey rivers in the north of England to the Thames Valley in the south; from the Welsh border in the west to the Fens in the east. His 'Dyke' (or the earthwork attributed to him) runs on or nearby the border between England and Wales, consisting of a ditch and rampart, with the ditch on the Welsh-facing side. When constructed it would have been around 89 feet wide; the rampart up to 26 feet high. About 80 miles of the original earthwork survive.

Offa's Dyke Path is classed as a National Trail, running for 177 glorious miles along or near the earthwork, through moors, river valleys and woodland from the Severn estuary just south of Chepstow in Monmouthshire to the north Wales coast at Prestatyn in Denbighshire.

Shropshire has two sections of the trail: up here in northwest Shropshire (from Bronygarth on the border with Wrexham down towards Llanymynech) and also in the south, heading down west of Bishop's Castle, past Newcastle (west of Clun) towards the path's halfway point at Knighton in Powys, where you'll find the **Offa's Dyke Centre** (see *Just over the border* on page 69).

If you're ready to take on King Offa there are numerous walking guides to aid and enhance your journey (the latest, Keith Carter and Henry Stedman's comprehensive *Offa's Dyke Path*, is published by Trailblazer). You'll also find circular walking routes taking in the National Trail at ⬧ www.shropshirewalking. co.uk/offas-dyke.

abandoned. But the loss of the races, of course, was nature's gain. Visit in spring for bluebells and tunnels of bracken, or in early autumn when rowan trees on South Common are at their bright berry best. Also look for holes burrowed by small mammals: moles, shrews, squirrels, rabbits, weasels and even polecats have made this grassland their home.

3 STONEHOUSE BREWERY

Weston SY10 9ES ✐ 01691 676457 ⬧ www.stonehousebrewery.co.uk ◔ bar & shop open 09.00–17.00 Mon–Thu, 09.00–19.00 Fri, 10.00–17.00 Sat; closed Sun & bank holidays

For traditionally brewed, highly drinkable cask beer, call in at the Stonehouse Brewery at Weston, just over a mile south of Oswestry, near Morda. This family business, started in 2007, is committed to *not* taking over the world; it supplies local pubs with SIBA award-winning beers whose names commemorate the old Cambrian Line on which the site is situated. You can buy bottle-conditioned beers (unpasteurised and fresh-tasting), polypins and jugs to take away, enjoy a pint in the brewery bar, or book a group tour and tasting session.

4 BRITISH IRONWORK CENTRE

Whitehall, Aston SY11 4JH ✆ 0800 6888386 ⌕ www.britishironworkcentre.co.uk ⊙ daily; free entry & parking ♿ fully accessible, although the ground outside is bumpy in places

Located off the A5 between Shrewsbury and Oswestry, the British Ironwork Centre provides a shopping experience with a difference – or just a happy afternoon out. Here you can browse the UK's largest collection of decorative metalwork: everything from life-size iron animals to ornate gazebos and carousel pavilions. The centre is also the site of the open-air **Museum of Steel Sculpture** (formerly located in Coalbrookdale, Ironbridge Gorge), showcasing the works of the late sculptor Roy Kitchin. Indoors, a packed but beautifully presented showroom stocks both functional and ornamental pieces for the home. The centre appears to be continually growing and evolving: recent additions are a café with chocolate counter, and **falconry displays** at weekends. Look out also for **experience workshops** in blacksmithing, farrier work and sculpting. The business has a strong social conscience and is dedicated to the preservation and creation of metalwork – a skill that could easily be lost with the decline in British manufacturing.

WHITTINGTON & NORTH OF OSWESTRY

Head north from Oswestry and you're in true marches territory. In early medieval times, before the 1536 Act of Union, Whittington was classed as being in Wales. There are some great – and too often overlooked – places to visit in this northwesterly patch of Shropshire, from the romantic ruins of **Whittington Castle** to the former mining town of St Martin's and its **nature reserve** reclaimed from spoil pits. From St Andrew's churchyard, set on the brow of the hilltop village of **Welsh Frankton** above the Montgomery Canal, you get wonderful views over north Shropshire, Cheshire and the Welsh hills.

5 WHITTINGTON

Whittington village and parish is dominated by the romantic ruins of its ancient castle: you can't miss the twin-towered outer gatehouse on your way through. The moat that half surrounds its hefty grey stone base is occupied by ducks and swans (and the occasional pike lurking beneath the water). Whittington is a worthwhile destination: the castle is free to visit and nearby **Park Hall the Countryside Experience** provides a fun day out for the very young.

Whittington International Chamber Music Festival takes place every May (𝒶 www.whittingtonmusicfestival.org.uk).

The nearest train station is Gobowen, two miles away. Whittington is also on the Arriva bus route D70 between Shrewsbury and Oswestry.

Whittington Castle

SY11 4DF ℰ 01691 662397 𝒶 www.whittingtoncastle.co.uk ☉ summer Wed–Sun, winter Fri–Sun 10.00–16.00; free public access to the castle grounds all year round; parking £1, reinvested in castle's upkeep

Welcome to England's first community-run castle. In 1998 the Whittington Castle Preservation Trust was granted a 99-year lease to protect the 12-acre site in perpetuity and manage it for educational and visitor benefits. The fabric of the ruins reveals many changes over time: the tower keep is 12th century but with later alterations, while the outer gatehouse was almost certainly built in the 13th century by Sir Fulk III Fitzwarin(e).

"Welcome to England's first community-run castle."

A nobleman who rebelled against King John and whose life as an outlaw inspired the French ancestral romance *Fouke le Fitz Waryn*, Fulk may also have influenced some of the Robin Hood legends.

Naturally, folklore about Whittington Castle abounds: one legend has it that the Marian Chalice – thought by some to be the Holy Grail – was once hidden in a private chapel of the castle. My favourite tale concerns a cursed Elizabethan wooden chest, allegedly given to the local parish council for safekeeping; its key lost in the moat.

As well as a **tea room** there's a small secondhand bookshop with proceeds going to the upkeep of the castle.

Park Hall the Countryside Experience

Burma Rd, SY11 4AS (for sat nav use Burma Rd) ℰ 01691 671123 𝒶 www.parkhallfarm. co.uk ☉ late Mar–late Sep 10.00–17.00 daily; Arriva bus 53 from Oswestry to Ellesmere stops nearby

Park Hall, a five-minute drive from Whittington (and only about eight minutes from Oswestry), feels to me faded yet thoughtfully run. Loved by its hordes of be-wellied young fans, it's predominantly a visitors' farm. With soft play, ride-on cars and small animal handling, families with children can easily fill a whole day here. Don't miss the comical pig races and, in spring, the chance to bottlefeed cade (orphaned) lambs. Park Hall is also home to a 'Victorian school' and museum as well as the Welsh Guards collection of uniforms and memorabilia. New for 2015 was an exhibition on World War I and II trenches. The **tea rooms** offer a good choice of freshly cooked food (including homemade cakes).

Walk to Selattyn Tower

Adapted from *Ron's Family Friendly Rambles*
with kind permission from Ron Bond

❄ OS Explorer map 240; start at small car park at Craignant ⚐ SJ254349; 2½ miles; moderately easy: track & field paths; stiles & gradual ascent uphill for over a mile, allow 1½ hours

This gentle and rewarding walk, close to the Welsh border, takes in a section of Offa's Dyke Path and the Shropshire Way to lead you to a Victorian tower built on the site of a Bronze Age burial cairn.

1 Leave the car park and turn right on the road. After 200 yards turn sharp right up the track which is signed from across the road as the Offa's Dyke Path. As you walk up the track you'll pass ancient quarry workings. Pass a sign for the Shropshire Way and instead keep going up the track. Arrive at a gate that has the notice, 'Woodside: please close gate'. Pass through the kissing-gate and continue up the track that becomes more grassy. Where the track goes right go straight on (the waymark is the acorn of the Offa's Dyke Path). The track now becomes totally grassy and passes between two tumbledown walls. When you arrive at another gate, go through it and head up into the open field to the corner of the hedge with a signpost. Go forward diagonally left to the corner of the wood with a signpost.

2 Go through the gate at the signpost – you're now leaving Offa's Dyke Path. At this point you'll see a Shropshire Way waymark. Look at the unusual information post. Pull the string and read the information about Selattyn Tower. You're now on the Shropshire Way. Walk ahead with the gorse and wood on your left until you reach a waymarked gate and stile in the left-hand corner. Go through it and right, across to Selattyn Tower. You get magnificent views at this point towards Cheshire.

3 Continue on the path right past the tower. Pass the information sign ('Selattyn Tower & Bronze Age Cairn') and head straight down across a track to small bench and a hidden kissing-gate. Go through the gate and down to the left-hand corner of a field. Go over the stile and walk with the wall on your right. At the corner of the wall continue down to the right-hand corner of the field. Go through the next kissing-gate and downhill left for a few yards to a waymarked post.

6 SELATTYN

🏠 **Springhill Farm Riding Stables & Accommodation** (page 250)

I've included Selattyn, three miles northwest of Oswestry, because of a special tower (to which the walk below will take you) and a cherished drinking pub. **Selattyn Tower** was built on a Bronze Age burial cairn by one Mr Crewe in 1847, to commemorate the 6th-century Prince Gwen

Look for the ruined remains of a shepherd's house. Pass the post into a grassy former drovers' road. Follow it down to the corner.

4 Cross to the left and then on the restricted byway walk across to the kissing-gate in the corner. The great views continue at this point. Go through the gate and walk on the enclosed path until it reaches a made-up track.

5 There's a large signpost here, pointing back towards Selattyn Hill. Turn left as indicated by the Shropshire Way waymark. Walk up the track to reach a large waymarked field gate on the right at a gate to the house ahead. Bear right through the field gate and head diagonally up the field to the far top-left corner. Arrived at another field gate. Go through it and head diagonally right to the stile in the far corner (it may be obscured slightly at first and the field may be very grassy). Head over the stile and walk left for ten yards. Turn right and, picking up the faint path through a scrubby area, cross to the large waymarked field gate. Go through it and walk ahead across a field below a house on left to a gate in the top-left corner. Go through the gate and straight ahead over a small field to a visible stile in the wall. Go over and down with the fence on your right. Keep going right down into the corner. Find the stile. Go over the stile and down the path to the track you started out on just after the car park.

6 Turn right and walk down to the road. Turn left and in 200 yards arrive back at the start.

killed at a nearby battle. In World War II the Home Guard used the tower to spot enemy aircraft heading for Liverpool.

The walk featured starts a few hundred yards away from Selattyn in the hamlet of Craignant, where a farming family in 2003 began bottling the fresh spring water they'd been drinking for three generations. Craignant Water is now sold all over the country.

¶¶ FOOD & DRINK

The Cross Keys Glyn Rd, Selattyn SY10 7DH ✆ 01691 653347. This cosy 17th-century inn is so loved that when landlord Phil Rothera was recovering from cancer a few years ago, locals stepped in to do unpaid shifts and keep the pub open. No food, but you'll often find live music in the evenings.

7 ST MARTIN'S

This former mining village four miles north of Whittington is a great destination for a walk followed by a hearty dinner, thanks to **Ifton Meadows Nature Reserve** and, north of the village on the B5069, a relaxed pub. The former is located on the old spoil heaps of Ifton Colliery, giving beautiful views of the Dee Valley and Welsh mountains. You can find it by taking the first turning left after Stan's Supermarket, then following brown Nature Reserve signs to the small car park (♿ accessible; Radar key needed for kissing-gate). The latter is the **Greyhound Inn** (SY11 3HD ✆ 01691 774307). So many menu options are scrawled on to the blackboards here, it's easy to assume they're bought in and heated up. But I checked, and almost everything is made from scratch. The chocolate brownie is a must.

"Ifton Meadows Nature Reserve is located on the old spoil heaps of Ifton Colliery, giving beautiful views of the Dee Valley and Welsh mountains."

MAESBURY & SOUTH OF OSWESTRY

This green and rolling pocket of northwest Shropshire lies snug against the Powys border, but is not to be overlooked on your way into Wales. One of my family's favourite days of an entire summer comprised lunch at the Navigation Inn at Maesbury Marsh followed by a horse-drawn boat cruise along the Montgomery Canal.

8 MAESBURY MARSH

The Stables (page 250), **St Winifred's Well**, Woolston (page 250)

About three miles southeast of Oswestry, the parish of Maesbury is fairly large, with the Montgomery Canal running serenely through it. The area featured here centres predominantly around **Maesbury Marsh**, which began life as a small cargo handling community where road meets canal. Just up the road at Maesbury village is the diminutive white corrugated iron **church of St John the Baptist**. Affectionately known as the 'tin tabernacle' (although presumably not to French Quebec speakers who would consider this a profanity of the rudest order), St John's is rumoured to have come from Harrods, arriving in kit form on a lorry in 1906 at a cost of £120 and assembled at its present site by two men.

Canal Central

Canal Central (page 249)

SY10 8JG ✆ 01691 652168 🖱 www.canalcentral.co.uk ◷ Wed–Sun

Cross a hump-backed bridge over the Montgomery Canal at Maesbury Marsh to reach this special place. Canal Central is focused around a **tea room** and **shop** in an environmentally friendly building, but represents a great deal more to holidaymakers enjoying the Montgomery Canal, and locals who appreciate having convenient access to local fresh produce (including bacon, sausages, organic eggs and milk – all of which feature in the wholesome tea room menu). A 7¼-inch **miniature gauge engine** running around a 400-yard track has recently been installed.

Bywater Cruises

Canal Central, SY10 8JG ✆ 01691 777738 🖱 www.bywatercruises.com ◷ Easter–Oct Fri–Sun & bank holiday Mon (cruises at 12.00, 14.00 & 15.30) ♿ phone ahead if you have accessibility needs

A force of 1hp would be decidedly unimpressive in the motoring world, but when 1hp is effected by a miniature shire gelding called Cracker and he's towing you along in a Victorian-style packet boat down the peaceful Montgomery Canal, suddenly it's all the speed you need. Bywater Cruises is run by Tim Barker and family, operating from the separately owned Canal Central site. Take an hour-long cruise in 35-foot *Countess*, or charter your own picnic or BBQ experience. The boat is party to seven miles of navigable canal, but for public cruises tends to head southwest for a mile and a half before turning around. 'It feels as though we've returned to a simpler age,' said one of my fellow passengers, travelling with her two grandchildren. All we could hear was birdsong – sedge warblers and reed buntings – and the swish of *Countess* gliding towards Redwith Bridge. In our eyeline were colourful barges, a proud duck leading her ducklings and, on the towpath, Cracker's companion, a Jack Russell called Rosie who scampered at his heels. Cracker the Boat Horse has his own Facebook page where he once corrected me on the colour of his coat: this little gelding is not grey, it seems, but a distinguished shade of strawberry roan.

¶¶ FOOD & DRINK

The Navigation Inn Maesbury Marsh SY10 8JB ⌀ 01691 672958. One of my favourite pubs in Shropshire: the atmosphere is laid back, wellies and well-behaved dogs are welcome, the beer is kept beautifully and the food is delicious and sourced locally and responsibly. You can choose from the rustic Bargee's menu (which includes sandwiches and warming favourites such as Welsh beef steak and chips) or choose the more formal Warehouse restaurant for upscale dining. Virtually everything served here is made in house, while the line-up of traditional cask ales changes weekly (the one constant being Cambrian Gold from Stonehouse Brewery). The pub also stocks local produce to take away – especially useful for canal boaters.

9 CAMBRIAN HERITAGE RAILWAYS AT LLYNCLYS

Llynclys South Station, Llynclys SY10 8BX ⌀ 07527 107592 ⌂ www.cambrianrailways.com
◴ see online timetable for open days

Five miles south of Oswestry is the small village of Llynclys where you'll find the second site of **Cambrian Heritage Railways**. On certain days you can ride in a vintage, usually steam-hauled carriage for about three-quarters of a mile between Llynclys and Pant (Pen-y-garreg halt). The journey doesn't take long, but nor does it cost much, and you'll be supporting CHR's efforts to reinstate the line between Oswestry and Pant and boost the region's economy. A **tea room** serving tea, coffee and toast operates from a stationary carriage run by friendly volunteers.

▣ SHOPPING

Llynclys Hall Farm Shop Llynclys Hall SY10 8AD ⌀ 01691 652434 ◴ daily (reduced hours on Sun). If you love farm shops to be authentically rustic, with radishes still field-bright and carrots topped and muddy, then stop at Llynclys Hall Farm off the A483. Richard and Lynda Jones sell their own crops in this charming shop, as well as produce from other local suppliers (including eggs, locally made pies and fresh bread, Jamie Ward's meats, Great Ness rapeseed oil and Welsh honey). In October this is the place for sourcing Halloween pumpkins.

10 LLANYBLODWEL

Seven miles southwest of Oswestry, in the valley of the River Tanat, is the village of Llanyblodwel and a church which Nikolaus Pevsner deemed 'bizarre' and 'unforgettable'. Thanks to work carried out by a Victorian vicar, St Michael the Archangel has a revivalist gothic stone tower which looks like a rocket about to zoom into space and, inside, bold stencilled decorations and passages of scripture.

11 LLANYMYNECH LIME KILN HERITAGE AREA

🏠 **Greystones**, Crickheath (page 249), **Penycoed Horse Riding Centre's log cabins**, Pant (page 250) ⛺ **Underhill Farm**, Pant (page 250)
Small car park at Underhill Lane, Pant (off the A483), SY22 6HD ⊝ free access; Shropshire Wildlife Trust

The village of Pant, whose name means 'hollow' in Welsh, is just a damselfly's wingtip into the English side of the Welsh border, nestling in the shade of the disused limeworks of neighbouring Llanymynech. Here, a unique coming-together of history, industry and nature means a site of former lime kilns and quarries, close to the Montgomery Canal, is now dense with natural woodland (ash trees swathed in wild clematis, or old man's beard). Its diverse wildlife includes pyramidal, common spotted and bee orchids, and peregrine falcons who build their eyries in the rock ledges (prompting restrictions on human climbers who understandably revel in the varied routes afforded by 100-foot quarry faces). The priority butterfly species, pearl-bordered fritillary, was reintroduced on the

"The village of Pant, whose name means 'hollow' in Welsh, is just a damselfly's wingtip into the English side of the Welsh border."

Welsh side of the reserve recently and is thought to be thriving, enjoying the new-found light created by carefully managed tree felling. Like the butterflies, you can pass freely between England and Wales: a wooden kissing-gate tells you where the border lies. Just into Wales, an attractive toposcope in hammered stainless steel highlights landmarks in the view over the serene Severn-Vyrnwy plain to the Breidden Hills and even The Wrekin.

Above you, surrounded by sheer cliff drops, is **Llanymynech Golf Club** and the only course in Europe to straddle two countries. On the fourth hole, you can have one leg in England and the other in Wales. Of special industrial interest are replica brake drum houses, which controlled the descent of blasted limestone-filled trucks, and the Hoffman Kiln down towards Llanymynech village (one of only three remaining in the UK and unique in retaining its chimney). In the past the kilns here were used for burning limestone to become the chalky substance calcium oxide (also known as quicklime) used as fertiliser and in mortar and plaster.

Three walks of varying ability are outlined on the interpretive panel at the Pant car park: ♿ the short walk has fairly level surfaced paths and on dry days would be suitable for buggies and wheelchairs. **Offa's Dyke path** runs close to the western side of the heritage area.

12 KNOCKIN

Seven miles southeast of Oswestry is Knockin, a quiet village of handsome old detached houses. The gigantic, alien-looking transmitter you might see in a field is one of the Jodrell Bank MERLIN radio telescopes, used to send data to the University of Manchester for the UK government's Science and Technology Facilities Council. As you travel through Knockin on the B4396, watch out for the Knockin Shop. Depending on their predilections, people are usually relieved or disappointed to hear that it's only a convenience store.

13 MULBERRY ALPACAS

Å Cranberry Moss, Kinnerley (page 249)
Mulberry Cottage, Knockin Heath SY10 8ED ✆ 01691 682757 ⌂ www.mulberryalpacas.co.uk ⊙ 10.00–16.00 Sat & by appointment

At Knockin Heath – which lies between Knockin and Nesscliffe – there's a family smallholding called Mulberry Alpacas. Harry and Roz Edwards bought their first three alpaca 'boys' when their daughter Chloe was five, as a way of enhancing family time and to guard their chickens from a persistent fox. Nearly ten years later, they have almost twenty huacaya alpacas, including a gentle black stud named Inca Grampian from whom they're breeding more.

'It's a hobby that's just expanded,' said Harry, who by day works as a chaplain for Severn Hospice. Judging by the love and care he,

Roz and Chloe lavish on their alpacas, I can tell he'd be comforting to have around during life's hardest moments. The family are closely involved with the British Alpaca Society which held a national show in Telford – and the show adopted Severn Hospice as its nominated charity.

Alpaca fibre is strong, silky, breathable, hypoallergenic and warmer than sheep's wool without being itchy. It's shorn once a year from the alpacas without hurting them. Mulberry Alpacas' **shop** sells gorgeously woven products (including hats, scarves, mittens, pillows and duvets) which are reasonably priced given the farm's relatively small yield of alpaca fur (and the intensive work that goes into spinning yarns, which is carried out at a mill in Scotland). The traceability is amazing: you can buy balls of yarn bearing the name of the alpaca they came from.

If you're interested in attending a spinning, knitting, felting or weaving class, do contact the Edwards family – or just drop by to say hello and meet their woolly beauties.

14 RUYTON-XI-TOWNS

This village on the River Perry – sometimes known as Ruyton of the XI Towns or simply as Ruyton – earned its unusual name in the 12th century when a castle established here became the manor for 11 local townships. Some of these townships survive as hamlets while others, such as Coton, are just a smattering of farm buildings. As a student of medicine Arthur Conan Doyle worked unpaid for a doctor in Ruyton for four months in 1878, later recalling that the place was 'not big enough to make one town, let alone eleven'. The castle stands as three ruined sandstone walls in the grounds of Ruyton's parish church, **St John the Baptist**. A local group secured Heritage Lottery Fund grants in 2007–08 to save the ruins from ivy and perilous neglect, and built new access paths. The elevated site no longer needs to defend England against plundering Welsh invaders, but it does offer a cracking view of the distant Welsh border, and Ruyton below. The small **post office and general store** along the road on Church Street stocks an impressive amount of local produce.

Ruyton-XI-Towns' parish war memorial takes the form of a cave, hewn from red sandstone; a tablet with the names of men from Ruyton who died during the two World Wars.

The village is served by the Arriva Midlands North **bus** route 70, which runs between Shrewsbury and Oswestry.

15 NESSCLIFFE HILL

Just off the A5 between Shrewsbury & Oswestry (♥ SJ390198). Arriva bus service number 70
stops outside the Old Three Pigeons (opposite); parking at Pine car park (♥ SJ389199)

Wonderful walking opportunities abound at Nesscliffe Hill, a sandstone
escarpment which is springy underfoot from the fallen needles of North
American redwoods and gloriously tangled with rhododendrons in
early summer.

With its proximity to the road running between Oswestry and
Shrewsbury, the hill was a handy 16th-century hideout for highwaymen,
including the notorious Humphrey Kynaston and Beelzebub his
steed, who are thought to have dwelt in a two-room cave carved from
the sandstone. Now home to Daubenton's, Natterer's and common
pipistrelle bats, the cave is closed to humans, but intriguing to view even
from a distance, especially when you know Kynaston's story (see below).
The vertical faces and exhilarating pitches around Nesscliffe make this a
popular spot for climbers.

'WILD' HUMPHREY KYNASTON THE HIGHWAYMAN

One of Shropshire's most dangerous characters may have lived in the red sandstone cave at Nesscliffe, alongside his trusty horse (who some say was named Beelzebub after the devil). Accounts of 'Wild' Humphrey Kynaston's colourful life vary but here are the most commonly collated 'facts' ...

Humphrey Kynaston was born a nobleman to Sir Roger Kynaston in c1474. He inherited Myddle Castle but through his reckless lifestyle and mounting debts it began falling into disrepair. Facing imprisonment for his part in the unprovoked murder of a man in Stretton Dale (Church Stretton), Kynaston fled to Nesscliffe with Beelzebub where he lived in the cave as an outlaw, using Nesscliffe Hill as a vantage point from which to apprehend merchant coaches on the Oswestry to Shrewsbury road.

The horse is as much of the legend as the highwayman. Kynaston's black steed is said to have jumped walls 12 feet in height, and once cleared the River Severn where the Montford Bridge was impassable. One story has Beelzebub's horseshoes shod back to front in order to confuse anyone trailing their movements.

Some say Kynaston lived like Robin Hood, robbing the rich to give to the poor, who repaid him with food. He regained his wealth and used his influence to support Henry VIII's military foray into France in 1513, an act which earned Kynaston a royal pardon in around 1516. He died in 1534, probably as an affluent man on his own estate in Welshpool.

FOOD & DRINK

The Old Three Pigeons SY4 1DB 🖉 01743 741279. This is where Humphrey Kynaston allegedly drank – and shot someone for sitting in his seat. His ghost is said to haunt the chair that's currently in the fireplace. Whether or not you believe the tales, this country pub exudes rural chic (low beams, polished wood, comfy sofas) and the homemade food is excellent. Tuesday night is gourmet burger night, while veggies will always find a separate and interesting menu just for them. Landlord Mike is establishing a microbrewery.

6 MELVERLEY

🏠 **Big Bear Lodge** (page 249), **River Cottage** (page 250)

At the confluence of the rivers Severn and Vyrnwy, offset by the inky silhouette of the Welsh Breidden hills, rests a very special church. Dating from 1406 (replacing an even earlier structure), **St Peter's** is black-and-white timbered inside and out; constructed from Melverley oak and pegged together in its entirety without use of a single nail. For this reason the gallery is sloping, a result of the mighty piece of wood settling over time. A bible on the lectern dates from 1727; chained because in the early 18th century people were reading more, yet books were still rare and expensive. Bats and small birds often fly into the church but must have a sense of reverence: they've never left droppings on the bible.

If you travel through Alberbury on your way to Melverley, look for the ruined castle tower (on private land).

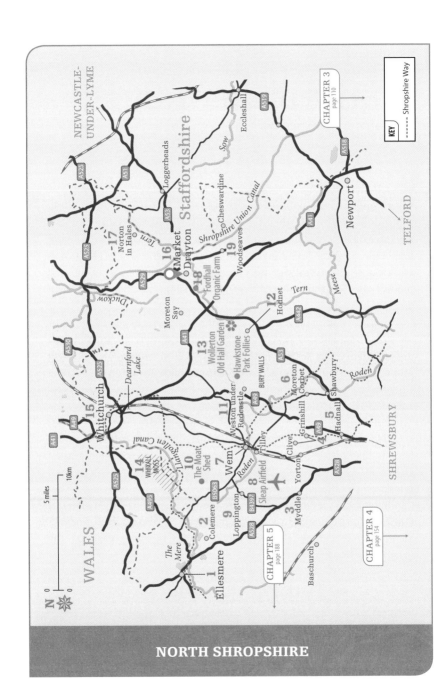

NORTH SHROPSHIRE

6
NORTH SHROPSHIRE

It may not have the pull of the Shropshire Hills Area of Outstanding Natural Beauty, the industrial legacy of Ironbridge Gorge or the romance of the Offa's Dyke Path through the Welsh Marches. But rural north Shropshire is full of natural wonders: nine glacial lakes known as **meres**, and scientifically important peat bogs (**mosses**) teeming with biodiversity. Its fertile soil and farming heritage yield delicious meat and produce.

North Shropshire has manmade beauty too: miles of canals and four market towns, Ellesmere, Wem, Whitchurch and Market Drayton, each distinctive in character. The latter is **Robert Clive** country, the stomping ground of a young ne'er do well who would grow up to become Commander in Chief of British India. It's also known for **gingerbread**: Clive is thought to have brought ginger back to the town from his travels.

In this region we have a **community-run organic farm** which won a David-and-Goliath battle against a multinational corporation, its tenants aged just 19 and 21 when their plight began. Nearby in Market Drayton is **Joule's Brewery**, reviving a tradition started by Augustinian monks (with a modern-day pledge never to sell to supermarkets). Other highlights include the Alice-in-Wonderland gardens of **Wollerton Old Hall**, 60 acres of landscaped splendour at **Hodnet Hall** and the country's first 'theme park', beloved by Victorian pleasure-seekers, at the mysterious **Hawkstone Park**.

GETTING THERE & AROUND

Wem and Whitchurch **railway** stations are on the Welsh Marches line, with regular trains running southbound to Shrewsbury and northbound to Crewe and, less frequently, longer distance services north to Manchester and south to Cardiff and eventually Carmarthen.

TOURIST INFORMATION

Ellesmere The Boathouse, Mereside, SY12 0PA ✆ 01691 622981 ☉ 10.00–17.00 daily
Market Drayton 49 Cheshire St, TF9 1PH ✆ 01630 653114 ☉ 09.30–16.00 Mon–Fri
Wem Town Hall, High St, SY4 5DG ✆ 01939 232299 ☉ 09.00–16.00 Mon–Sat, 08.00–16.00 Thu
Whitchurch Heritage Centre, 12 St Mary's St, SY13 1QY ✆ 01948 664577 ☉ 11.00–16.00 Tue, Thu, Fri

Trains run less frequently on Sundays. Yorton station on the same line is a request stop and perfectly positioned if you want to head out from Shrewsbury to explore Clive and Grinshill. Four fairly important towns in north Shropshire mean the area is well served by **buses**; I've listed routes where available under individual place listings. The Arriva bus service 511 between Shrewsbury and Whitchurch is useful, with stops at Hadnall, Clive and Wem, while the number 64 between Shrewsbury and Market Drayton stops conveniently at Battlefield and Hodnet.

Canals provide an alternative means of transport. The Shropshire Union Canal runs through Market Drayton, or you can navigate the Llangollen Canal branch through Whitchurch and Ellesmere, which joins the Montgomery Canal at Lower Frankton. Narrowboats can be hired from Whixall Marina. ♿ If a member of your party has a disability, illness or injury, or is very elderly, you may like to look up the **Lyneal Trust** (⚓ www.lyneal-trust.org.uk) which provides affordable day trips and holidays on accessible canal boats.

WALKING

The meres are great places to walk, with flat pathways and plenty of wildlife to spot. **The Mere** at Ellesmere is the obvious starting point, but I prefer **Colemere** for a circular, and somehow more satisfying, stroll. My small son loves this walk, finding dens in the trees and looking out for squirrels.

Towpath walks are another possibility: level, easy to navigate and with plenty of interest along the way. Do try the Market Drayton and Shropshire Union Canal walk on pages 240–2, which follows in the footsteps of the young Robert Clive. You could also follow Victoria Jubilee Park out of Whitchurch to reach the **Whitchurch Waterways Country Park**, an important site for water voles.

Heading down towards Shrewsbury, I love the thickly wooded **Grinshill** area for a ramble or amble – the view from the top is almost certain to lift you – followed by refreshment at the Inn at Grinshill. Completely different, but equally beautiful and very wild, is **Whixall Moss**, north of Wem. Visit the 9,000-year-old peat bog for level walking conditions amid an untouched landscape, with stories of grisly 19th-century discoveries and World War II decoys.

CYCLING

North Shropshire has fewer hills than the rest of the county, so cycling is more of a relaxed pastime up here. For a route through lanes relatively free from traffic you could take National Cycle Route 45 (known in Shropshire as the **Mercian Way**) up to Whitchurch from Shrewsbury, and then onwards into Cheshire. See also the North East stretch of Shropshire Council's **Shropshire Cycleway** routes which passes through Whitchurch and Market Drayton before heading south towards Newport. Both routes are outlined at ⏴ www.shropshiresgreatoutdoors.co.uk.

BIKE SALES

Brenin Bikes 79 Cheshire St, Market Drayton TF9 1PN ✆ 01630 656614 ⏴ www. breninbikes.co.uk. For high-end bikes and accessories – as well as fairtrade coffee for when you need a brew.
Jack Davies Cycles 58 High St, Wem SY4 5DW ✆ 01939 235485 ⊙ closed Wed & Sun. Sales and accessories.

HORSERIDING

At **The Moat Shed** near Wem (pages 228–9), riders can pay a small fee to access a cross-country course around the farm: there are seven wickets and five adjustable jumps, open when livestock and arable schedules permit.

Route 8 of the **Humphrey Kynaston Way** passes through the southern part of this region, near Harmer Hill and up to **Grinshill**: see ⏴ www. shropshireriding.co.uk for a detailed guide.

WET-WEATHER ACTIVITIES

Ellesmere Heronwatch and lunch at **the Boathouse** (page 218)
Mythstories museum in Wem (when open; page 226)
Sleap Airfield for plane spotting from the Lock Lounge (page 227)

ELLESMERE & SHROPSHIRE'S 'LAKE DISTRICT'

The word 'mere' crops up often on maps of this watery part of the country. Meres were formed in the last Ice Age when glaciers retreated, leaving gaping holes in their absence. No streams flow in or out of a mere – rather the water is leached from surrounding land, giving us a lake that is rich in nutrients and therefore diverse in plant, animal and insect life.

The area in and around Ellesmere has nine such glacial lakes and I'm sure whoever first came up with 'Shropshire's Lake District' to describe it was much congratulated. I'm not crazy about the name, though, feeling that it cannot help but draw unfair comparisons to the rugged fells and wild beauty of Cumbria, the landscape that fed Wordsworth's 'lofty speculations'. Besides, Ellesmere and its surroundings have a charm all their own – and the twin attraction of a canal heritage.

1 ELLESMERE
⌂ Mereside Farm (page 251)

Ellesmere was once an important trading town on the Llangollen Canal – so vital that the famous port at Merseyside, where canal meets estuary, was named in its honour. So as well as **The Mere** (page 217), which draws walkers and ducks to its shimmering presence, Ellesmere has the Welsh branch of the Shropshire Union Canal, attracting narrowboaters in need of refreshment.

Ellesmere's **market day** is Tuesday and the town has held regular markets since 1221, when its first charter was granted by Henry III. Today the high street feels a little run down but the shops that thrive here are mostly independent and family run. Look out for **Ellesmere Food Festival** in June.

Ellesmere's **church of the Blessed Virgin Mary** is usually closed outside worship times, but the churchyard – in its elevated position overlooking The Mere – is a peaceful spot. One area is kept as natural meadow, cut only in the summer by hand with a scythe. A profusion of wildflowers grows here, and lichen on many of the gravestones is indicative of the clean air. Notes on the churchyard (available inside for a small fee) recount an 18th-century challenge to keep rats out of the church: in 1760 buttered crumpets 'with ArsenNick' were left for the critters. On display inside are small mammal bones discovered in

JUST OVER THE BORDER

- **Audlem** Visit this village for canal towpath walks and a 15-lock drop
- **Barn Books** ⬦ www.barnbooks.co.uk
- **The Dorothy Clive Garden** ⬦ www.dorothyclivegarden.co.uk
- **Hack Green Secret Nuclear Bunker** ⬦ www.hackgreen.co.uk
- **National Waterways Museum** ⬦ www.canalrivertrust. org.uk/national-waterways-museum
- **Norbury Wharf** For day boat hire (⬦ www.norburywharfltd.co.uk)

the tower during restoration work in 1904, thought to be crusader's relics brought back from the Holy Land in the 13th century (possibly by a Knight of St John). You can also see the 1598 charter granted by Elizabeth I, allowing Ellesmere to hold a market on Tuesdays and a fair every November, with a Piepowder Court to deal with offences committed and disputes arising at the fair.

Eglantyne Jebb was born to a wealthy family in Ellesmere in 1876 and would go on to found the charity Save the Children.

The Mere & around

Shropshire's largest and most dramatic glacial lake is at the east end of Ellesmere and known simply as The Mere. Perhaps inevitably, a myth has grown up about The Mere's formation. It seems a mean old woman named Mrs Ellis wouldn't share the water pump on her property, inflicting hardship on her neighbours. As is usually the case in folklore, selfishness did not go unpunished and one night Mrs Ellis's well overflowed. In daylight, neither she nor the water pump could be found, but an enormous lake had appeared. Ellis's mere. Although the legend was contrived to fit the place name, it's intriguing to think that Ellesmere almost certainly does mean 'lake belonging to Ellis' (or maybe Elli or Elia).

The benches by The Mere provide a great spot to sit and listen to ducks laughing. You can buy grains to feed the waterfowl (and an ice cream for you, perhaps) from the kiosk near **the Boathouse**. On sunny Saturdays and Sundays you can hire charmingly old-fashioned rowboats.

Look out to the heron island in the middle of The Mere. This was formed when spoil, cut to create the Garden Terrace, was tipped into the frozen mere. When the ice thawed a mound of earth was left protruding from the water. The 'island' appeared in the same year Napoleon invaded Russia (1812) and hence it's called **Moscow Island**.

To learn more about the herons and watch them nesting, call in to the Boathouse where **Ellesmere Heronwatch** (⊙ Feb–Jun 10.30–15.30 daily;

JOHN 'MAD JACK' MYTTON (1796–1834)

John Mytton was a Shropshire squire, daredevil and rake. A neighbour named him Mango as a child – the king of the Pickles – and, according to Mytton's friend and biographer Charles James Apperley (writing as Nimrod), 'he proved his title to the honour even to the end of his life'. Which was short even by the standards of his day (Mytton was 38 when he died) but surprisingly long given his appetite for danger.

Among the thousands of animals Mytton kept at Halston Hall, there lived a bear named Nell (whom he once rode into the drawing room; she responded by biting him on the calf) and a monkey with a drinking habit. Mytton guzzled several bottles of port a day and thought nothing of jumping field gates with a horse and gig – he positively enjoyed 'accidents'. Once, after a parson and doctor bade him farewell from dinner, Mytton too mounted a horse and, armed with a brace of pistols loaded with blanks, took a circuitous route to meet them on the road before letting fly both barrels, declaring 'Stand and deliver!'. One night, in an attempt to cure a bout of hiccups, he set his own shirt on fire.

Mytton was a jealous husband whose conduct in marriage, even Nimrod admitted, was 'in great part indefensible' and whose amours were 'too numerous to recite'.

As profligate as he was lustful and drunken, Mytton squandered £10,000 to get into parliament and lasted only half an hour in his seat, while much of his remaining fortune was frittered on fine clothes. He died in a debtors' prison, his mother at his side. Three thousand people are said to have attended his funeral: showing, perhaps, that for all Mytton's faults he was considered 'faithful to his friends, an indulgent landlord, and a most kind master'.

He was buried in the chapel at Halston Hall, which is privately owned (look out for open days through English Heritage), but you can find Mytton's legacy throughout Shropshire. There's the Jack Mytton Way, the Mytton & Mermaid pub in Atcham where his funeral cortege halted (and his ghost is said to haunt on his birthday, 30 September) and the Jack Mytton Inn in Hindford near Whittington, which was undergoing renovation at the time of writing. Look for numerous roads and avenues bearing the Mytton name – and of course the bridleway (page 74).

Across the Atlantic, at the University of Minnesota, an annual streaking event called the Jack Mytton Run recalled the squire's decision to leave his house in *puris naturalibus* one night to shoot ducks. The run was stopped by police in 2009.

free entry ⊘ www.heronwatch.org.uk) offers video links and telescopes over to Moscow Island. **Shropshire Wildlife Trust** also has an information point and small shop in the Boathouse where you can collect trails and activities for children.

Turn right out of the Boathouse's main entrance for a flat, fairly accessible walk partway around The Mere. Soon you'll come to **Cremorne Gardens**, traditional Victorian pleasure gardens overlooked by Wellingtonia trees (given to Ellesmere by Lord Brownlow; see below), and **Tricia's playground** for little ones. As you proceed around The Mere you can also view some of the **Ellesmere Sculpture Trail** installations, created by international artists in response to this special location (⊘ www.ellesmeresculpture.co.uk).

¶¶ FOOD & DRINK

Vermeulen & Son 6 Cross St ⊘ 01691 622521. A cheerfully old-fashioned bakery and delicatessen.

The Boathouse Mereside, SY12 0PA ⊘ 01691 623852 ⊙ café daily 08.30–17.30; restaurant 12.00–15.00 (Fri–Sun afternoon tea from 15.00 & bar & supper from 18.00). The mere-side Boathouse has been here since the 1930s, installed by philanthropic landowners Lord and Lady Brownlow to provide refreshments to visitors and passing motorists. (Lord Brownlow was a close friend to Edward VIII, supporting him through his 1936 abdication.) As well as being a visitor information centre, it's a great place to eat. The café menu is ideal for a quick stop (scones, cakes, excellent coffee) while the sunny restaurant serves well-presented yet unfussy steaks, burgers and plates of pasta, salad and seafood, making use of local specialities (for example, Stonehouse beer, Hereford beef and Perl Wen brie).

2 COLEMERE

Å **Colemere Caravan Park** (page 250), **Nink's Wagon**, English Frankton (page 250)

Colemere is two miles as the canal flows from Ellesmere, or three miles heading southeast down the A528 by car. You can also undertake a tranquil seven-mile walk along the towpaths of the Llangollen branch of the Shropshire Union Canal (see Walk 4 in the Meres Meander at ⊘ www.shropshirewalking.co.uk).

You can park for free at **Colemere Country Park** (SY12 0QW ♀ SJ435328), almost diagonally opposite the **church of St John the Evangelist**, a gothic beauty shared with neighbouring Lyneal. Cole Mere, from which the old village of idyllic thatched cottages takes its name, is surrounded by mature woodland and meadows. It's the only place in England where the **least water lily** grows, a tiny yellow relic of the post-glacial age. Cole Mere is also the only mere in Shropshire to offer a perfect circular walking route (about a mile long), with level footpaths. Head anti-clockwise around the mere to cross Yell Field through a kissing-gate into sun-dappled **Yell Wood**, where you'll see the remains of kilns from the days when horse-drawn barges transported coal and lime down the Shropshire Union Canal. The canal runs behind the north end of the mere: you can follow the steps up through the woods to see it. As you near completion of the circuit you'll pass through Boat House Wood and the black-and-white headquarters of **Colemere Sailing Club** (⊘ www.colemeresailing.org) which organises races on the mere most Sundays and Thursday evenings in summer.

TOWARDS SHREWSBURY

We may be in north Shropshire, but to the south of this region you're only a few minutes' drive down the A49 to Shrewsbury. Before you exit for Shropshire's county town, take some time to explore the wooded, mysterious landscape around Clive and Grinshill …

3 MYDDLE

On Castle Farm, a private property in the middle of Myddle (on the A528 from Shrewsbury to Ellesmere), exist the remains of a stair turret from **Myddle Castle**, built in 1307 by Lord Lestrange of Knockin and left to decay by a hard-up Humphrey Kynaston (page 210). You can catch a glimpse of the ruin from the main road through Myddle, by the church, but there is no direct public access.

Even with a piece of old castle Myddle would be, while pleasant, unremarkable in guidebook stakes were it not for the lovely **Red Lion** and the work of a yeoman who lived 300 years ago. Richard Gough began *The History of Myddle* in 1700 when he was a 66-year-old widower living with two of his daughters. He finished the first part, *Antiquityes and Memoryes of the Parish of Myddle,* within a year. It concerns mainly manors, parishes, boundaries – rather dull unless you're into the topography and administrative arrangements of a Salop parish in the late 17th century. But where Gough's work gets juicy is with the second part, nearly three times as long as the first: *Observations concerning the Seates in Myddle and the familyes to which they belong.* In it Gough wrote,

CHURCH GOSSIP

Richard Gough wrote of lascivious husbands, illegitimate children, disgruntled parents and ill-advised marriages. Take Richard Cleaton, an 'untowardly person':

> He married Annie, the daughter of William Tyller, a woman as infamous as himself. *Pares cum paribus facilime congregantur.* [Like are most easily brought together with like.] The parents on both sides were displeased, (or seemed soe,) with this match, and therefore allowed the new marryed couple noe maintenance. Richard Cleaton soon out run his wife, and left his wife bigge with child.

Historians, with records available today, confirm that Gough did indeed write about almost everyone – although he sometimes confused names and relationships, and details about early generations of even his own family are inaccurate.

One of my favourite of Gough's observations is about Richard Wicherley, who was 'put to schoole' with Mr Suger of Broughton:

> Hee was very dull at learning, which caused Mr. Suger to say very often hee had noe gutts in his braines, but it seems he had geare in his britches, for hee got one of his uncle's servant maids with child.

Anyone who thinks debauched Saturday nights are a new ill of British society should look to drunken Elizabeth Kyffin whose husband came to 'fetch her from the ale-house in a very darke night'. Unwilling to leave, she:

> pretended it was soe darke that shee could not see to goe; hee told her hee would lead her by the arme, and got her away almost halfe way home, and then shee pretended shee had lost one of her shoes; and when he had loosed her arme, and was groaping for the shoe, shee ran backe to the ale-house, and boulted him out, and would not come home that night.

I wonder what the 'man that they called Welch Franke' might have made of Gough's pronouncement that 'Hee could speake neither good Welsh nor good English'. *The History of Myddle* was first published in 1834 and therefore brought Gough no fame in his lifetime. Perhaps this was just as well.

pew by pew, about the families who attended the church in Myddle, their histories and their intrigues. In doing so he painted a detailed local picture of life in rural Stuart England. You'll find more information about Gough in **St Peter's Church** in Myddle. The original manuscript is in the archives of Shropshire Council and modern published editions are out of print, but you can read a digitised version for free: follow the link from ⌖ www.myddle.net.

The **bus** service 501 running between Shrewsbury and Ellesmere stops outside the Red Lion.

¶¶ FOOD & DRINK

Moor Farm Shop Ruyton Rd, Baschurch SY4 2BA ℐ 01939 262632 ⌖ www.moorfarmshop. co.uk ⊙ closed Sun & Mon. Just under four miles away from Myddle (on the way to Ruyton-XI-Towns) is this spacious farm shop, run by a family who've been farming in Baschurch since World War I. The fact that Moor Farm Shop employs a full-time butcher, a shop chef (making sausage rolls, pork pies and fresh bread) and a tea room chef should tell you that this is a worthwhile place to stop.

The Red Lion SY4 3RG ℐ 01939 290171. You can't miss the Red Lion as you travel through Myddle: it's huge and L-shaped, with lattice windows and characterful red brick nogging – the inviting epitome of a 17th-century inn. The inside is both understated and comfortable: exposed beams, cosy nooks, woodburner and chesterfield sofas. The food pays due attention to provenance: properly aged steaks, delicate fish dishes and pan-roasted chicken, and always a couple of creative veggie options. I found the waiting staff knowledgeable and caring too.

4 GRINSHILL & CLIVE

🏠 **Amblewood Cottage & Woodpeckers** (page 251), **The Inn at Grinshill** (page 251)

Three miles south of Wem, the parish of Grinshill is known for the quarries that provided the stone for some of Shropshire's finest buildings, including the mansion house at Attingham Park, and St Chad's Church in Shrewsbury. Easily worked, durable and attractive in appearance, **Grinshill stone** is a Triassic sandstone which weathers to a greenish grey or brown. Roman builders were on to its useful properties first, of course, as evidenced in the remains at Wroxeter. Notable modern use of the stone includes the lintel and door surrounds of 10 Downing Street.

Although mining still takes place at Grinshill, many of the old quarries have returned to nature, giving us dense conifer and broad-leaved woodland to explore. After a spell of rain in late summer this place is mysterious, alive and humming with insects and the insistent chirrup of coal tits and warblers. Wear sturdy shoes because it can be muddy and rough underfoot. You'll find exhilarating viewpoints over south Shropshire, quite out of proportion to the minimal effort in wandering to the top of the hill. If driving, you might find it best to start at **Corbet Wood Countryside Heritage Site** (♀ SJ525238) where there's free parking: follow signs from the A49. A family-friendly walking route starts here, taking in the site where fossil skeletons and imprints of rhynchosaurs have been discovered: see ✑ www.shropshirewalking. co.uk and search for 'Grinshill'.

Grinshill village waits sleepily at the foot of the sandstone slopes, where **the Inn at Grinshill** is an excellent place to reward yourself with lunch. The area is served by Yorton station in the next village, with **trains** running twice an hour (Monday to Saturday) between Shrewsbury and Crewe and some early morning and late evening services which travel as far as Manchester Piccadilly and Cardiff Central. On Sundays there are five trains in each direction. Yorton is a request stop, so you'll need to wave at the train as it approaches.

Half a mile west of Grinshill is **Clive**, an attractive village made from Grinshill stone, with the tall sharp spire of **All Saints Church** lancing the sky over the hilly landscape. The name Clive derives from the Old English *clif*. This is the birthplace of the Restoration dramatist **William Wycherley**, renowned for his good looks, bawdy plays and a quarrel with Alexander Pope over, among other things, the 'improvements' Pope made to some of Wycherley's poems. Wycherley is still a strong Shropshire family name: I've encountered several in this part of the county. The churchyard (where you'll find a memorial to the Wycherley family, although there's no evidence William is buried here) is delightful, with a winding pathway around its sloping terrain and interpretive signs pointing out interesting graves. Visit in May for a dazzling display of crocuses.

"The churchyard is delightful, with a winding pathway around its sloping terrain and interpretive signs pointing out interesting graves."

Arriva's 511 **bus** service from Shrewsbury to Whitchurch stops at Clive.

¶¶ FOOD & DRINK

The Inn at Grinshill High St, SY4 3BL ✑ 01939 220410. Kevin and Victoria Brazier have created a destination pub at the Inn at Grinshill, equally suited to a special birthday lunch or a lost afternoon spent by the fire with ale and newspapers. Don't be intimidated by the formal Georgian frontage: walkers in wellies and dogs are welcome and the ambience inside is elegant yet unpretentious. There are no highchairs, although you're welcome to bring your own booster seat. The menu is British fine dining, always seasonal and as local as possible (part of the Inn's rose-filled garden has been turned over to growing produce). For those days when fine dining isn't quite right, smaller plates and sandwiches are available in the bar. If you find yourself getting comfy, you can stay over.

5 HADNALL

Five miles north of Shrewsbury, located off the A49, is the village and civil parish of Hadnall. The body of Sir Rowland Hill (second in command to the Duke of Wellington at the 1815 Battle of Waterloo: see *Lord Hill's Column* on page 170) is interred with his two sisters in a crypt at the **church of St Mary Magdalene**.

Country Garden Roses

SY4 3DH ✆ 01939 210380 ⌨ www.countrygardenroses.co.uk ⊙ Mar–Oct 10.00–17.00 daily, Nov–Feb 10.00–16.00

This independent garden centre is a pleasant place to stop, if you're travelling through on the A49. The signs are confusing as they refer variously to Country Garden Plant Centre, The Garden Plant Centre or even Black Birches. (The centre is in the grounds of **Black Birches**, a timbered house dating back to the 12th century, now the headquarters of a care company.) This is essentially a garden centre specialising in roses (look for the personalised rose service if you need a special gift to take home) with a welcoming **tea room**. You'll find homemade cakes, all-day breakfasts, gardening books to browse, and free Wi-Fi. And when the pace just gets too much, you can take yourself off to the potting shed-style loos for a few moments' peace.

6 MORETON CORBET

St Bartholomew's in the quiet village of Moreton Corbet, about 9½ miles north of Shrewsbury, is a treasure among English churches. Corbet knights lie cold in stone chest tombs, topped with painted effigies, while fine stained-glass windows filter in the Shropshire sun. It's next to **Moreton Corbet Castle** (SY4 4DW; free) the ruined shell of a medieval stronghold and an ambitious Italianate mansion begun in the late 15th century. This is a romantic and peaceful picnic spot on the right day, but watch out for the ghost of Paul Holmyard, a Puritan cast out by his neighbour Sir Vincent Corbet. ✋ Go to ⌨ www.bradtguides.com/corbetcastle to find out more.

WEM TO WHITCHURCH

The town of Wem, on the banks of the River Roden, is about ten miles north of Shrewsbury. Between here and Whitchurch it's all rural, open and green as Shropshire's landscape rolls towards the plains of Cheshire. This is where you can explore the astonishing follies of **Hawkstone Park** or watch light aircraft taking off and landing at the small **Sleap Airfield**. If you're lucky enough to be in Shropshire during their limited opening hours, you can wander in the luxuriant **gardens of Hodnet Hall**.

7 WEM

🏠 **Aston Lodge** (page 250), **The Old Rectory** (page 250), **Soulton Hall** (page 250)

People chuckle about how nothing ever happens in Wem, but even in affection that serves an injustice to this dignified market town. It doesn't help that Royal Mail insists on using Shrewsbury as Wem's postal address file code; as well as causing no end of trouble for parcel and letter deliveries, it gives the smaller town an inferiority complex. But with its curving high street, topped and tailed with a train station and solid-looking 19th-century church, Wem has a pace and quiet charm all its own.

The Sunday market charter granted by King John in 1202 was revised to a Thursday market in 1351 – and you'll still find a market here on Thursdays in Market Square and **Town Hall**. The latter makes huge efforts to lift Wem from snoozing obscurity with an independent cinema, café bar and plenty of community events. And perhaps Wem (called Wamm in Saxon times, meaning 'marsh') deserves its peace after centuries of unrest. The town was torn to the ground during the Wars of the Roses by the Earl of Salisbury on behalf of the Yorkists, then rebuilt in around 1500 by the Baron Sir Ralph Greystoke. During the Civil War 5,000 Cavaliers attacked Wem. A Parliamentary garrison of just 40 men was so outnumbered that the local women rallied around - and together they successfully held the town. This gave rise to a couplet:

> The women of Wem and a few musketeers
> Beat Lord Chapel and all his Cavaliers.

One of Wem's sweetest boasts is that it is home of the modern sweet pea. In 1887 the horticulturalist Henry Eckford, who lived on Noble Street, cultivated a beautifully blooming specimen of the

Grandiflora variety – transforming the humble sweet pea into what is known in gardening circles as Queen of the Annuals. The Eckford Sweet Pea Society is still going strong in Wem today, holding the **Annual Sweet Pea Show** every July.

 If you have a penchant for a ghost story, go to ⊘ www.bradtguides. com/wem to read about the Wem ghost.

Mythstories
Aston St, SY4 5AU ℰ 01939 235500 ⊘ www.mythstories.com ⊙ limited: see website for latest dates; free entry

Mythstories museum in Wem's former Morgan Library deserves lots more funding, not least for its curators' commitment to promoting literacy and storytelling. It's a place to hear Shropshire folk tales from resident storytellers: Wild Edric (pages 50–1), Mrs Ellis (page 217), the apocalyptic whistlers of the Stiperstones (page 50). For a museum of the intangible – the telling of stories – Mythstories offers plenty to look at, including two processional giant puppets, Bertilak the Green Knight and Morgan le Fey. The museum also houses the **Society for Storytelling Library**. Admission is free, but you could always slot a donation into the fairytale cottage box.

 SHOPPING

Wem is a town where I offset my guilt about impulse shopping by telling myself how important it is to support local traders. To give you an idea of who needs your money and mine: there's an old-fashioned sweet shop called **the Treacle Mine** (22A High St) harking back, of course, to the days when treacle mines flowed thick and sweet beneath Shropshire's untapped soil (and we were all a little more gullible). It's owned by the incumbent Mayor of Wem Councillor John Murray and his family, who are passionate about promoting the town. Just along the road, the **Fruitful Deli** (17 High St) stocks the feted Coopers Gourmet Sausage Rolls (page 197) and there's a prettily laid out gift and craft shop called the **Soul Bird Gallery** (7 High St). At the other end of the street, just when you think you've run out of shops, you'll find the small and welcoming **Wem Bookshop** (81 High St) whose selection of new children's books is particularly pleasing.

FOOD & DRINK

While there's no current Wem establishment that would send food critics racing northbound from London (and perhaps many people would consider that a good thing), nor have I ever had a bad meal here. With two Joule's pubs on High Street you're guaranteed a great pint:

The Castle ✆ 01939 236088) is the oldest pub in town, with a friendly atmosphere complemented by cosy beams and polished wood floors. Landlords Dee and Rich serve good value, proper pub grub (and Dee is vegetarian so you'll find decent veggie options). If you like cocktails paired with well-cooked food head for the **Drayton Gate Restaurant & Bar** (2 Aston St ✆ 01939 235654). **Maypole Court Café Bistro** (8 Maypole Court (✆ 01939 235802) is a tucked-away bistro serving comforting home-cooked food (think lasagne, stroganoff, warm salads, crispy fishcakes) and has a pleasing wine selection. I like the Welsh dresser of local produce and handmade gifts to take away.

For a special but reasonably priced Sunday lunch, **the Old Rectory** (Lowe Hill Rd ✆ 01939 233233) is less than ten minutes' walk from Wem: head up High Street with the church on your left, and take the right fork to Lowe Hill Road. The kitchen at this Georgian hotel uses home-grown vegetables and herbs.

About a mile south of Wem is the black-and-white timbered hamlet of Tilley. Housed in an 18th-century inn building, **the Tilley Raven** (SY4 5HE ✆ 01939 234419) is family owned and food-oriented with a big menu of pub favourites, as well as being CAMRA-listed. You'll find fair prices, gluten-free options, and live music on Friday evenings.

8 SLEAP AIRFIELD

Sleap SY4 3HE ✆ 01939 232882 🖱 www.shropshireaeroclub.co.uk

Three miles south of Wem is a little secret. At Sleap (pronounced 'Slape') Airfield you can watch nifty two-seaters taking off and landing on the breezy runways of the Shropshire Aero Club. If you'll forgive the pun, the atmosphere in the club and control tower is entirely without airs, and you can enjoy a generous portion of lunch or the famous Flying Start breakfast for a bargain price in the **Lock Lounge café** (🕓 09.00–17.00 daily). Be prepared for a wait on Sundays. It's likely that your fellow diners will just have zoomed in from Wales or Herefordshire for a bite to eat. Harrison Ford is a lifetime member of Shropshire Aero Club, having rented an aircraft while shooting the latest *Star Wars* movie at Pinewood Studios in Buckinghamshire.

The site is also home to the **Wartime Aircraft Recovery Museum** (🕓 10.00–17.00 w/ends; free entry) which remembers the 'forgotten young' RAF, Royal Navy and US Army Air Force pilots who lost their lives in training flights over Shropshire during World War II. The twisted fuselage and charred seats were grimly revelatory for me and not a little shaming: I'd never thought about airmen dying in training, only in combat. The museum content is sensitively presented and interpreted.

9 LOPPINGTON

About four miles west of Wem, the village of Loppington has the only remaining bull ring in Shropshire. Don't go searching for an arena, though, as I did: it's an iron ring to which bulls were tethered for baiting by dogs, in front of the Dickin Arms.

The churchyard of **St Michael and All Angels** has been deliberately run to meadow in order to nurture biodiversity. Inside the 14th-century church, peep behind the protective curtain to see the colourful Millennium Tapestry. An unfortunate placement of window leading makes it look as though a stained-glass depiction of Jesus reads 'Risen he is not'.

¶¶ FOOD & DRINK

The Dickin Arms (✆ 01939 233471) has been an inn since the 1660s, taking its name from local landowners. Current landlords Phil and Norma Kelly serve homemade pub grub (with bargain price lunchtime deals). Their menu doesn't shout about local ingredients, but I know they look to nearby farms and smallholdings for eggs and produce. Phil knows his beer, and his music. If you like gin, you'll like the bar: there are over 120 different types to try.

10 THE MOAT SHED

🏠 **The Moat Shed's 1960s vintage house truck** (page 250)
Northwood Hall, Newtown SY4 5NU 📍 SJ491312. If you're driving, look for signs when you near the destination as it is some way further than a sat nav may indicate ✆ 01939 236252 🖰 www.themoatshed.co.uk 🕐 09.00–17.00 Thu–Mon

Early medieval Shropshire had a high number of moated farmhouses – that's what comes of being a border county, threatened by Welsh invaders. Many of the houses have survived but lost their moats. Northwood Hall, about three miles from Wem, is sort of the opposite: while there is no building now, the site has retained not just a moat but a double moat. This extraordinary scheduled ancient monument, protected by English Heritage, is home to the Moat Shed, a tucked-away **café** serving hearty breakfasts and lunches (including a roast of the day), sourced from an impressive list of local suppliers. More like a restaurant in ambience, the café manages to feel equally welcoming to walkers, cyclists, riders (there are hitching posts for horses), and special occasion diners.

"While there is no building where Northwood Hall once stood, the site has retained not just a moat but a double moat."

The interior is warmed by underfloor heating and a wood burner (which nestles on cornerstones reclaimed from Northwood Hall); in sunnier weather you can dine outside on the 70-foot covered deck overlooking the moats. Booking is essential: The Moat Shed may feel like a secret but locals sure do know about it.

11 WESTON UNDER REDCASTLE

The Barn at Maynards Farm (page 251), **The Citadel** (page 250), **Windmill Cottage Guesthouse** (page 250)

Six miles east of Wem by road, and about halfway between Whitchurch and Shrewsbury, is the enchantingly green and wooded village of Weston under Redcastle. In Saxon times it was known just as Westune: the Redcastle came about when the marcher lord Henry de Audley built a red sandstone castle on a crag jutting out of the Shropshire plain. In the late 18th century the castle's ruin would inspire Richard Hill of Hawkstone to begin creating Hawkstone Park, full of grottoes and follies.

Hawkstone Hall was separated from the rest of the estate in the 1930s: it's now the Redemptorist International Pastoral Centre England, providing a retreat for priests and religious laypeople, but open a few days each year to the public (www.hawkstone-hall.com).

Weston under Redcastle also has a famous **golf course**, restored to its pre-war condition by Alex Lyle in the 1950s. Alex's son is **Sandy Lyle**, the first British golfer to win the US Masters. He maintains close ties with the club, where a trophy competition is named in his honour.

Hawkstone Park Follies

SY4 5JY 01948 841700 www.hawkstoneparkfollies.co.uk Mar– website for events outside this time

If you've never before visited Hawkstone Park Follies, I envy you your first glimpses of this mysterious place, just east of Weston under Redcastle. Pack a torch, drinks and lunch and wear sturdy shoes because you're not venturing out on an ordinary walk. You're embarking on an adventure through a restored 200-year-old pleasure garden of which **Samuel Johnson** described: 'its prospects, the awfulness of its shades, the horrors of its precipices, the verdure of its hollows and the loftiness of its rocks … above is inaccessible altitude, below is horrible profundity'. Walking where whimsy and fabricated surprises meet with naturally dizzying cliffs and crags, it's pleasing to imagine the reactions of Georgian and Victorian visitors who weren't spoiled as we can be today by theme parks and manufactured thrills.

Of course Hawkstone Park is not nearly as dangerous as Dr Johnson's comments suggest it may have felt to his contemporaries. I highly recommend it for families with children who enjoy walking and exploring. There's something exhilarating about following one of the trails up sandstone cliffs and often slippery steep steps, over crags and through caves so dark your eyes may as well be closed, to discover the follies created by the Hill family of Hawkstone. Ascend the 150 steps in the spiral staircase of the 100-foot high monument, raised by Sir Richard Hill in 1795 to commemorate the first Protestant Mayor of London (who bought Hawkstone in 1556), and you'll have views over 12 or 13 counties. Its dramatic scenery made Hawkstone Park the BBC's film location for that late 1980s Sunday teatime staple, *The Chronicles of Narnia.*

♿ Visitors need a certain level of fitness and the hilly terrain makes Hawkstone Park unsuitable for pushchairs or wheelchairs, although users of those could still enjoy the level grassy Grand Valley area. The **tea room** is also accessible (although I found it overwhelmed in peak season). There are different trails for people's varying levels of stamina. 'Silver safaris' can also be booked for people who are less mobile. Dogs kept on leads are welcome.

🛍 SHOPPING

Maynards Farm Weston under Redcastle SY4 5LR ✆ 01948 840252 ⌂ www. maynardsfarm.co.uk ⏲ 09.00–18.00 Mon–Sat. If you're heading up the A49 from Weston under Redcastle, do stop at Maynards – one of Rick Stein's Food Heroes – where you can buy bacon and sausages, freshly baked bread, cheese, pâté, eggs, milk and other treats. It's more than a farm shop: you can take **courses** in butchery, curing and cookery, and the owners host the occasional **supper club**.

12 HODNET

Bigger than a village but smaller than a town, half-timbered Hodnet (about six miles east of Wem as the crow flies) is centred around Hodnet Hall and, at its highest point, the village church. **St Luke's** 14th-century tower is octagonal from the ground to the top, said to be the only one of its kind in the country. The Norman building was restored in 1846 and the Heber-Percy Chapel added in 1870: look for the spooky marble effigy of Blanche.

Bishop Reginald Heber, who was for a time rector of Hodnet, wrote the hymn 'From Greenland's Icy Mountain'. His sister was the novelist **Mary Cholmondeley**.

Hodnet Hall Gardens

TF9 3NN (entrance gates to the left of St Luke's Church: car parking inside; pay cash at gate)
⌀ 01630 685786 ◈ www.hodnethallgardens.org ☺ Apr–Sep Sun, bank holiday Mon & certain Weds (see website)

For more than half a century, visitors have been able – on certain days in summer – to wander the glorious 60 acres around Hodnet Hall, the ancestral home still occupied by the Heber-Percy family. I recommend a visit to these tree-canopied grounds, set in a gentle valley. The forebears of the lofty oak and beech trees above you once surrounded a Norman motte-and-bailey castle, the earthworks for which you can see near the car park. Other features include the Water Gardens, fed by underground springs and dominated by Main Pool upon which Australian black swans glide; a dovecote built in 1656, and a magnificent tithe barn from the same century. You can buy plants, flowers, vegetables and shrubs from the **kitchen garden**.

The black-and-white stable building is all that remains of the Heber-Percy's Tudor mansion (the current Elizabethan-style red-brick house was built in the 1860s); it's now a **restaurant** with an alarming array of big game trophies, collected mainly in the 1920s and 1930s. If you don't fancy eating alongside dead animals, you can sit on the lawn outside in dry weather: ploughman's lunches and sandwiches are very reasonably priced, and the delicious cakes are from Maynards Farm.

The Rocking Horse Workshop

TF9 3NF ⌀ 01630 685888 ◈ www.therockinghorseworkshop.com

While you're passing through Hodnet, peep through the windows of the Rocking Horse Workshop (on the main road) where, alongside a showroom filled with future family heirlooms, you'll see glass eyes, hair for manes and tails, leather bridles and other accessories required for the loving construction and restoration of rocking horses. David and Noreen Kiss began their business in Wem in 1987 and it is now recognised as one of the world's leading manufacturers of these traditional toys. Indeed David's painstakingly written directory of pre-1950 British makers means his name has been adopted as a collective noun:

a *kiss* of rocking horses. If the showroom is open, it's worth going inside: David and Noreen are warm and welcoming; their passion for preserving old skills is palpable. Kiss rocking horses are exquisite too (models from the deluxe range cost up to £5,000); an antidote to mass-produced toys.

13 WOLLERTON OLD HALL GARDEN

Abdo Hill Farm, Rosehill (page 250)
Wollerton TF9 3NA 01630 685760 www.wollertonoldhallgarden.com Good Fri–end Aug 12.00–17.00 Fri, Sun & bank holiday Mon (& Fri only in Sep)

Around three miles southwest of Market Drayton, Wollerton Old Hall Garden is the four-acre private family garden of Lesley and John Jenkins, open for a couple of afternoons each week in warmer months. Lesley spent her childhood in the house and gardens, happening upon the site again in the early 1980s when an estate agent's sign indicated it was for sale. John put in an offer, sight unseen, and they've spent the decades that followed creating what is widely regarded as an important formal garden in the English tradition, with precise attention to colour, form, shape and scale.

Developed along three north–south and three east–west vistas, now divided by neat, overlapping hedges, half-concealed red-brick walls and inviting arched oak gates, the garden unfolds before you as a series of rooms. It's said to follow the Arts and Crafts style, although the planting style is modern and represents, in the Jenkinses' words, 'controlled exuberance'. Towering yew pyramids and enormous box ball topiary, always symmetrical, bring an element of theatre to your stroll, while clever water features – including two rills – give the classic English country garden sound of falling water, despite Wollerton Old Hall standing on a sloping site above nearly 200 feet of sand. The wide range of species includes significant collections of rambling clematis, star-shaped, blooming phlox, roses (including the creamy peach, myrrh-scented Wollerton Old Hall variety cultivated by David Austin Roses) and almost a hundred types of salvias, especially loved by head gardener Andrew Humphis.

You can buy plants in the **nursery** by the entrance, propagated and nurtured on site. Salad and chilli plants are available too.

Wollerton Old Hall is off limits to visitors, but its gently beautiful presence of weathered timber frames and creamy yellow-painted brickwork gives context and backdrop to the garden.

Look out for special events, including lectures, walks with the head gardener and Wollerton Old Hall's evening **Summer Stroll** with wine, a salmon supper and talk.

At the road junction at the top of Wollerton you can see an 18th-century brick **animal pound** into which wandering cattle were corralled.

FOOD & DRINK

The estate produce supplies Wollerton Old Hall's **tea room**. Home-cooked, freshly prepared hot and cold lunches (such as good quiches, soups and salads), cakes and drinks are available; there's an orchard area outside for warm days or, if the garden is not too busy, you may be able to take your tea tray to one of the arbours or the summerhouse.

14 WHIXALL MOSS

Follow brown signs from the A495 south of Whitchurch to the Morris's Bridge car park; free car park closes at dusk ⅙ ramps allow easy access from the car park along an even-surfaced towpath & boardwalk on to a restored part of the moss

Fenn's, Whixall and Bettisfield Mosses National Nature Reserve is Britain's third-largest lowland raised bog – a fascinating place to walk. The site stretches into Wales (Bettisfield and Fenn's Mosses are several miles north) but by following the directions above you'll enter Whixall Moss at the Shropshire end.

The bog was formed around 9,000 years ago when a large meltwater lake became inhabited with swamp and fen plants before sphagnum bog moss set in, acidifying the water and stopping plant remains from decaying. Over time this built up a huge dome of peat. The result today is rich biodiversity and an extraordinary landscape from a different age, wild and mysterious.

Interpretive panels are dotted around the site, but to enhance your walk I'd recommend downloading the 'Fenn's and Whixall Mosses History Trail' leaflet from Natural England (⊘ publications.naturalengland.org. uk). Through this you'll learn about the three Bronze Age and Iron Age **bog bodies** found on the English/Welsh border in the late 19th century. Possibly examples of human sacrifices, the corpses' bones had dissolved but the acidic bog had essentially 'pickled' their hair and skin.

Another incredible story is that of **Strategic Starfish** in World War II. Decoy fire baskets were remotely lit on Fenn's Moss, fooling German pilots into thinking they were bombing the burning factories and cities already set alight by their pathfinders.

It's sensible to wear wellies because there may be adders in the long grass. Between June and August you may see **round-leaved sundew** in crimson bloom, a carnivorous (insect-devouring) plant, and Shropshire's county flower.

From nearby **Whixall Marina** (SY13 2QS) you can collect beautifully equipped narrowboats for holidays on the Llangollen and Montgomery canals: see ⊘ www.hireacanalboat.co.uk and ⊘ www.peagreenboats.co.uk for information and advance booking.

15 WHITCHURCH

⌂ **Oakpond Cottages** (page 251)

Don't be put off by the imposing brick gateway to Whitchurch from the A41 which gives one the impression of entering a business park (and whose jaunty design of WWWs comically predates the worldwide web). Shropshire's northernmost market town has many independent shops and characterful pubs, and a long history belied by its modern amenities (such as the shiny new Civic Centre which hosts the popular **Friday market**). In fact, Whitchurch is the oldest continually inhabited settlement in the county: a Roman fort on its site called Mediolanum ('town in mid plain') served as an overnight stop after a day's march between Uriconium (Wroxeter) and Deva (Chester).

Whitchurch's more recent history is horological – from the late 17th century it was home to **JB Joyce & Co**, manufacturer of world-renowned turret clocks – although that chapter has all but closed now too. The brand name is upheld by parent company Smith of Derby, but JB Joyce & Co's Edwardian premises on Station Road, distinctive with its green and gold clockface, was recently acquired by a firm of auctioneers.

In an eminent location at the town's centre, **St Alkmund's Church** is in its fourth incarnation, the third version having fallen down in 1711. Consecrated in 1713, the 'latest' model is an elegant Neoclassical building with vast windows that make the interior feel light and airy. Notable features include the tomb of Lord John Talbot (d1453), the first Earl of Shrewsbury, whom Shakespeare had the Countess of Auvergne in *Henry VI Part I* refer to as 'the scourge of France'. A plaque commemorates Whitchurch-born Sir Edward German, composer of the comic operas *Tom Jones* and *Merrie England*.

From Victoria Jubilee Park at the western end of town you can access miles of countryside via **Whitchurch Waterway Country Park**.

RANDOLPH CALDECOTT (1846–86)

Randolph Caldecott was a Chester-born artist and illustrator who spent his late teens in Whitchurch, working in a bank. These were formative years for young Caldecott's artistic style, for many of his later illustrations included scenery and buildings from north Shropshire and around. One of his most famous works is an illustrated version of the nursery rhyme The House That Jack Built (1878). Many local people claim that Cherrington Manor, a privately owned half-timbered manor with outside malt house in Cherrington near Newport, is the original house that Jack built, although the Randolph Caldecott Society says it is more likely to be Brook House Farm in Hanmer near Whitchurch.

In America the prestigious Caldecott medal is awarded annually to an outstanding children's picture book published the previous year.

A footpath follows Staggs Brook (an important site for rare water voles) to Greenfields Nature Reserve and on towards the Llangollen Canal, where you'll find Grindley Brook, a flight of seven locks.

Whitchurch Heritage Centre

12 St Mary's St ✆ 01948 664577 ⬙ www.whitchurch-heritage.co.uk ⊙ 11.00–16.00 Tue, Thu, Fri; free ♿ fully accessible

This smart white-painted former chapel incorporates the town's **visitor information service** and a museum of local history, focusing on Sir Edward German and the Victorian artist and illustrator **Randolph Caldecott**, who spent some years working in Whitchurch. It has information about Whitchurch's clock-making heritage, as well as medieval and Roman artefacts.

If you exit through the rear courtyard to St Mary's Street you'll find craft units including the **Down to Earth Gallery** (⊙ Tue–Sat) which sells British-made (often Shropshire-made) jewellery, ceramics, textiles, glass and paintings. An excellent place to source an unusual gift or souvenir.

¶¶ FOOD & DRINK

The Black Bear 4 High St ✆ 01948 663800. This Tudor building with low ceilings and inviting nooks has been a pub since at least 1667 and was an important coaching stop for 19th-century travellers. Today it's run by real-ale fans. Expect good beer and hearty portions of well-cooked, responsibly sourced food: local suppliers of meat and cheese are frequently name-checked in the menu.

Dearnford Lake

⋏ Dearnford Lake glamping pod & campsite (page 250)

Tilstock Rd, SY13 3JQ ✆ 01948 665914 (café) ⌂ www.dearnford.net

A mile south of Whitchurch is one of those special Shropshire places that manages to be lots of things to lots of people. Essentially Dearnford is a serene spot with a lake, and a relatively modern lake at that. Created by extraction work that began in 1991 to build the Whitchurch bypass,

> *"A mile south of Whitchurch is Dearnford Lake – one of those special Shropshire places that manages to be lots of things to lots of people."*

the spring-fed lake was deemed best for trout – and so a fly-fishing location was established by the Bebbington family, who own the land. Thoughtful landscaping with gentle slopes complemented by woodland and wildflowers have made Dearnford Lake a lovely place to walk: you can circumnavigate the water to work up an appetite for a locally sourced breakfast, lunch or afternoon tea in **Dearnford Café**. From spring to autumn the lake is open daily for wild swimming, group fishing (♿ accessible via a specially designed vessel from The Wheelyboat Trust for people with disabilities) and model boats. Canoeing and raft building are available by arrangement and the lakeside is also a launch spot for hot-air balloons. Cyclists receive a 10% discount in the café.

The 511 **bus** from Shrewsbury to Whitchurch stops adjacent to the site.

MARKET DRAYTON & AROUND

🏠 Old Colehurst Manor, Colehurst (page 250), **Goldstone Hall** (page 250), **The Shooting Folly**, Lipley (page 251), **Ternhill Farm House**, Tern Hill (page 250)

In and around the Tern Valley, as north Shropshire makes way for Cheshire, the land is flattish and fertile – perfect for farming. It's here, just outside Market Drayton, you'll find **Fordhall Organic Farm**, with its extraordinary story about the battle between a small family business and a multinational corporation.

A notable village is the flower-filled **Cheswardine** (mentioned in the Domesday Book as Ciseworde), located on a hill with the Shropshire Union Canal below. The views over the Stretton and Clee Hills and The Wrekin from **St Swithin's** churchyard are as lovely as the epigraphs on the gravestones are morbid.

16 MARKET DRAYTON

Dratuine was a Saxon settlement which appeared in the Domesday Book. There's been a market here for more than 760 years: a market so good, they say, the modern town was named after it. Indeed the streets of Market Drayton used to be named after the animals traded there: Cheshire Street was Horsemarket Street, Stafford Street was Sheepmarket Street and Great Hales Street was the amusingly named Beastmarket Street. Wednesday is still market day and it remains a busy affair:

CLIVE OF INDIA (1725–74)

Robert Clive, one of Shropshire's most famous sons, was born to Richard and Rebecca Clive at Styche, an Elizabethan manor house near Market Drayton. Their lineage was distinguished but times were hard. Styche was falling apart, and crowded: Richard and Rebecca had 13 children, although six died in infancy.

As a boy, Robert was plucky and wilful – to put it politely. Once he climbed the steeple of St Mary's in Market Drayton and perched on a gargoyle to scare people below. He was expelled from three schools.

No-one could have predicted the man he would become. Least of all his father, who packed 17-year-old Robert off on a Madras-bound ship to work as a clerk for the East India Company. Ten years later Robert Clive returned home extremely wealthy, happily married to Margaret Maskeylne, and a national hero. Of his many achievements he had saved the East India Company from destruction at the hands of the French and helped secure India for the British crown. The Prime Minister declared him a 'heaven-born general'. For a balanced perspective the writer and historian William Dalrymple has called Robert Clive an 'unstable sociopath', pointing out that a 'proportion of the loot of Bengal went directly into Clive's pocket'.

Robert Clive settled in Britain, was awarded the title Baron of Plassey and rebuilt Styche for his father. For his own growing family he bought Walcot Hall (page 49). But while Clive's political career continued to flourish, his health did not. He had long suffered from depression, possibly having the condition we now know as bipolar disorder, and had a gallstone problem. He took opium and laudanum. As MP for Shrewsbury he was increasingly attacked for his defence of the Prime Minister, William Pitt.

Robert Clive died in London, aged 49; probably by his own hand.

I visited the church of St Margaret of Antioch in **Moreton Say** to see where Robert Clive was baptised and buried. The fact that his body was interred within the walls suggests his death was not by suicide, although his grave is unmarked; his wall plaque overshadowed by larger and more ornate Clive memorials. He's a controversial character for many reasons, but one that Shropshire is unlikely to forget.

cheerful traders along Cheshire Street and plenty of meat, fish and deli goods in the covered market.

With thanks to Clive of India (page 237) Market Drayton is the self-professed home of **gingerbread** (best served, apparently, dunked in port) but despite having four gingerbread bakers in the early 20th century, only one remains today. Image on Food has its production line at a nearby business park.

As well as its market, Drayton retains a medieval street pattern and a good number of black-and-white buildings, alongside the red sandstone so typical of the county. I like the old grey sandstone buttercross (c1824) on Cheshire Street, with its wooden bellcote and two copper fire bells. The Shropshire Union Canal runs south of the town.

Arriva bus number 64 travels between Market Drayton and Shrewsbury (stopping also in Hodnet) and the 341 links the town with Wellington (at certain times Telford too), taking just over an hour.

Market Drayton Museum & Resource Centre

53 Shropshire St ☉ Apr–Oct 10.30–13.00 Tue, Wed, Fri & Sat; free

In 1908 a Market Drayton bicycle maker called Arthur Phillips built a prototype 'vertical takeoff aircraft'. His vision was that one day everyone would own a personal aircraft, landing and taking off from the roofs of houses. He patented the Phillips Matchless Flying Machine in 1909, a single-engine craft with variable pitch blades on adjustable propellers. It wasn't powerful enough to lift both pilot and contraption, although a smaller (probably half-scale) unmanned model did take to the air briefly at nearby Peatswood, lifting, it is said, on a gust of wind and blowing into a nearby beech tree. It seems Arthur was inspired by other pioneering aviators: his eldest sons from his second marriage were named Wilbur and Orville.

You can learn more about Mr Phillips – as well as Clive of India, the town's gingerbread heritage and other Market Drayton titbits – at the super-local museum on Shropshire Street.

Joule's Red Lion Brewery Tap

Great Hales St, TF9 1JP ✆ 01630 652602; free parking at the back of the brewery

The Joule's brewery draws soft mineral water from the Triassic pebble beds below its site on Great Hales Street to brew craft beers from a tradition started by Augustinian monks in Staffordshire. The building has been sensitively extended from a 16th-century inn, the Red Lion, incorporating a spacious bar and the woodburner-warmed 'mouse room' where you're treated to a live view of the brewery. The renovations are typical of the Joule's estate as it expands into previously unloved sites in Shropshire and Staffordshire; the sanded floors, polished tiles and restored stained glass of Joule's-owned pubs illustrating a new chapter in the brewing company's story. The Joule's offering is simple: three core craft beers and a seasonal beer every three months. Joule's is only available on draught, so the brewery never sells to supermarkets.

On Fridays from 17.00 the bar offers complimentary sausage rolls and there's a jazz night on the last Thursday of each month. Brewery tours take place from 19.30 on the first Wednesday – you get a pork bap at the end. If you're driving, four-pint carry-out cases are available.

The physicist James Prescott Joule, who gave his name to the standard unit of energy, was a relative of the original Joule's founder.

ARTS

Festival Drayton Frogmore Rd ✆ 01630 654444 ⬦ www.festivaldraytoncentre.com. Market Drayton's community-owned arts centre is used as a cinema, theatre and exhibition space. The garden and patio area has frescoes celebrating scenes from the town's history.

SHOPPING

Craft Revolution 18 Shropshire St ✆ 01630 654347. Alison Fellows is a champion of Shropshire craftspeople. I recommend her shop for unusual gifts and its regularly changing wall of local artistry (not just photography and paintings – once it was cross-stitch).
Tuesday's Fine Confectionery 2 Wilkinson Walk ✆ 01630 652332. Tuesday's has the ambience and enticing aroma of a Belgian chocolatier's shop, which is amazing when you realise 75% of its produce is made in this little Shropshire store. From May to October part of the premises are turned into an Italian-style ice-cream bar.

FOOD & DRINK

The Buttercross Tearoom 22 Cheshire St ✆ 01630 656510. 'Never trust a man who, when left alone with a tea cosy, doesn't try it on.' Those words by Billy Connolly adorn the bill of fare at the Buttercross. If you're still not persuaded: this café has well-dressed tables, big windows, proper coffee and reasonably priced, home-cooked food – along with toys for toddlers on the top floor. It's cash only; there's an ATM across the road at HSBC.
Joule's Red Lion Brewery Tap Great Hales St, TF9 1JP ✆ 01630 652602. The food dished out at Joule's flagship pub is deliberately not fancy – just well-presented and satisfying,

239

Shropshire Union Canal walk

Kindly supplied by Keith, Meg & Kate Pybus

✽ OS Explorer map 243; start in the churchyard of St Mary's, Market Drayton ♀ SJ675340.
4 miles; easy, with well-surfaced tracks & towpaths; allow 2 hours

This walk leaves Market Drayton in the sometimes rebellious footsteps of the young Robert Clive (page 237) and also follows part of the Shropshire Union Canal, past a peaceful flight of five locks at Tyrley.

1 Fortified with a packet of the town's gingerbread (page 238), start in the churchyard of St Mary's, just off Church Street. In his boyhood, Clive climbed the church tower and, straddling one of the gargoyles, waved to the townsfolk below. The gargoyle is preserved in the museum in Powis Castle near Welshpool. Follow the path around the church. The Old Grammar School was the first of several schools to expel young Bob before he was shipped off, aged 17, with the East India Company – 'the grandest society of merchants in the universe' – to Fort St George, Madras.

Follow the path past the school and down Clive Steps. Glancing to your left before crossing to the Joule's Brewery, there is another scene from Clive's scapegrace youth. His gang had a sort of protection racket. When one of the shopkeepers refused to pay the levy of sweets or pennies, Clive planned to flood his premises by damming the gutter. When the dam broke, Clive threw himself bodily into the breach.

2 Go down Great Hales Street. Pass the cottages and the church of St Thomas Aquinas. Follow the curve of the high red-brick wall on your right and turn into Berrisford Road. On your left is Grove School. In 1830 Grove House was bought by Charles Wilson, canal contractor and friend of Thomas Telford. Building the neighbouring canal, Wilson employed more than two thousand navigators, or 'navvies'. The Wilson family lived in Grove House for over a hundred years.

3 Being wary of oncoming traffic, cross the Tern over the little stone bridge. Ahead of you is the Forty Steps Aqueduct, which carries the canal over both road and river. Take the sandstone steps up the right-hand side to the canal. Take the towpath to the right.

When the Birmingham and Liverpool Junction Canal opened in 1835, the threat from the railways was already apparent. Rather than linking one town to another, now the emphasis had to be on providing the most direct link. To cut down the journey time, Telford drove this canal across the landscape, ignoring the contours. His pioneering cut-and-fill technique created dramatic cuttings and massive embankments. Rock from the cuttings went to build embankments further along, just what the railways ordered! The race was lost. However, the achievement remains phenomenal; especially when you consider the only tools were the pick and shovels of the navvies.

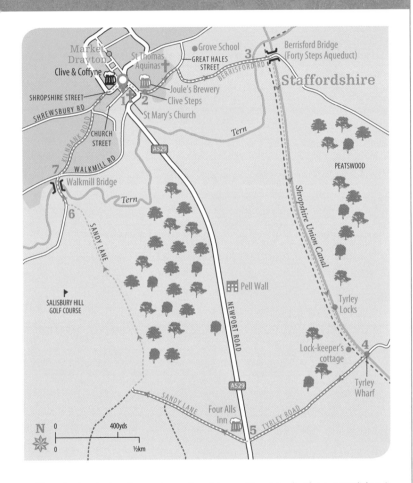

After a few hundred yards you enter a red sandstone cutting stained with sea-green lichen. It now forms homes for bats and kingfishers. You will also pass a flight of five locks at Tyrley which raise the canal a total of 33 feet.

4 Before Bridge 60 is a lock-keeper's cottage. Go under the bridge and make a hairpin turn to the right. The attractive wharf and cottages were built in 1837 for shipment of milk from the nearby Peatswood estate. Turn left up the lane; after half a mile cross the busy A529. ▶

Shropshire Union Canal walk (continued)

◄ Should you have developed a navigator's thirst, the Four Alls Inn (🕾 01630 652995) marks the halfway house of the walk.

5 Take the lane running down the left side of the inn, until it veers off to the right down a lane Sandy by name and nature. This is your route.

On your left is Salisbury Hill, now part of the golf course. In 1489, during the Wars of the Roses, the Earl of Salisbury and his 5,000-strong Yorkist army camped here. Two and a half miles east they met the Lancastrians at Blore Heath. At least 2,000 Lancastrians were killed, with the Yorkists losing nearly a thousand, and the Hemp Mill Stream ran red with blood.

At a dip in the lane, to the right, you will see a low red-brick house and walled garden. This was the gardener's house and kitchen garden of the Neoclassical Pell Wall, the last domestic building of the architect Sir John Soane. His best-known design was the Bank of England. Continue down the track past a veteran gnarled sweet chestnut on your left.

6 You will come to road; turn right towards the sound of rushing water. This stretch of the River Tern is so clear that you may see trout basking on the river bed.

7 At the junction cross the road. Two roads lie straight ahead. Take the one to the right, Kilnbank. It's a fairly steep climb through the sandstone cutting, but you are only minutes away from a drink. You emerge from Kilnbank Road on to Shropshire Street. Turn right into the town centre. The turning for Church Street is on your right.

featuring delicious cheese from super-local Mr Moyden's (🖉 www.mrmoyden.com) and meat from Fordhall Organic Farm. In a neat arrangement which feels very Salopian but should be the norm everywhere, Fordhall Farm feeds its 'Joule's herd' of free-range Gloucester Old Spots with spent grains from the brewery.

17 NORTON IN HALES

In the positively floral **Norton in Hales** (regularly scooping Britain in Bloom awards), just over four miles north of Market Drayton, on the neat triangular green by the church, you'll find the **bradling stone**. According to folklore, any man or boy found working after noon on Shrove Tuesday would be bumped or 'bradled' against this glacial boulder. The **Hinds Head** (Main Rd 🖉 01630 695555) has the convivial atmosphere of a local pub and a menu worthy of a great city brasserie; as many ingredients as possible are sourced within a 30-mile radius.

18 FORDHALL ORGANIC FARM

Å Fordhall Organic Farm yurts (page 250)

Tern Hill Rd, Market Drayton TF9 3PS ☏ 01630 638696 🖥 www.fordhallfarm.com

🕓 09.30–17.00 Tue–Sat, 10.00–16.00 Sun & bank holidays; free ♿ indoors highly accessible; community garden accessible for sturdy wheelchairs & buggies. See ad, 4th colour section.

Clearly signposted off the A53 outside of Market Drayton, next to the massive Müller Dairy factory, is England's first community-owned farm. Here in 2004, Charlotte and Ben Hollins faced losing their family's beloved organic farm to aggressive development from their neighbours. Just two days before the Hollins family was due to be evicted, Charlotte and Ben, aged only 21 and 19, secured the short-team lease of the farm. But the future of Fordhall remained fragile. In the shadow of the loss of their father Arthur Hollins, a passionate pioneer in organic farming, the brother and sister team had until 1 July 2006 to raise £800,000 and purchase the land. At the time Ben was studying agriculture at Harper

THE FIGHT FOR FORDHALL FARM: TEN YEARS ON

Charlotte Hollins

The last ten years have been a rollercoaster. Fordhall has been transformed from a rundown farm – about to be buried under concrete by industrial development – to a community asset. Our offices have moved from draughty temporary cabins (we had to run outside in the rain to use the compost toilet!) to our ecologically renovated Old Dairy building, with hemp walls, renewable energy, a green roof, clay paints and recycled newspaper. Don't worry, we now have a deluxe compost toilet should visitors wish to experience it . . .

Our education programme has grown. A 'care farm', working with adults with learning disabilities, is established in our community garden, while a youth project supporting young people at the point of school exclusion is flourishing.

Most recently we renovated our yurts, which were opened by the Queen's cousin, His Royal Highness the Duke of Gloucester. Available for glamping, these Shropshire-built structures are insulated with sheep's wool, have a lovely wood-burning stove and their own deluxe compost toilet. Rented as one unit, they sleep up to six guests and are privately situated in the peace and quiet of the Tern Valley.

The last of our large projects will be a straw-bale bunkhouse for our volunteers and visitors.

Being in community ownership is a privilege and an honour. We love sharing our journey with our 8,000-plus community shareholders and look forward to sharing it with our visitors too.

Adams University and Charlotte was working in a nursing home. 'I think we were living so much in the moment trying to get everything done, we didn't realise how hard it actually was,' Charlotte said, when I asked how on earth they'd coped.

What happened next was extraordinary. Taking advice from a cooperative consultancy in Gloucestershire, Charlotte and Ben established an industrial and provident society called the Fordhall Community Land Initiative and began selling not-for-profit £50 lifelong shares in the farm. The shares could not be traded but instead represented an investment in the future of Fordhall. The idea was that the trust would hold the land, protecting it from development for the benefit of the community. Without wishing to ruin a great story (which unfolds beautifully in Charlotte and Ben's book, *The Fight for Fordhall Farm*), their plight attracted the attention of journalists, conservationists, educationists and thousands more caring people across the world. The pop star Sting gave a £2,000 donation, while Prince Charles donated a tour of Highgrove as an auction prize. Now the thriving organic farm you can visit today has an inspirational strapline: '1 Farmer, 8000 Landlords'.

To enhance your visit, it's fun following one of the **free farm trails** (named after Charlotte, Ben and Arthur) to work up an appetite for a late breakfast, lunch or afternoon tea at **Arthur's Farm Kitchen**. Free guided walks are available for groups of over ten people. You'll find a picnic area outside (including covered seating for wet days) if you prefer to bring your own food. Or you could buy something from the **farm shop** run by tenant farmer Ben (which has an organic butchery and sells many more local and organic goods, including cheese and ice cream). Festivals, craft and farming workshops, ceilidhs, hog roasts, wild play and volunteer weekends take place throughout the year. You can still buy community shares today.

🍴 FOOD & DRINK

The name of Fordhall Organic Farm's restaurant, **Arthur's Farm Kitchen**, commemorates Charlotte and Ben's late dad Arthur Hollins, whose 1986 book on his personal experiences of organic farming, *The Farmer, the Plough and the Devil,* shows how ahead of his time he was. You're unlikely to find higher quality or better cared for meat anywhere else: all of Fordhall's sheep and Aberdeen Angus and Hereford cattle are reared to Soil Association organic standards, grazing year round in the clover-rich meadows. Fordhall uses a local abattoir and butchers and hangs the slaughtered meat back on the farm. You can enjoy it in a full Shropshire breakfast, chunky beef burger, sausage sandwich or perhaps a pie or slow-cooked cawl (Welsh stew). Vegetarians are well catered for too, with warm salads and daily specials created from local, often organic produce and the region's finest cheese.

Of course you can always just call in for organic coffee or a locally brewed beer and a homemade treat. Eating lemon drizzle cake in Arthur's one clear February day, I was even able to watch via webcam a live link to a sparrows' nest.

All profits from Arthur's are reinvested in the farm's education and community work.

█9 WOODSEAVES GARDEN PLANTS WITH WOODSEAVES MINIATURE RAILWAY

Woodseaves, Market Drayton TF9 2AS ✐ 01630 653161 ✆ www.woodseavesminirail.co.uk
◷ nursery 10.00–18.00 Mon, Tue, Fri, Sat & Sun. Trains run from Mar to Sep & in Dec on Sun & bank holiday Mon (10.30–16.30). Free entry & parking; train rides in exchange for donations

Tucked away in Woodseaves, a hamlet just over two miles south of Market Drayton (not to be confused with the Staffordshire village), is a 2.2-acre slice of happiness where one couple – Bill and Jean Haywood – are living out their individual dreams alongside each other. A talented gardener, Jean has created a **nursery** where all fruit trees, shrubs, climbers and bedding plants for sale are also featured in pockets of gardens, allowing visitors to see them in context. Jean, whose rose collection displays the year each specimen was first cultivated (the earliest being Maiden's Blush from the 1400s) also makes up baskets to customers' budgets.

On Sundays and bank holiday Mondays in summer, hauling delighted passengers around Jean's gardens and through a willow tunnel, is Bill's 7¼-inch **miniature railway**, complete with a green Roanoke-made engine called Sydney and a burgundy steamie named after Jean. Bill built the narrow gauge track himself: it covers 400 yards although the clever layout gives the illusion of a longer journey; a trick Bill told me he learned from working on model railways. You'll find one of those operating on the second Sunday of summer months too.

A shed-cum-**tea room** supplies refreshments, including Jean's homemade cakes.

SHROPSHIRE ONLINE

For additional online content, articles, photos and more on Shropshire, why not visit ✆ www.bradtguides.com/shropshire.

ACCOMMODATION

Below is a list of B&Bs, camping and glamping sites, self-catering options, lodges and boutique hotels that I consider to be special – perhaps for their location, ethos, ambience or history, or a mixture of all those things. For more full descriptions of these places listed, see ⊕ www.bradtguides.com/shropshiresleeps. Throughout this guide B&Bs, self-catering cottages and hotels are indicated by 🏠 under the heading for the nearest town or village in which they're located. The ▲ symbol covers everything from no-frills field pitches to luxurious glamping.

1 SOUTH SHROPSHIRE

B&Bs

Broome Park Farm
Catherton Rd, Cleobury Mortimer DY14 0LB
𝒥 01299 270647 ⊗ www.broomeparkfarm.co.uk

Castle View B&B
Stokesay SY7 9AL 𝒥 01588 673712 ⊗ www.castleviewstokesay.co.uk

Hopton House B&B
Hopton Heath SY7 0QD 𝒥 01547 530885 ⊗ www.shropshirebreakfast.co.uk. See ad, 4th colour section.

Orchard House
Ashford Bowdler, near Ludlow SY8 4DJ 𝒥 01584 831270 ⊗ www.orchard-barn.co.uk (cottage also available for self-catering)

The Poppy House
20 Market Sq, Bishop's Castle SY9 5BN 𝒥 01588 638443 ⊗ www.poppyhouse.co.uk

The Porch House
High St, Bishop's Castle SY9 5BE 𝒥 01588 638854 ⊗ www.theporchhouse.com (also available for self-catering)

The Quarry House
Church Rd, Newcastle-on-Clun SY7 8QJ 𝒥 01588 640774 ⊗ www.quarry-house.com

Timberstone Bed & Breakfast
Clee Stanton SY8 3EL 𝒥 01584 823519 ⊗ www.timberstoneludlow.co.uk (house also available for self-catering)

Victoria House
48 High St, Church Stretton SY6 6BX 𝒥 01694 723823

B&Bs with horse accommodation

Long Mountain Centre
Rowley, Pleasant View SY5 9RY 𝒥 01743 891274 ⊗ www.longmountaincentre.co.uk

Middle Woodbatch Farm
Woodbatch Rd, Bishop's Castle SY9 5JS 𝒥 01588 630141 ⊗ www.shropshirehillsriding.co.uk

Camping & glamping

Brow Farm Campsite
Ratlinghope SY5 0SR 𝒥 01588 650641 ⊗ www.browfarmcampsite.co.uk

Feather Down Farm
Acton Scott SY6 6QQ ✆ 01420 80804 ⌂ www.
featherdown.co.uk/farm/acton-scott.html

Foxholes Castle Camping
Montgomery Rd, Bishop's Castle SY9 5HA
✆ 01588 638924 (email through website
preferred) ⌂ www.foxholes-castle.co.uk

The Green Caravan Park
Wentnor SY9 5EF ✆ 01588 650605 ⌂ www.
greencaravanpark.co.uk

**Shropshire Hills Mountain Bike
and Outdoor Pursuit Centre**
Marshbrook, near Church Stretton SY6 6QE
✆ 01694 781515 ⌂ www.camping-shropshire.
co.uk

Complete experiences

Westhope College
near Craven Arms SY7 9JL ✆ 01584 861293
⌂ www.westhope.org.uk

Hostels

YHA Bridges
Ratlinghope SY5 0SP ✆ 01588 650656 ⌂ www.
yha.org.uk/hostel/bridges

YHA Clun Mill
Clun SY7 8NY ✆ 0845 3719112 ⌂ www.yha.org.
uk/hostel/clun

Hotels

Fishmore Hall
Fishmore Rd, Ludlow SY8 3DP ✆ 01584 875148
⌂ www.fishmorehall.co.uk

Pubs with rooms

The Baron at Bucknell
Bucknell SY7 0AH ✆ 01547 530549 ⌂ www.
baronatbucknell.co.uk (camping also available)

The Bridges
Ratlinghope SY5 0ST ✆ 01588 650260 ⌂ www.
thebridgespub.co.uk

Castle Hotel
Bishop's Castle SY9 5BN ✆ 01588 638403
⌂ www.thecastlehotelbishopscastle.co.uk

Charlton Arms
Ludford Bridge, Ludlow SY8 1PJ ✆ 01584 872813
⌂ www.thecharltonarms.co.uk

The Crown Country Inn
Munslow SY7 9ET ✆ 01584 841205 ⌂ www.
crowncountryinn.co.uk

The Crown Inn
Wentnor SY9 5EE ✆ 01588 650613 ⌂ www.
thecrowninnwentnor.com

Restaurants with rooms

The Clive
Bromfield SY8 2JR ✆ 01584 856565 ⌂ www.
theclive.co.uk

Self-catering

Annie's Cabin
Caynham Mill SY8 3BH ✆ 07977 091928
⌂ www.ludlowecologcabins.co.uk

The Bindery Flat
12 Old St, Ludlow SY8 1NP ✆ 01584 876565
⌂ www.trevorlloyd.co.uk/thebinderyflat/
location.html

Bromfield Priory Gatehouse
Bromfield SY8 2JU ✆ 01628 825925 ⌂ via www.
landmarktrust.org.uk

Buckshead Eco-cottage
Newcastle, near Clun SY7 8QU ✆ 07799 681134
⌂ www.buckshead-ecocottage.co.uk

Castle House Apartments
Ludlow Castle, Ludlow SY8 1AY ✆ 01584 874465
⌂ www.ludlowcastle.com/accommodation

Criggin Cottage
Melin-y-Grogue, Llanfair Waterdine LD7 1TU
✆ 01547 510341 ⌂ www.criggin.co.uk

The Dick Turpin Cottage
Cockford Hall, Clun SY7 8LR ✆ 01588 640327
⌂ www.dickturpincottage.com

Eaton Manor Country Estate
Eaton-under-Heywood, Church Stretton SY6 7DH
✆ 01694 724814 ⌂ www.eatonmanor.co.uk

Henley Cottage
Acton Scott ✆ 07976 839997 ⌂ www.english-
country-cottages.co.uk/cottages/the-acton-scott-
estate-henley-cottage-roo4

Middle Farm Cottages Betchcott near Church Stretton SY6 6NP 𝒟 01694 751232 ⌖ www.middlefarmcottages.co.uk. See ad, 4th colour section.

Pooh Hall Cottages
Woodside, Clun SY7 0JB 𝒟 01588 640075 ⌖ www.pooh-hallcottages.co.uk

The Pottery
Overbatch, Castle Hill, All Stretton SY6 6JX 𝒟 01694 722121 ⌖ www.thepotteryshropshire.co.uk

Redford Farm Barns
Nash SY8 3BA 𝒟 01865 764087 ⌖ www.sheepskinlife.com/holiday-home/redford-farm-barns

Upper Heath Farm
Heath SY7 9DS 𝒟 01584 823845 ⌖ www.upperheathfarm.com

Walcot Hall
Lydbury North SY7 8AZ
𝒟 01588 680570 ⌖ www.walcothall.com (glamping also available)

2 SOUTHEAST SHROPSHIRE

B&Bs
The Old Rectory
Wheathill WV16 6QT 𝒟 01746 787209 ⌖ www.theoldrectorywheathill.com

Wenlock Pottery
Shineton St, Much Wenlock TF13 6HT 𝒟 01952 727600 ⌖ www.wenlockpottery.co.uk

Hostels
YHA Wilderhope Manor
Longville TF13 6EG 𝒟 01694 771363 ⌖ www.yha.org.uk/hostel/wilderhope-manor

Pubs with rooms
The Down Inn
Ludlow Rd, Bridgnorth WV16 6UA 𝒟 01746 789539 ⌖ www.thedowninn.co.uk

Restaurants with rooms
The Hundred House
Norton TF11 9EE 𝒟 01952 580240 ⌖ www.hundredhouse.co.uk

Raven Hotel
Barrow St, Much Wenlock TF13 6EN 𝒟 01952 727251 ⌖ www.ravenhotel.com

Self-catering
End Barn
Sheinton St, Much Wenlock TF13 6HU 𝒟 Please use enquiry form on website ⌖ www.shropshire-guide.co.uk/places/united-kingdom/shropshire/much-wenlock/accommodation/end-barn/

Live the Adventure House
1 Manor Farm Barns, Stottesdon DY14 8UA 𝒟 01746 718436 ⌖ www.ovac.co.uk

Mose Cottage & Big Mose Bunkhouse
Dudmaston Estate, Quatt WV15 6QN 𝒟 01746 780866 ⌖ National Trust

Temple of Diana
Weston Park, Weston-under-Lizard TF11 8LE 𝒟 01952 852100 ⌖ www.ruralretreats.co.uk/England/Shropshire-Holiday-Cottages/Temple-of-Diana_SH027

3 IRONBRIDGE GORGE & THE WREKIN

B&Bs
The Library House
11 Severn Bank, Ironbridge TF8 7AN 𝒟 01952 432299 ⌖ www.libraryhouse.com

Hostels
YHA Coalbrookdale
1 Paradise, Coalbrookdale TF8 7NR 𝒟 0845 3719325 ⌖ www.yha.org.uk/hostel/ironbridge-coalbrookdale

YHA Coalport
John Rose Building, High St, Coalport TF8 7HT 𝒟 0845 3719325 ⌖ www.yha.org.uk/hostel/ironbridge-coalport

Self-catering
Coalport Station Holidays
Station House, Coalport TF8 7JF 𝒟 01952 885674 ⌖ www.coalportstation.com

Iron Bridge House
34 High St, Ironbridge TF8 7AG ✆ 01628 825925
⌂ www.landmarktrust.org.uk
Morrells Wood Farm
Leighton SY5 6RU ✆ 01952 510273 ⌂ www.
morrellswoodfarm.co.uk

4 SHREWSBURY & MID SHROPSHIRE

B&Bs
Brompton Farmhouse B&B
Brompton SY5 6LE ✆ 01743 761629 ⌂ www.
bromptonfarmhouse.co.uk
Ferndell Bed & Breakfast
14 Underdale Rd, Abbey Foregate, Shrewsbury
SY2 5DL
The Old Station
Leaton near Bomere Heath SY4 3AP ✆ 01939
290905 ⌂ www.theoldstationshropshire.co.uk

B&Bs with horse accommodation
The Isle Estate
Isle Lane, Bicton SY3 8EE ✆ 01743 851218
⌂ www.the-isle-estate.co.uk
Wenlock Edge Riding Centre B&B
Hughley SY5 6NT ✆ 01746 785645
⌂ www.millfarmridingcentre.co.uk

Hotels
Lion & Pheasant Hotel
49-50 Wyle Cop, Shrewsbury SY1 1XJ ✆ 01743
770345 ⌂ www.lionandpheasant.co.uk

Pubs with rooms
The White Horse
Pulverbatch SY5 8DS ✆ 01743 718247 ⌂ www.
thewhitehorseinnpulverbatch.co.uk

Restaurants with rooms
Drapers Hall
10 St Mary's Place, Shrewsbury SY1 1DZ ✆ 01743
344679 ⌂ www.drapershallrestaurant.co.uk/
contact

The Golden Cross
14 Princess St, Shrewsbury SY1 1LP
✆ 01743 362507 ⌂ www.goldencrosshotel.co.uk
Porterhouse SY1
15 St Mary's St, Shrewsbury SY1 1EQ ✆ 01743
358870 ⌂ www.porterhousesy1.co.uk

Self-catering
Caro's Cottage
1 Higher Netley, Dorrington SY5 7JY ✆ 01244
345700 ⌂ www.caroscottage.co.uk
Haymakers Cottage
Minsterley SY5 0HG ✆ 01743 891412 ⌂ www.
gleaningscentre.co.uk/holiday-cottage
The Old Police Cells
4 The Old Police Station, Swan Hill, Shrewsbury
SY1 1NN ✆ 01743 272544 ⌂ www.
theoldpolicecells.co.uk
Pitchford Estate
Three sites near Pitchford ✆ 0870 5851155
(bookings) ⌂ www.pitchfordestate.com. See ad,
4th colour section.

5 OSWESTRY & NORTHWEST SHROPSHIRE

B&Bs
Big Bear Lodge
Hendre Villa near Melverley SY108PH
✆ 07711 312103 ⌂ www.bigbearlodge.co.uk
(self-catering and camping pods also available)
Greystones
Crickheath SY10 8BW ✆ 07976 740141 ⌂ www.
stayatgreystones.co.uk

Camping & glamping
Canal Central
Maesbury Marsh SY10 8JG ✆ 01691 652168
⌂ www.canalcentral.co.uk (first floor self-
catering accommodation also available)
Cranberry Moss
Kinnerley near Knockin Heath SY10 8DY ✆ 01743
741118 ⌂ www.campingandcaravanningclub.
co.uk/campsites/uk/shropshire/oswestry/oswestry

ACCOMMODATION

Underhill Farm
Pant near Llanymynech SY10 9RB ✉ enquiries@
underhillfarm.org ⌕ www.underhillfarm.org

Hotels
Pen-y-Dyffryn Country Hotel
Rhydycroesau near Oswestry SY10 7JD
☎ 01691 653700 ⌕ www.peny.co.uk

Restaurants with rooms
Sebastians
45 Willow St, Oswestry SY11 1AQ ☎ 01691
655444 ⌕ www.sebastians-hotel.com

Self-catering
River Cottage
Church Lane, Melverley SY10 8PJ ☎ 01938
580286 ⌕ www.rivercottagemelverley.co.uk
The Stables
Maesbury Marsh SY10 8JB ⌕ www.
holidaylettings.co.uk
St Winifred's Well
Woolston near Maesbury SY10 8HY ☎ 01628
825925 ⌕ www.landmarktrust.org.uk

Self-catering with horse accommodation
Penycoed Horse Riding Centre's log cabins
Llynclys Hill, Pant SY10 8LG ☎ 01691 830608
Springhill Farm
Riding Stables & Accommodation
Springhill Farm, Selattyn SY10 7NZ ⌕ www.
penycoedridingstables.co.uk

6 NORTH SHROPSHIRE

B&Bs
Aston Lodge
Soulton Rd, Wem SY4 5BG ☎ 01939 232577
⌕ www.aston-lodge.co.uk
The Citadel
Weston under Redcastle SY4 5JY ☎ 01630
685204 ⌕ www.thecitadelweston.co.uk

The Moat Shed's 1960s vintage house truck
Northwood Hall, Newtown SY4 5NU ☎ 01939
236252 ⌕ www.themoatshed.co.uk
Soulton Hall
Soulton near Wem SY4 5RS ☎ 01939 232786
⌕ www.soultonhall.co.uk
Ternhill Farm House
Tern Hill, Market Drayton TF9 3PX ☎ 01630
638984 ⌕ www.ternhillfarm.co.uk
Windmill Cottage Guesthouse
Weston under Redcastle SY4 5UX ☎ 01939
200219 ⌕ www.windmillcottage.co.uk

Camping & glamping
Abdo Hill Farm
Rosehill TF9 2JF ☎ 07928 910091 ⌕ www.
abdohillfarm.co.uk
Colemere Caravan Park
Colemere SY12 0QL ☎ 01939 272999 ⌕ www.
colemerecaravanpark.co.uk
Dearnford Lake glamping pod & campsite
Tilstock Rd, Whitchurch SY13 3JQ
☎ 01948 665914 ⌕ www.dearnford.net
(B&B also available)
Fordhall Organic Farm yurts
Tern Hill Rd, Market Drayton TF9 3PS ☎ 01630
638696 ⌕ www.fordhallfarm.com. See ad, 4th
colour section.
Nink's Wagon
English Frankton SY12 0JX ✉ jess@quirkyaccom.
com ⌕ via www.quirkyaccom.com/nink-s-wagon

Hotels
Goldstone Hall
Goldstone Rd, Market Drayton TF9 2NA ☎ 01630
661202 ⌕ www.goldstonehall.com
Old Colehurst Manor
Colehurst, Market Drayton TF9 2JB ☎ 01630
638833 ⌕ www.colehurst.co.uk
The Old Rectory
Lowe Hill Rd, Wem SY4 5UA ☎ 01939 233233
⌕ www.oldrectorywem.co.uk. See ad, 4th colour
section.

Restaurants with rooms

The Inn at Grinshill
High St, Grinshill SY4 3BL ✐ 01939 220410
✦ www.theinnatgrinshill.co.uk

Self-catering

Amblewood Cottage & Woodpeckers
The Vineyard, Grinshill SY4 3BW ✐ 01939 220214
✦ www.amblewoodcottages.co.uk

The Barn at Maynards Farm
Weston under Redcastle SY4 5LR ✐ 01948
840252 ✦ www.maynardsfarm.co.uk

Mereside Farm
Ellesmere SY12 0PA
✐ 01691 622404 ✦ www.meresidefarm.co.uk
(also available on B&B basis)

Oakpond Cottages
Ightfield, Whitchurch SY13 4BL ✐ 01948 890245
✦ www.oakpondcottage.com

The Shooting Folly
Lipley, near Cheswardine, Market Drayton TF9 2SQ
✐ 01747 828170 ✦ www.hideaways.co.uk

INDEX

Entries in **bold** refer to major entries.

INDEX OF ADVERTISERS

HOPTON HOUSE B&B

A relaxed and friendly rural retreat with more than a touch of luxury.

Within walking distance of Hopton Heath train station and Hopton Castle, Hopton House B&B is the perfect base for exploring south Shropshire. This comfortable converted granary combines a strong environmental policy with linen-soft luxury, welcoming you home from the hills with a super king-size bed, double-ended bath and powerful shower. The famous Hopton House breakfast (served 08.30–10.00 to encourage lie-ins) eases you into the day with local bacon and sausages, and free-range eggs from the resident hens.

Hopton House B&B
Hopton Heath, SY7 0QD
Tel: 01547 530885
Email: info@shropshirebreakfast.co.uk

@HoptonHouseBnB
Hopton House B&B Shropshire

www.shropshirebreakfast.co.uk

MIDDLE FARM COTTAGES

Sumptuous, Enjoy England Gold Award cottages on a smallholding near Church Stretton.

With rare-breed sheep, pigs and chickens, this small farm offers a perfect getaway for couples or families. Try the home-reared pork and fresh eggs and pick your own veg when in season, or walk half a mile to the much-loved Bottle and Glass pub.

Middle Farm
Betchcott, Church Stretton SY6 6NP
Tel: 01694 751232
enquiries@middlefarmcottages.co.uk

MIDDLE FARM COTTAGES

www.middlefarmcottages.co.uk
🐦 @MiddleFarm1
📘 Middle Farm

FORDHALL ORGANIC FARM YURTS

Luxurious, Shropshire-made yurts on a delightful community farm near Market Drayton.

A romantic and private hideaway or a family adventure? Fordhall Organic Farm's two interconnecting Mongolian-style yurts sleep up to six and are equipped with kitchen, wood burner and everything else you need for a cosy glamping break in the Tern Valley.

Fordhall Organic Farm Tern Hill Road, Market Drayton TF9 3PS
Tel: 01630 638696 Email: project@fordhallfarm.com www.fordhallfarm.com
🐦 @fordhallfarm 📘 Fordhall Organic Farm

PITCHFORD ESTATE

Luxurious self-catering with access to 1,000 acres of private Shropshire countryside.

Pitchford Estate is a dairy, sheep and arable farm in extensive woodland, six miles south of Shrewsbury. Hide away in a stunning barn conversion: Windy Mundy Farm (sleeping 16), Stockbatch Granary (14) or Tree House Barn (four). The latter has views of the 17th-century Pitchford tree house, once visited by Queen Victoria. The estate is part of Natural England's Higher Level Stewardship scheme, working to improve habitats and increase biodiversity. Income is reinvested in preserving the estate's historic buildings.

www.pitchfordestate.com

🐦 @PitchfordEstate   📘 Pitchford Estate   📷 www.instagram.com/pitchfordestate